THE MEN
IN OUR LIVES

BY ELIZABETH FISHEL

The Men in Our Lives
Sisters

THE MEN
IN OUR LIVES

**FATHERS
LOVERS
HUSBANDS
MENTORS**

by
ELIZABETH
FISHEL

WILLIAM MORROW AND COMPANY, INC.

NEW YORK

Grateful acknowledgment is made for permission to reprint the following:

Introduction: Andrew Turnbull, letter dated August 8, 1933, from F. Scott Fitzgerald. Copyright © 1963 by Francis Scott Fitzgerald Lanahan, reprinted by permission of Charles Scribner Sons.

Chapter 7, "Mr. Wrong & Mr. Right": "For My Lover Returning to His Wife" by Anne Sexton from *Love Poems;* copyright © 1967, 1968, 1969 by Anne Sexton. Reprinted by permission of Houghton-Mifflin Company. "The Man Under the Bed" by Erica Jong, from *Fruits & Vegetables;* copyright © 1968, 1970, 1971 by Erica Mann Jong. Reprinted by permission of Holt, Rinehart & Winston, Publishers. The lines from "The Big Heart," words by Jamie Bernstein and music by Jamie Bernstein and David Beck; copyright © 1980 by Pick Lip Music and Art Street Music. Used by permission. All rights reserved.

Some portions of Chapter 7 ("Mr. Wrong and Mr. Right") appeared in slightly different form in *Cosmopolitan*.

Library of Congress Cataloging in Publication Data

Fishel, Elizabeth.
  The men in our lives.

  Bibliography: p.
  1. Fathers and daughters—United States. 2. Men—United States. 3. Masculinity (Psychology) 4. Women—United States—Psychology. I. Title.
HQ756.F57 1985   305.3   84–8984
ISBN 0–688–03960–X

Printed in the United States of America

First Edition

1 2 3 4 5 6 7 8 9 10

BOOK DESIGN BY ABBY KAGAN

To Robert Houghteling

ACKNOWLEDGMENTS

ABOVE ALL, I WOULD LIKE TO THANK THE NEARLY TWO HUNDRED women from all over the country who shared with me their stories about the men in their lives, both in person and in written autobiographies. Without their passionate concern and frankness in exploring these relationships, my work on this book could not have begun.

I would also like to thank my editor, James Landis, whose interest and involvement in my work was always an important source of support, and whose thoughtful responses guided its progress at every stage. And thanks to my agent, Pat Berens, whose enthusiasm for this project was also very much appreciated.

During the four years of work on this book, many other people made valuable contributions to its development. I would especially like to thank the psychologists and psychoanalysts whom I consulted about the underlying issues of this book and who gave generously of their time and expertise: Mary Dwan, marriage and family counselor; Rudolf Ekstein, training analyst and clinical professor at the University of California at Los Angeles; Suzanne Gasner, clinical psychologist; John Munder Ross, clinical associate professor of psychiatry at Downstate Medical Center and editor most recently (with Stanley Cath and Alan Gurwitt) of *Father and Child: Developmental and Clinical Perspectives;* Philip Spielman, child psychiatrist and director for many years of the Child Psychiatry Service of Mount Zion Hospital in San Francisco; Lora Heims Tessman, clinical psychologist at the Massachusetts Institute of Technology Psychiatric Service and author of *Children of Parting Parents.*

Thanks as well to the friends who encouraged me and kept up my spirits: Sheila Ballantyne; Josie Gerst; Phyllis Koppelman; Binnie McMurtry; Margaretta and Frederick Mitchell; B. K. Moran; Dusky Pierce; Leah Potts; Merry Selk.

Thanks also to the women's groups who supported my work and contributed provocative ideas to it: the Women's Research Caucus, the Radcliffe Club of San Francisco and the East Bay; and special thanks to the members of my writers' group, past and present, who offered both serious advice and much needed laughter: Carolly Erickson, Jeremy Joan Hewes, Mollie Katzen, Janet Peoples, Linda Williams.

My appreciation also to Meg Holmberg, who tirelessly and expertly transcribed my interview tapes, and also to Chris Endo, Jenny Falloon, and Ann Irving, who typed parts of the manuscript. Special acknowledgment to Lynn Coulter, who generously helped out with an important piece of library research early on in my work.

Finally I give my deepest thanks to my family: to my parents, Edith and James Fishel, who encouraged me in countless ways both during my work on this book and for all the years leading up to it. As the first and most influential man in my life, my father was the first inspiration for this book, and I hope only that now completed, it does him justice. Thanks also to my sister, Anne Fishel, who was not only a crucial source of support and a sympathetic ear, but also, as a clinical psychologist, offered me invaluable ideas, suggestions of books, and most helpful commentary along the way. And thanks to my parents-in-law, Fiora and James Houghteling, whose clippings and enthusiasm were always welcome.

As I researched and wrote about the men in our lives, my husband, Robert Houghteling, was the man in my life who accompanied and bolstered my journey. His astute comments and careful reading of the manuscript—and his wonderful dinners—nourished this journey at every stage. This book is dedicated to him with great pleasure and love.

CONTENTS

12 / CONTENTS

Things to worry about:
  Worry about courage
  Worry about cleanliness
  Worry about efficiency
  Worry about horsemanship . . .

Things not to worry about:
  Don't worry about popular opinion
  Don't worry about dolls
  Don't worry about the past
  Don't worry about the future
  Don't worry about growing up
  Don't worry about anybody getting ahead of you
  Don't worry about triumph
  Don't worry about failure unless it comes through your own
    fault
  Don't worry about mosquitoes
  Don't worry about flies
  Don't worry about insects in general
  Don't worry about parents
  Don't worry about boys
  Don't worry about disappointment
  Don't worry about pleasures
  Don't worry about satisfactions

Things to think about:
  What am I really aiming at?

—F. SCOTT FITZGERALD in a letter
to his daughter, Scottie,
August 8, 1933

INTRODUCTION

THE WORLD I GREW UP IN WAS A WORLD OF WOMEN—MOTHER, sister, schoolmates, friends. Against this landscape, boys and men stood out both mythic and mysterious. In relation to them, the girls at my New York City girls' school were loving and fearing, yearning and retreating. We daydreamed about phantom princes and used our wiles to please, when the rare opportunity permitted. But more often we hurried back to the haven of comfort and safety provided by the other girls. I saw the world of men refracted through our shared lens, and the distorted image both protected and frightened me. In our world women held sway. We were the rule, men the exception. Women articulated ideas, created art, unearthed discoveries, set the tone, called the shots. In our own world I believed we women were perfectly powerful, and among them I, too, could reach as far as I dared.

But I also sensed that outside the safe boundaries of our school, this power was undependable. In the "real" world— the world of men—our strength did not count for much. To share power with men was to lose it. I marked how vigilantly men were excluded from our school (in my thirteen years there, I remember only three who pierced the barriers: an elevator man, a choral conductor, and one lone math teacher who lasted a year under trial-by-fire of the girls). Perhaps this vigilance masked fear, camouflaged envy, curtailed threat. But being excluded, men became infinitely more dangerous and more desirable. They were intruder and enemy, but to find one, to tame one was to have an entrée into a forbidden and seductive world. They seemed unattainable, but to be without one was to be incomplete. They were undefinable in the terms of our world, but to define one would be to define oneself.

My connections with the women in my world were from the first palpable in body and blood. For I could see how like my mother I was in my hands, my hopes, my habits. (Even now, using Jergen's on my hands every night, as she does, I am linked with her. That faint smell of almonds in the lotion brings her immediately to the room.) I could hear myself even in my younger sister's voice, her laugh, her mannerisms. I could imagine in my teachers images of the women I might become, with their beads and boots and Marimekko dresses and the sureness of their opinions about Woolf and Wordsworth and the world. I could feel my sympathies lighting effortlessly on the shoulders of my girlfriends, as we chattered and cried through childhood, stumbled and spread our wings through adolescence.

But as tangible as this bond with women, so intangible was the bond with men. How the men in my life left their imprint on me was not as definite as the shape of my hands; how they influenced me, what they taught me was not as recognizable as the lessons of mother and sister, nor as accessible as the wisdom of my teachers. The women's voices spoke clearly from faces like my own. The men's were more muffled, as if coming from behind masks or across vast continents.

On the terrain of my childhood the men whom I loved loom larger than life. Their shadows are as tantalizing as their images, their messages as provocative unspoken as spoken. First, I see my grandfathers. One had been a financial wizard, but was already past his heyday when I knew him. Setbacks took their toll on him, and he withdrew into the privacy of his thoughts. My father showed me his father's picture as a younger man, wanting me to remember him that way: dapper and debonair on a boardwalk in Atlantic City, flushed with possibilities for the future. But I knew him only afterward, when the possibilities had not led where he hoped. A child of three, awed and puzzled by his silence, I circled round him and murmured to myself, "Not a word, not a word."

My other grandfather I knew to be a doctor whose specialty was helping women conceive. Women flocked to him from around the world, and I saw them in his waiting room in various stages of expectancy and fulfillment. On his desk was a bronze sculpture of his hands, just his hands, and lining the office walls were photographs of babies, emblems of his patients' gratitude, symbols to me of his omnipotence. When he died, I was still too young to understand death, and for years afterward I would see a shock of white hair, a certain elderly gait and be convinced it was he. From my grandfathers I learned about the grandeur of wishes and the disappointment of loss. Their lives suggested that life was fragile, that it was grand, that it could last forever, that it would have to end.

But in these early years no one stands taller than my father. Hero and protector, he would carry me on his shoulders into the summer ocean, and when the waves rose on the horizon, he would cry, in mock despair, "What *shall* we do?" Then he would sink beneath the water, effortlessly as Neptune, carrying me with him, while the waves crashed over our heads. When we rose—I terrified and delighted, he victorious—the sea was calm as a baby's blanket. This was his role in my childhood: magician, savior from storms, calmer of the sea.

I saw him living in a house of words: buried beneath *The New York Times* at the breakfast table, hunched over his mahogony desk writing ad copy for products he swore the world did not really need but were magical to me (trees that bore lemons and oranges on the same branch, a glass globe over a tiny replica of the White House—shake it, and it filled with snow). And most of all I saw him reading, reading from evening until the still center of the night, reading books and papers and magazines (running his fingers through the pages of the *New Yorker,* he would say, "Feel the paper, it's like silk"). Is it any wonder that when I was old enough I wanted to make my way into that kingdom of words? There was my father, incessantly reading, smoking his cigars, dreaming his dreams. From him I learned how to pursue my own.

His was a tall figure to fill. Looking back over the young men in my life, I realize that for a long time I did not truly wish to replace him. When I looked for love, I had an unerring instinct for picking out the fey, the wild, the dangerous—in short, the inappropriate. I spent my adolescence refining (if not finding) my romantic type, from the whimsy of the Little Prince to the intensity of Dean Moriarty (asked in high school to write about "The Most Attractive Man in English Literature," I chose without hesitation Kerouac's antihero, a character as far beyond the confines of our school as I could find). The first boy I fell in love with knew all the words to "Blonde on Blonde" and carried his treasures in a box lined with black velvet. To me, at sixteen, this was the stuff of poetry. That he loved me gave me the first inkling I was lovable. That he left me, left me wondering.

After him came a succession of long-haired drummers, leather-jacketed revolutionaries, dreamers of dreams. One introduced me to Marx, another to Buddha, another to Antonioni. Some read poetry to me; few read the poems I wrote. There were those who loved me more than I loved them, who courted me as avidly as I courted others—the ones who would not love me back. What separated these two groups was more than chemistry but less than reason. In memory these men exist almost more in the telling, the rehashing, than in reality, in themselves.

I measured myself against them, with them and without them. I gauged their world against the world I might find on my own. I listened to their messages, their pearls of wisdom, delivered always with utter self-seriousness and conviction. And I wondered to myself how their words—then the words of boys, but all too soon to be the words of men, of my father and grandfathers—would ever apply to me. For me, growing up meant moving from the cozy certainty of the world of women to that foreign country, men, whose language I did not speak, whose customs I did not know, whose currency I surely did not own. All I felt sure of was that everything we women were, men were not. They were brash, we were gentle. They were competitive, we were conciliatory. They thought with their heads, we felt with our hearts. They were indescribably mysterious—opposite and other. Along with most women of my generation, I would be unlearning this particular lesson many times over, as my search to unravel the mystery of men became more and more the search to unravel my own.

My own experience growing up, raised and schooled by women, is by no means typical. But my sense of living in a world apart from men—with different language, habits, customs—is, I believe, shared by many women and leaves many of us wondering, as we approach adulthood, how our worlds can ever overlap, how we can retain our identity while sharing common ground. Much has been written about woman-as-other, about men's love and fear of her mysteries. My intention in this book is to pursue the alternate course: to begin with the mystery that father presents to daughter, the awesome otherness of his presence, which then in various ways is echoed and embellished by other crucial men in her life: grandfathers and brothers, lovers and husbands, teachers and mentors. And from there I want to examine the subtle, complex, and lifelong process by which the daughter comes to understand and define the world of her father, and then the world of men, and gradually decides which of its teachings, its messages and mores to adapt for her own. (Concentrating on the daughter's formative years of development around the issues of love and work, I decided to stop before the daughter becomes a parent herself. At least another book could be written about mothers and sons).

My exploration of the panorama of men who share a woman's journey began, of course, with questions about her father, that first giant in her life. I was surprised at how haltingly and hazily the initial responses came. When I had interviewed women for my first book, *Sisters,* the memories rushed out, colorful and detailed, stories recounting years of shared times and territory. But this time, the stories were sketchier at first. The figures drawn often seemed more mythic than flesh and blood.

The most striking fact about father was, of course, his absence. (Here I should point out that for the most part the women in my study came from traditional families in which father worked outside the home and was the champion of that province and mother stayed at home with the children and was the linchpin there.) For most daughters father was simply gone all day working; many admitted not knowing, as children, where or at what. One woman in her thirties recalled a father who worked three jobs, gone from eight one morning till one the next morning. Her relationship with him was a nightly phone call at seven. Another woman spoke of how the "family must have seemed like a photo album collection" to her father, so distanced was he from their everyday lives. So the daughter may often seem as much an illusion to her father as he is an enigma to her.

Even at home the fathers of early memory were often absent, hidden behind books or newspapers, not to be disturbed from their important thoughts, their well-earned rest. For one woman in her fifties the image of her father was of a man deep in reverie behind his evening paper. Once able to stand the distance no longer, she threw herself in a rage on his newspaper. "Darling," he said, emerging from that faraway place where daughters were not allowed to tread, "you're everything to me." And as if those words closed the case forever, he retreated once more, leaving his daughter still ruffled and unsoothed, to face a future of tearing down that paper time and time again, as she searched for a man who would finally listen to her, let her into his world.

Writing about the father's role in his daughter's formative years, Simone de Beauvoir underlines his mythic presence:

> The life of the father has a mysterious prestige: the hours he spends at home, the room where he works, the objects he has around him, his pursuits, his hobbies, have a sacred character. He supports the family, and he is the responsible head of the family. As a rule his work takes him outside, and so it is through him that the family communicates with the rest of the world: he incarnates that immense, difficult and marvelous world of adventure; he personifies transcendence; he is God. This is what the child feels physically in the powerful arms that lift her up, in the strength of his frame against which she nestles.[1]

De Beauvoir was of course writing for a generation that recognized only subliminally its status as second sex. But for contemporary women who have begun to articulate their outrage, the struggle against father nevertheless remains an ancient one. For most daughters part of growing up means coming to terms with the mystery that surrounds father, decoding and learning his language, challenging his prestige, confronting his very godliness in a way that may be both terrifying and liberating. In the wake of the Women's Movement many of us have found ourselves at once rebelling against but also coveting our fathers' world. In the earliest throes of feminist anger we may have resisted its patriarchal values with zealous fury. Liberation often translated as emancipation from father. The early stages of struggle necessitated criticism and rage, distancing and separation from father, his male cohorts, and the patriarchy they stood for.

But in more recent years this clear and cleansing, but also tiring anger has been transformed into a more complex and unsettling ambivalence—about fathers whose approval is sought in the midst of turbulent rebellion, about lovers and husbands whose affection is needed in the midst of rage, about teachers and mentors whose counsel is valued in the midst of disdain for the hierarchy they may represent. After the last decades of change many of us have seen the world of our fathers—the world of work, of power, of money—gradually opening up for us, and the possibility is both tantalizing and frightening. Many of us wish to enter this formerly all-male territory, yet fear the stranglehold of its edicts and pressures. Or we would like to share its prizes and adventures, but question our entitlement to them or are all too wary of the risks and pitfalls that accompany them. Or beckoned by the world of our fathers, we feel guilty about deserting our mothers and their world of home and nurturance and family. Still, for many women who for years have defined ourselves in opposition to men, it is oddly disconcerting to find that men's choices may be becoming our own.

So the women I have chosen to study are those for whom personal and social changes have collided in various complicated ways that create conflict but also dazzling leaps of growth. For many of us, coming to adulthood has meant reexamining and renegotiating mother and father's lessons, questioning the old models they presented and beginning to fashion new ones, new images of masculine and feminine and what is appropriate or possible for each. "The central struggle for women of this generation," observed Stanford sociology professor Ann Swidler in an interview, "is to redefine the categories of male and female, father and mother, nurturer and nurtured. Our task is to reorganize the psychic elements of the early years into something more plausible for maturity."

My interviews for this book focus on women immersed in this process of redefinition of male and female, of themselves and the men in their lives. They are women in transition, women on the cusp of change. In all, I spoke with about seventy women in lengthy, detailed and intense personal interviews. They are women primarily in their twenties, thirties, and forties, because I felt that their life decisions were most dramatically altered by the tumultuous changes of the past decades. But I also talked with women at either end of the life cycle who are most certainly feeling the fallout from these changes as well. I also looked for a variety of background and history, of education and occupation, of sexual preference and family style. There are lawyers, secretaries, actresses, students, and mothers. Some of the women are well known for their recent achievements; some are daughters of celebrated fathers. But most are unknown and remain anonymous, except, I hope, in the power and persuasiveness of their stories.

Besides personal interviews, I also sought written autobiographies from women around the country, both through requests after lectures I gave and through ads placed in numerous publications, including *Mother Jones, The New York Review of Books,* the newsletters of Union W.A.G.E. and several other women's networks. This gave me broader access to women of disparate backgrounds whom I could not meet in person.

This excerpt from one of the letters in response to my ad explains the kind of dilemmas that drew women toward my subject:

I am married, pregnant with my first child, and an architect at a well-known design firm. The pressures were conflicting while I was growing up and are still. Before I became pregnant, my father used to call me out of meetings at work to ask when I was going to have a baby. He would then hang up, call my sister, who had her first child last summer, and ask when she was going to get a job and *do* something with her life!

In all, I heard from some one hundred women from all over the country, who wrote voluminous and passionate autobiographies, about their relationships with men from father forward and the influence of these relationships on their choices in love and work.

A healthy person, goes Freud's often quoted dictum, is one who is able to work and love. Indeed, working and loving were the two pivots of my interviews and provide the design of this book. For the women I am studying are preoccupied with this double quest. They yearn for satisfaction in both work and love, and most of the time feel entitled to it. Yet too often they feel that success in work and happiness in love are at odds with each other or that having one means having to go without the other.

My research suggests that the girl's relationship with her father is enormously influential on her chances for fulfillment in loving and working. My major interest in this book is to explore the father's influence on his daughter in these two important realms from earliest childhood forward and then to explore what she makes of this influence as an adult in her relationships and in her work.

In loving and working the father is his daughter's first and most magnetic male model. Lora Heims Tessman, clinical psychologist at the Massachusetts Institute for Technology Psychiatric Service, has coined useful terms to describe the father's potential influence in love and work. From a very early age, Tessman suggests, a daughter needs her father to recognize and respond to her "erotic excitement" and "endeavor excitement." "Endeavor excitement," according to Tessman, includes the daughter's work and play efforts, any task-oriented goal she has set for herself aside from personal relationships, where the pleasure is in creation or mastery either privately or out in the world. Her father's ability to take her efforts seriously enables her to do the same, from her first awkward mudpies to science projects to poems to legal briefs.

By "erotic excitement" Tessman has in mind the daughter's blossoming sexual feelings about herself, her father, and the opposite sex. In his response to his daughter's erotic excitement, she says, "A father walks a tricky fence. Ideally if he can respond with tender interest, without denying that [his daughter] is lovingly involved with him and has many fantasies about him, it helps her both to de-sexualize the intensity of her feelings and yet keep the notion that passions are good and to be looked forward to in later life." How the father treads this fine line has a great deal to do with how his daughter will fare choosing and loving men later on.

There is a further delicate balance between supporting the daughter's erotic excitement and her endeavor excitement, and some fathers may feel more comfortable or secure acknowledging one rather than the other. Some fathers may enjoy the erotic quality of their daughter's devotion but perhaps be threatened by her growing competence and unable to encourage her endeavors. Other fathers might be thrilled by their daughter's achievements but feel awkward about or threatened by her girlish sexuality.

As I reviewed the interviews and autobiographies, paying special attention to these messages about love and work, five distinct categories of father-daughter relationships emerged. They are: the Patriarch, the Pal, the Bystander, the Charmer, and the Absent Father.

In Part One of this book, "Fathers and Daughters," after an overview of important developmental issues, each of five chapters will explore the prominent father-daughter types.

The Patriarch is the authoritarian father whose messages about work and love are law. The Pal is the comrade father, the playmate and intellectual companion who is often more comfortable with his daughter's mind than with her blossoming sexuality. The Bystander stands aside from his responsibilities as a father, and his lessons about love and work are often too fuzzy to be discernible. The Charmer is another incarnation of the Pal, who often from disappointment in his own marriage makes his daughter into his plaything, or in the most extreme cases his lover. He is usually more nurturing of his daughter's sexual self than of her developing competence. Finally the Absent Father, removed by death, divorce, or desertion, often leaves his daughter in a vacuum of guidance about love and work, leaves her perpetually searching to replace the intimate connection she has lost. Beyond each particular father, each type also epitomizes a more archetypal image of masculinity, a certain kind of man whom the daughter must confront as she moves forward into the world.

I defined the father-daughter types in terms of the kind of model of masculinity each father provided, the kind of marriage each was part of, and the kind of relationship each forged with his daughter from infancy to adulthood. I paid particular attention to the messages each father passed on to his daughter about love and work and to the emphasis he gave to supporting endeavor excitement, erotic excitement, or both. If the daughter's early image of masculinity was significantly modified by a relationship with brothers, I considered that influence as well. I also considered each daughter's relationship with her mother and the counterbalance it provided. Finally, given these profound early influences, I then followed up the daughter's later choices in love and work. Did the men she chose to love follow in her father's footsteps? How did the work she chose show the influence of father's work or his guidance?

Each of the father types can be seen in a kind of continuum from the most ideal and balanced to the most distorted and troubled examples. For the Patriarch, for instance, this covers a range from an ideal father who might be a steady, guiding mentor to one who might be a rigid and punitive authoritarian—and numerous combinations in between. The five types often overlap, the same father falling into different categories, given his age or stage or daughter's shifting perception of him.

The portraits in this book are drawn primarily from the daughter's point of view to emphasize how daughters see and define their fathers and make use of their messages to define themselves. If at times these portraits seem unduly harsh or angry, this focus may have more to do with the distortions of daughters' fantasies than with the realities of fathers' limitations. The shifting nature of children's perceptions of father (echoed in the memories of grown daughters as well) is explained in an essay, "The Forgotten Father," by psychologist John Munder Ross:

> The nature of internalization is such that no father is ever swallowed whole by his child. Rather, our fathers are composite sketches based on many encounters with us and on images of these drawn by a childish hand. . . . In psychic reality [there is not] any one father. The moments with father are many, and since he is human, he is also changeable. Moreover, during the earliest years of ego development each shift in mood and attitude is hugely exaggerated and concretized, making for many different persons. These characteristics are subject to alterations in the child's ego states, which seize on certain impressions as abiding certitudes: the feeling that father loves us may make him all good and all powerful; an instant of anger harshly expressed may suggest an ogre. Children may want to forget certain of the father's vicissitudes, to deny and later repress them, although the engrams endure at some level and cannot be erased.[2]

I interviewed a number of fathers as well as daughters, and their side of the story will also be included. I often found the fathers to be more guarded and protective than their daughters, as if looking back on their actions and decisions they had a higher stake in proving they had done right. But our conversations also humbled me to the deeply challenging nature of the task of fathering and the awesome lack of preparation most fathers feel. I was haunted by this admission from philosopher and futurist George Leonard, the father of four daughters, who I believe speaks for many of the generation of men who fathered my generation of daughters:

> We came back after World War Two supposedly men of the world. I've been an officer and pilot—flown missions. I must really know what's going on, right? I knew nothing. But the thing is we were given a sanction. Not only the sanction, but the imperative to have children. The message we got in World War Two—fight this war, you brave men, come back to this golden future, all kind of misty and Vaseline over the lens. You came back and married this beautiful blonde and you were going to have these children and a house and a car and you were going to have this wonderful life. You'd done it all now. That's all you need. We came back thinking we knew something, and we knew nothing. We were totally ignorant. We didn't have the faintest training in parenting. Or in being married. Or in communication skills. I now look at some of these things that are often associated with California, new modes of communication, being open and so forth. And they are largely joshed about—but if only I'd had some of those. It wasn't even available. It wasn't even known that you could reveal yourself. To reveal a weakness is to be weak. To reveal ignorance is to be ignorant. Therefore, nothing is revealed. Therefore, we become absolute menaces to the countryside.

Listening to both sides of the story, I tried to stay tuned to the difficulties of the father's challenges as well as to the depths of the daughter's needs. I realized that every daughter might yearn for a father with the conviction of a Patriarch, the enthusiasm of a Pal, the detachment of a Bystander, and the magic of a Charmer. But, meanwhile, every father can respond only within his own capabilities and his own limitations, doing the best he can while juggling his own needs and uncertainties.

As I explored the strengths and drawbacks of each of the father-daughter pairs, the points of connection and the pangs of separation, I began to delineate a model of a healthy, balanced meeting of father and daughter, where each could thrive. I looked for the ways the father could encourage his daughter to bloom in love, prosper in work, to the benefit of both, the detriment of neither. I sought an ideal in which, as Rudolf Eckstein, training analyst and clinical professor at UCLA has put it, "The father can maintain the relationship with his daughter, but can let her go without feeling deserted or deserting." Or as marriage and family counselor Mary Dwan suggested, "A successful father is one who lets everyone in his family know that all the individuals in the family are equally important to him and that his work is important also. To grow up healthy, children have to feel they are more important than the work. In the future I envision, there would be no difference between a good father and a good mother. Both would give their children the sense that the children are more important than any other work."

Against the backdrop of the father-daughter relationship, Part Two of this book—"Daughters, Lovers, and Others"—will explore several of the significant men in the lives of grown women and their influence on adult development in love and work. A chapter on Mr. Wrong and Mr. Right will investigate these two powerful figures of reality and fantasy, these potent —and often debilitating—images in women's love lives. The one is the cad, the man who can be counted on to treat a woman badly—and is often chosen for this very reason. The other is the prince, the idealized hero who, the woman fantasizes, will make life perfect and will save her from herself. These Bastard and Prince fantasies (like their counterparts of Whore and Madonna) are often psychologically intertwined and have their roots in the daughter's early distorted images of her father, as this chapter will discuss.

A chapter on mentors will then illuminate these influential guiding figures in the working lives of many contemporary women. The central question of this chapter will be how the mentor-protégée relationship repeats and synthesizes aspects of the daughter's relationship with father and the lover's with her beloved yet becomes more complex than an amalgam of both.

Taken together, the chapters in Part One on the father-daughter types and those in Part Two on these later influential male figures will, I hope, create a kind of contemporary collage of masculinity. Piece by piece, the interviews will put together a composite portrait, the face a woman sees when she thinks of maleness. First it is her father's face or her brother's; later its features bear more of a resemblance to lovers and husbands, or its demeanor is modified by teachers and mentors. Jung puts the name "animus" to this face and calls it "The deposit, as it were, of all woman's ancestral experiences of man . . . rather like an assembly of fathers or dignitaries of some kind who lay down incontestable . . . ex cathedra judgments."[3] Father's messages may often become the inner tapes ascribed to the animus.

But this face, this animus, which is often projected onto the faces of the men in our lives, may perhaps be more deeply fathomed when we are really able to see ourselves. For the search that begins when we are nestled by father, continues when we are enhanced by lovers and comforted by husband, then changes when we are supported by teachers and mentors does not finally take wing until we're on our own, facing our own joys and demons. The Conclusion of the book, "The Men in Our Inner Lives," will discuss the complex images of masculinity we incorporate into our image of ourselves, culling from father's messages and lovers' affections, brothers' teases and mentors' wisdom, from wildest fantasies and most inexplicable dreams, from darkest nightmares and most luminous wishes.

Emma Jung has written tellingly of the woman's path to discover this animus. That she wrote these words fifty years ago emphasizes only that each generation must redefine this quest for itself:

> Woman has learned to see that she cannot become like a man because first and foremost she is a woman and must be one. However, the fact remains that a certain sum of masculine spirit has ripened in woman's consciousness and must find its place and effectiveness in her personality. To learn to know these factors, to coordinate them so that they can play their part in a meaningful way, is an important part of the animus problem. . . .
>
> The first stage on the right road is, therefore, the withdrawal of the projection by recognizing it as such, and thus freeing it from the object. This first act of discrimination, simple as it may seem, nonetheless means a difficult achievement and often a painful renunciation. Through this withdrawal of the projection we recognize that we are not dealing with an entity outside ourselves but a quality within; and we see before us the task of learning to know the nature and effect of this factor, this "man in us," in order to distinguish him from ourselves.[4]

This book begins as a story of women's relationships with men, how we are taught and led and influenced by our fathers and brothers, lovers and mentors. But this book ends as a story of women's autonomy, how we integrate from these relationships what is useful, discard what is not, move forward in the world on our own. This book begins with our dependence on our fathers but ends where we are learning to take care of ourselves. It begins with our fantasies about our lovers' largess but ends where we are appreciating what we can provide for ourselves. It begins with our lessons from our mentors but ends where we are learning to guide and trust ourselves.

PART ONE

Fathers and Daughters

CHAPTER

FATHER-DAUGHTER SINGLES/ FATHER-DAUGHTER DOUBLES

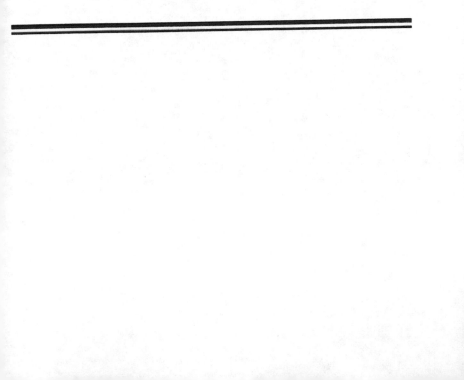

On the courts of childhood, father teaches daughter how to play the game. At first she is all fingers and feet, swooshing at air while the ball sails behind her, and the game seems a caricature of itself. He must repeat the most basic clues, the rudiments of the game. "Hold the racket tight, as if it were an extension of your arm," he must say. "Get the racket back," he must urge, while in her childish hand the racket feels immense, unwieldy. But he keeps hitting the ball back to her until the pace becomes familiar, the racket almost manageable, aiding her strength, not sabotaging it.

And then she begins learning the ground strokes, stepping low and deep into the forehand, pivoting for the backhand, always watching him for clues, mirroring his moves. At times she hears the solid and satisfying ping of the ball hit squarely in the center of the racket, and then she knows she is getting the knack, hardly even needs his "Good shot, Lizzy," because gradually her own voice is telling her that, building her confidence in whispers. But other times the game is all frustration. Every backhand stutters into the net, every forehand loops miles upward into the air, over the fence, lost in grasses, ruined in puddles. She is a failure. She will never master the game. She is enraged and despondent. That is when she most counts on him not to leave her, not to let her down. That is when she most depends on his patient repetitions, his steady return of the ball.

Slowly, then, her limbs grow stronger and her eye grows shrewder, and father begins to train her to use her power in the game. Back at the base line he has her practicing her serve, tossing the ball into the air higher than her height and bearing down on it from above, feeling energy and will converge upon it. And then he brings her volleying to the net, and the pace quickens, suddenly more dangerous. She learns to grab the velocity coming from the other side and turn it to her advantage.

And finally, as the years pass and he sees her becoming a woman, getting ready to leave him, his teachings become most subtle and complex. Now he must teach her strategy and technique, gamesmanship and finesse. "Play the alleys," he advises, or "Drop a shot just over the net after a hard volley to the base line." Sometimes she follows his tips and makes the point, wins the game. Other times she strikes out on her own, eyeing her own shots, devising her own plans, trying out her wings. For just as he is fervently using these last precious moments of childhood to teach her the rules of the game, she is dead set on proving that there are no rules. Or if she admits to rules, she must somehow make them her own. And this is by far the most difficult and painful part of the lesson. For he has spent all of this time—loving and confused, jubilant and angry time—training her to play the game, and now in order to see what she has learned, he must allow her other partners, other matches, her own victories and defeats. The wisdom of his training will become apparent only when he lets her go.

On the courts of childhood summers my father and I keep the ball in endless play. We do not compete, only rally. Back and forth in the brittle weekend heat, back and forth in the murky shadows of late afternoon, everything I hit comes back to me: the shots that miss by a mile ("Just over, just over," he says, forever indulgent), the lobs that run amok in the air. As wild as my game is, his game is utterly steady, graceful, imperturbable. The secret of his teaching is to let me use his strength until I find my own, to take advantage of his steadiness until I generate my own.

"Move your ass," he says. "Keep your eye on the ball." I dash for the ball, panting, hair flying, face blazing red. He stretches out his racket, and his reach seems to span the court. Hardly moving his feet, he is always, effortlessly at the ball. This is part of his magic, part of his style, and tumbling and fumbling, at sixes and sevens, I yearn to copy it.

The other secret of his game is this: Even on the hottest day, with the sun unrelenting upon us, my father does not take off his sweater. On my side of the court, I may be melting in a pool. On his side he's playing as if tropical breezes are gently cooling him. A matter of pride, of technique, of character: The sweater stays on. My father stays cool and keeps his cool. On the fingers of one hand could I count the times I have seen him lose his temper, even raise his voice. Indeed, in later years he is personified by a reporter for *The New York Times* as a "pipe smoker so placid that he gives new meaning to the expression soft-spoken." This is part of the mystique, part of the mythology that he brings to the game. And it is also part of what I struggle so valiantly to mirror, meanwhile trying to tune out the childish, contradictory voices churning inside.

But there are other crannies in his mythology, other stories passed and repeated until they become fused with my own memories, although strictly speaking I do not remember them myself. One of them concerns the day I was brought home from the hospital, a day in early May, warm with spring, high expectations, and, presumably, apprehension. My mother carries me tight in her arms, a squirmy, red-faced bundle. My father carries the formula, just the right amount to launch me through the weekend. But at the door of their apartment suddenly he drops the bottle onto the floor. The milk spills in every direction, bathing the neighbors' stoops in pools of sustenance forever lost. I howl; mother howls; I imagine father howls, too. And on each of my birthdays after that the story is repeated, passed like a torch from year to year, and with each year glowing brighter, funnier, less cataclysmic.

So this is another father beneath the implacable tennis sweater. The one who cannot for the life of him hold on to the formula, the one who cannot open a can of tuna fish or boil an egg, the one who will doze in an armchair for half an hour after dinner, wake up in a daze, asking "What was I doing?" and then not be able to sleep again until dawn. And I, as an infant, as a toddler, as a girl, must get to know the cool father as well as the flustered father, the capable father as well as the awkward father, the father who knows everything as well as the father who is learning, one step forward, two steps back, three to the side, just as I am. I must get to know him by mirroring and rebelling, by identifying and rejecting what I see in him, what I need for myself. And I also get to know him, to join him and retreat from him by finding his resonances in boys and other men and naming that journey love. But all this is the work of a lifetime, only dimly visible to the young girl, as if peering through a door just ajar, she tries from the swirl of a cocktail skirt, the clatter of glasses, a few false laughs to know what it means to be a grown-up. It would take years to fling that door wide open, years to know my father's many selves, to try to see the whole man, and in seeing him, to try to see myself.

"Bend your knees," my father says. "Don't let the ball get behind you." Weekend after summer weekend we are on these courts, honing my skills. Often he has already played an hour or two of doubles, my mother his partner, their styles divergent but finely meshed after years of marriage. They play politely, with laughter, but with concentration, determination. They play to win and often do.

Sometimes my mother sits on the sidelines and watches my father and me play afterward. Sometimes she takes photographs, recording and interpreting the game. Tennis and pictures are motifs of their marriage, and when my father turns sixty my mother makes him a collage of tennis photographs from thirty years of marriage. Some are snapshots from these formative summer games, others from vacations around the world. Always the same pose: the two of them, arms around each other, rackets poised, on a court in the Caribbean, on a court flanked by the Alps. In one they are wearing hats I gave them, his-and-hers hats that say Hemingway and de Beauvoir. Sporting the hats, they look sheepish but proud.

Tennis is their game, but my sister and I are also allowed to share it. Even when my mother leaves us alone to practice ground strokes on the courts of summer, she remains a crucial part of the game. She is always there between the lines, singles and doubles, interpreting, encouraging, offering her own set of rules, her own world view.

Of the many father-daughter excursions of early childhood, one stands out and seems to sum up the others, those special times when just the two of us ventured together into the wide world. I am about two. My father is to take me downtown to visit his men's club and have a treat. My mother stays behind, but first she dresses me for this special public appearance. And I am dressed to the nines—a hand-knit Parisian dress of the fluffiest wool, and over that a navy and green plaid coat and a pair of velvet leggings. It is winter, and I am not supposed to feel the slightest chill.

Papa's club is a wonderland of high ceilings and gilt-edged chandeliers, leather armchairs and overstuffed couches.

Everywhere there are men smoking and playing cards, reading magazines and discussing unfathomable matters. I toddle around this grove of pants legs as if in an enchanted forest, wide-eyed and spellbound. My father greets some friends, and then we head to the restaurant. I am skittish with expectation.

I order vanilla ice cream. But when it comes, there is something grossly wrong. It is French vanilla, and it has tiny black flecks all through it. I take one look at it, my favorite vanilla ice cream now suddenly so foreign and tarnished, and burst into tears. "What is the matter?" my father asks, alarmed and confused. I cannot bear to say. I continue to sob. Men in three-piece suits turn disapprovingly in our direction. Waiters gather around. "What is it?" my father presses again. Finally I gather my courage. "It's dirty," I cry. Everyone is silent. Several laugh. I am mortified and undone. And I am thinking that in my mother's world the ice cream would be clean. Having ventured into my father's realm on wings of desire and expectation, I no longer feel like flying. No amount of paternal sympathy or cajoling will change the course to which I am inalterably bound: home to mother.

The pull between the world of mother and the world of father is one of the basic rhythms of childhood, and nowhere is it felt more intensely and ambivalently than in the years from one to three that are considered the pre-oedipal period. Until fairly recently—and certainly in my own childhood and those of the women I am studying—the line between mother's and father's realms has been rigidly drawn. On one side lies the cozy safety of the world of mother, the known and circumscribed world of home, where needs are met with reasonable certainty, where activities are controlled, where strangeness is at a minimum, where, in short, the ice cream is kept clean. On the other side lie the unknown reefs of the world of father, that remote and mysterious world beyond the front door into which he strides every morning and from which he emerges, battle-weary and worn, every evening. In his world strangeness predominates, choice is everywhere; the lack of control makes events in his world both dazzling and dangerous. His world may be a wonderland, but in it even ice cream becomes unfamiliar, contains the possibility of threat. But as differences are accepted and threats faced, leaps of growth also take place that are at the heart of this period.

The pre-oedipal period is one of separation and individuation between mother and daughter, and the father is a necessary facilitator of this process. He provides an alternative to the snug symbiosis between mother and child. Explains theorist Ernest Abelin, who with Margaret Mahler has extensively researched this period, "From the fact that the vital task of a child [at this stage] is to achieve individuation through a process of intrapsychic separation from the symbiotic mother, it does not necessarily follow that this is an affair between just mother and child. Quite to the contrary, the task might be *impossible for either of them to master without their having the father to turn to.*"[1]

Psychoanalytic thinking has shifted in its perception of the father's role in this period of his daughter's development. Child psychiatrist Philip Spielman observes, "The previous attitude was that the father was an intruder into the relationship between mother and child, disturbing the intimacy between them. But more recently, the father is seen to provide an escape from that bond, a support for the budding ego against reengulfment. In Phyllis Greenacres's phrase, the father represents the child's 'love affair with the world.' " More recent, but still traditional psychoanalytic thinkers view the father of this phase as drawing and attracting the child into the wide world of things and people. Margaret Mahler dubs him "the knight in shining armor" who at times may be a "rescuer from the 'bad' mother," or at least another buffer against the child's emerging fears of being abandoned or punished by the mother. States Mahler, "The father image comes toward the child . . . 'from outer space' as it were . . . as something new and exciting, at just the time when the toddler is experiencing a feverish quest for expansion."[2]

Most recently theorists have begun to speculate about the impact of the changes in family roles on the daughter's development and identification with her parents. New research must grapple with the changes brought about now that traditional parental roles are no longer so severely circumscribed. Now it is more and more likely that both parents work or that mother works, while father stays home as the main care-giver, or again, that one parent becomes the head of a single-parent family and is both the main care-giver *and* the main breadwinner. But the result of these changes will be the story of the generation of women who are the daughters of my own generation, and for now remain beyond the scope of this book.

Looking at the lives of women in their twenties, thirties, and forties, psychologist Lora Tessman considers the "feverish quest for expansion" during individuation from mother a fertile time for excitement between father and daughter to develop. First she describes an "endeavor excitement," a burgeoning interest in work and play efforts, which begins during the child's second year and comes to be associated with autonomy and competence and influences her later confidence and direction in work. (Again, in a family where mother works and cares about her work or indeed in a family where mother stays home—but has the time and inclination to stimulate her daughter's efforts—she, too, will inspire endeavor excitement. But the focus of this book will be on the particular ways that father generates this kind of excitement.)

Tessman also postulates an "erotic excitement," a child's blossoming sexual feelings about herself, her father, and the opposite sex, which begin in the third or fourth year, gather momentum during the oedipal period, and subtly influence later choices of lovers and pleasure in sexuality. Infantile excitement, Tessman feels, needs soothing and relieving from one or the other parent as a prerequisite to establishing the "foundations of the sensuous self." But as the child's sexual identity evolves during the pre-oedipal period, a different quality of excitement, directed primarily at father, begins to emerge. Explains Tessman:

As the little girl progresses in her individuation from the mother it seems to me that she develops a different kind of excitement, one that involves wishes more complicated than being soothed or sated. By age 3 or 4 years focal excitement toward the father appears to include both an active, loving exuberance and passive wishes to adapt to a new kind of mutuality with him. This inner excitement is not to be soothed, for it seeks not only acknowledgment and acceptance by the father as a feeling toward him, but in addition its utilization in a variety of loving collaborations. In her fantasy these may emphasize erotic, domestic, companionable, or "joint endeavor" adventures and may be based on a beginning appreciative or hopeful perception of both similarities and differences between father and self.[3]

As the inner excitement of the pre-oedipal period continues to percolate, the daughter's fantasies of "joint endeavor" adventures with her father become more and more passionate, more and more preoccupying. Her perceptions of the similarities and differences between herself and father and mother grow in clarity and intensity. By the time the daughter is three or four, the pull between the world of the mother and the world of the father seems to become concentrated into the psychodynamics of the family triangle. The torrid and tumultuous oedipal drama has begun.

By the time I am five, my relationship with my father is in ritualized full bloom. Every night he comes home at exactly seven o'clock, and every night for about an hour before, I prepare for his return. First I sit on the side of my mother's tub while she takes a bath, and we chat together in steamy privacy. I savor these moments as co-conspirators in the world of women. Then I take my own bath, and in later years my sister presides over me the way I preside over mother, keeping me company, handing me towels, completing the circle. I put on a nightgown and always the frilliest of robes, and usually the doorbell sounds just as I am tying the bow at my neck.

Through the corridors I dash—no bride ever fluttered faster—and opening the door, I greet my prince with hugs and kisses. My mother greets him, too, but I see to it that my exuberance overshadows hers. Then, as he hangs up his coat and hat, I take his briefcase from him, and it is there I unleash the full force of my excitement. For every morning he leaves with his briefcase only half full of papers, but when he returns every night he has it filled to the brim with magazines. Even before I can read, these magazines are magical. They are totems of the world he works in every day, the strange and beckoning world beyond the front door. I pull them out of the briefcase one by one, each fairly incandescent with promises, lure and taboo, and I pore over them on the living-room floor. First I head for the pictures: the rainbow-colored spreads of other people's houses in the decorating magazines; the exotic fashion photographs; the drama of the newsweeklies, where my eyes widen at pictures of strewn battlefields and starving children, images I seek out, yet somehow feel sullied for seeing, old before my time. My father shows me the difference between the articles and the advertisements, some of which he has written. The ads are no less magical than the rest. Possibly they are more so.

As I learn to read, I begin to make sense of the captions, and soon I am reading the articles, too. Reading them, but never entirely understanding them, I piece together a skewed and myopic picture of the world where wives learn "Ten Warning Signs of Your Husband's Affair" and husbands learn "Ten Ways to Hustle to the Top." This is what I imagine the grown-up world to be, ordered by rules that are different from the ones I know at home—and scandal when the rules are undermined. This is also the world I imagine my father moves in when he leaves the cozy chambers of our apartment, and there is nothing I both want and fear more than to join him there. Sitting on the floor, riffling through my father's magazines, I do join him there in my fantasies. And one of the ways I join him, I now believe, is by imagining, by imperceptibly foreshadowing the day when I will write for these very magazines myself. That will be my key into the magical and forbidden world in which my father moves.

The oedipal period, the years from about three to five, is an intense and romantic one between father and daughter, rife with fantasies that leave tracings on daughter's later choices in love and work. The most potent of these fantasies is described by Freud's classic formulation of the realignment of the family triangle. In Freud's view, when, around age three, the little girl discovers she has no penis, she blames her first love, her mother, for this lack and turns away from her with anger, hostility, and contempt. She turns toward her father, who not only has the desired appendage, but, she imagines, will provide her with one as well. Eventually she makes an unconscious symbolic equation, and the wish for a penis from father becomes a wish for a baby from him. Later she will gradually abandon the fantasy of having a child with father, pay attention to her identification with mother as another adult sexual woman, and turn toward the more realistic goal of bearing a child with a beloved man of her own. But for now during this oedipal phase, in her fantasies she and father are romantically and sexually linked, and mother becomes a feared and hated rival as well as a symbol of the helplessness and dependence of an earlier infantile time.

But contemporary psychoanalytic theorists do not believe that the daughter simply transfers her affection and interest from mother to father during the feminine Oedipus complex and gives up her mother entirely. Rather, recent psychoanalytic research suggests that the relationship between mother and daughter continues from the pre-oedipal period to be crucial and that the relationship to father is woven in with it, both as addition and alternative. As Nancy Chodorow explains in her recent reappraisal of psychoanalytic material, *The Reproduction of Mothering*, "The oedipal girl alternates between positive attraction to her father as escape from her mother, and reseeking of her mother as a safe and familiar refuge against her father's frustrating and frightening aspects."[4] The high charge of oedipal fantasies results from the essential ambivalence of the triangle: for the daughter at once wishes to get rid of her mother and yet also wishes to have her to herself. She feels herself to be caught in the middle of not one, but two powerful romances, dazzled by her father but also deeply needful of the bond with her mother. These complex configurations of feelings dominate the oedipal period, but are often not resolved until adolescence or even later.

Some psychotherapists refer to this period as one of "family integration," choosing to emphasize the struggle to bring the family together rather than the oedipal strife pulling it apart. Marriage and family counselor Mary Dwan explains, "During these years, the child learns to be attracted to a person of the opposite sex. The daughter learns to see something special about the opposite sex because the person of the same sex—her mother—finds her father special. But she also learns that her attraction and love must be shared. The struggle of these years is to integrate and share." Child psychiatrist Richard Gardner, who specializes in the treatment of children of divorce, further illuminates these issues by describing his clinical approach with children of this age:

I try to help [the child] gain a more accurate picture of [her] parents, their assets and liabilities, the areas in which they can provide [her] with meaningful gratifications and those in which they cannot. [She] is helped to accept the fact that [she] cannot completely possess either of [her] parents and that the affection and attention of each of them must be *shared* with other members of the family. This sharing concept is an important one to impart. The child must be helped to appreciate that no one can possess another person completely: [her] father shares mother with the children; [her] mother shares the father with the children; and [she] has no choice but to share [her father] with [her mother] and siblings. In the context of sharing, however, [she] *must be reassured that, although* [she] *may not get as much as* [she] *might want,* [she] *will still get something.* [5]

How mother and father handle the ambiguities of the realigning family triangle of course influences how the daughter is able to handle her own ambivalence and gradually resolve it. Philip Spielman explains how the emotional climate in which the shift from mother to father takes place is a vitally important factor:

Optimally, the mother permits the shift, particularly when it takes on sexual overtones; she neither pushes the girl toward premature heterosexuality nor abandons her watchful care of the child. The father's attitude to the shift must be equally appropriate, both sexually and nonsexually. This same shift must then be repeated during adolescence when the nature of the emotional climate is again a crucial factor.[6]

Summarizing contemporary psychoanalytic thought on this delicate and double-edged transition, Nancy Chodorow writes:

Every step of the way, as the analysts describe it, a girl develops her relationship to her father while looking back at her mother —to see if her mother is envious, to make sure she is, in fact, separate, to see if she can in this way win her mother, to see if she is really independent. Her turn to her father is both an attack on her mother and an expression of her love for her.[7]

Just as the girl's mother during the oedipal phase walks a fine line between showing her daughter love and giving her permission to seek love from her father, so, too, the father must keep a delicate balance. His role is to make himself available to his daughter and her fantasies and yet, paradoxically, not overly available. He must let her know that he loves her and finds her attractive, but this affection must be offered in an appropriately paternal manner, neither too withdrawn nor too sexualized.

In her important essay "Fathers and Daughters: The Significance of 'Fathering' in the Psychosexual Development of the Girl," psychologist Marjorie Leonard describes the effect on the daughter when the father is insufficiently involved at this critical stage:

> When a father holds himself aloof there is insufficient opportunity for day-to-day comparing and testing of the fantasied object with the real person. Moreover, consistent lack of attention is experienced as rejection which is destructive to the sense of self-esteem derived from the knowledge of being loved by an admired object. Ignored by the father, the girl has no real basis for competition with her mother and lacks incentive to relinquish her pre-oedipal attachments.[8]

Writer Anne Roiphe, reminiscing in a magazine essay about her relationship with her classically remote father, adds personal testimony to Leonard's observations:

> Oedipus is a cruel master and makes us love our fathers even if they are absent, away at war, hurried in work or sealed off in their cocoons of masculine activities—their clubs, their sports, their politics. . . . My love was unrequited, not only in the oedipal sense but in the paternal sense as well; and when I grew up and chose a man for myself, I did the very thing I intended to avoid. I married a man handsome like my father—tall and immaculately dressed—who did not and could not love me.[9]

In the ambivalences of the oedipal years, in the push and pull between the safety of mother and the allure of father, between adoring father and casting off mother, between needing mother and scorning father, the daughter makes a blueprint of attitudes that affect later choices in love, later decisions about work. Family therapists Lily Pincus and Christopher Dare in their book *Secrets in the Family* call this oedipal time a "tangled and bewildering mixture of love, hate, jealousies, rivalries, sexual wishes, fears, and expectations."[10] In the untangling lie clues to the daughter's future. Will the daughter of the absent father, like writer Anne Roiphe, try to resolve her unrequited love by seeking a man exactly in her father's image? Or will she hold herself aloof from men, making sure she is not abandoned the way her mother was? Will she, if the daughter of a writer, choose to become a writer herself, wanting to emulate him, identify with him, join his world, never lose him? Or will the same daughter of a writer—if her mother never worked as most mothers of daughters in my sample did not—choose her mother's route instead, feeling cozier that way, safer, less guilty, wanting to join her mother's world, never lose her? In the oedipal drama, will she cast her lot with father or mother, with neither, or—pulled in opposite directions—with both? These are some of the questions that the chapters on the five father-daughter types will consider.

Eventually the daughter wrenches away from the feverish familial involvement of the oedipal years and moves into another realm—school. At six I take that quantum leap into another world, propelled by reading, writing, and arithmetic. At seven I am spending my first nights away from home, sleeping over in the widening world of my peers. And at eight I am making ritual of the world of school with the energy and excitement I used to unleash on father, the intensity and curiosity I used to save for mother. Every day I come home from school and sequester myself in my room, door closed against intrusion. My new desk, procured from one of my father's clients, is in place by the window. When I sit down at it, my status immeasurably increases. I have glimmers of the omnipotence I imagine my father feels at his own grand mahogany desk. (One day my straitlaced first-grade teacher visits our apartment, and showing her around, I proudly point to my father's desk. "This is where my father chases the buck," I say, not knowing what I'm saying, mimicking the phrase my father uses, leaving my teacher stunned.)

Sitting at my desk every day after school, I enter my own world, my own ritual. I run my fingers lovingly over the smooth wood surface, past the sharpened pencils that boast "Lizzy, Lizzy, Lizzy," in red, green, and blue, the erasers in the shape of elephants and pandas. Then my hands rest on the oversized looseleaf notebook beckoning me in the middle of the desk. I pick it up, turn in my seat to face the empty room, and my fantasy begins.

In my fantasy I am the teacher and the empty room is a sea of pupils. My notebook is a rollbook that I have arranged exactly the way I see my teacher does: all the girls in my class listed in alphabetical order along with their grades on imaginary papers I have pretended to assign. Every day I turn toward the empty room and teach the imaginary students exactly what I learned that day in school. I question them, I correct them, I lecture them unflaggingly on what is right and what is wrong. Every day I replay the day's events, shifting my role from the powerless to the powerful. In this way I reinforce the limits of my new terrain, reminding myself of its rules and messages, readying myself for the time when I will be leader rather than led. Slowly I am also building an identity, a world that is separate from the world of my parents. The wrenching tugs of the oedipal triangle have for the moment gone underground.

From the time the daughter goes to school till she reaches puberty—these are the years Freud called the latency period. During latency, Freud felt, sexuality recedes as an issue, and oedipal drives and fantasies stay dormant. More recent psychoanalytic theorists have redefined latency as a time when, perhaps, no *new* instinctual urges or issues develop, rather than one in which sexual concerns do not exist at all. If the issues of the oedipal period have, at least for the time being, been ameliorated, during latency the daughter may begin to have fantasies not about father, but about boys her own age. Reports Eleanor Galenson after a meeting of contemporary psychoanalysts:

> The general psychoanalytic proposition is that the onset of latency is signalled by the relinquishment of oedipal wishes as the result of fear of loss of the mother's love, fear of penetration by the father's penis, and realistic disappointment in the wish for a child, and that there is usually a concomitant decrease of sexual drive intensity and shift to peer relationships.[11]

Latency is typically circumscribed by the opportunities of the world of school: learning and role training, making friends, mastering games and skills, developing a conscience, delineating what is right and wrong. For Erik Erikson, the central struggle of this stage concerns "industry versus inferiority":

> With the oncoming latency period, the normally advanced child forgets, or rather sublimates, the necessity to "make" people by direct attack or to become papa and mama in a hurry: he now learns to win recognition by producing things. . . . He has experienced a sense of finality regarding the fact that there is no workable future within the womb of the family, and thus becomes ready to apply himself to given skills and tasks. . . . He develops a sense of industry—i.e., he adjusts himself to the inorganic laws of the tool world.[12]

But if the child cannot develop this sense of industry, then, Erikson feels, the danger lies in feelings of inadequacy and inferiority:

> If he despairs of his tools and skills or of his status among his tool partners, he may be discouraged from identification with them and with a section of the tool world. To lose the hope of such "industrial" association may pull him back to the more isolated,

less tool-conscious familial rivalry of the oedipal time. . . . Many a child's development is disrupted when family life has failed to prepare him for school life, or when school life fails to sustain the promises of earlier stages. . . .[13]

Between father and daughter the intensity of the earlier years is often put on hold during latency. But even if erotic excitement has cooled, endeavor excitement still flourishes. Father may foster his daughter's budding sense of competence and of industry by sharing his skills with her, taking her on trips, including her from time to time in the activities of his workplace, so that she begins to sense her possibilities expanding, her capabilities strengthening. As at earlier stages, father may facilitate his daughter's movement away from home and out into the world, specifically into the world of school.

Lora Tessman reports a patient's testimony to her father's encouragement during a pivotal juncture of latency—her first day of school. "My father had a fine sense of humor and a lot of energy," this patient told Tessman. "And yet he was able to understand what people needed. Like on the first day of school, he packed a stick of gum in my pocketbook, and then I was able to be on my way. It was like he added a friendly touch to each event."

Tessman's interpretation underlines the sexual and symbolic implications of this gesture: "Already one catches a glimpse of father's supporting her first major separation from home and mother. Holding onto the symbolic nurturance of the stick of gum, she could go confidently, without holding onto an adult. Putting his 'stick' in her 'pocketbook' seems a charming version (in her fantasy or his action or both) of his adding his 'friendly touch to each event' remembered by her."[14]

The sexual issues and reverberations from the oedipal triangle, which seem to recede during latency, reemerge rather powerfully with puberty. Between father and daughter the relationship is once again stormy and passionate, rocky and idyllic. During adolescence both players take up the old game with renewed intensity, trying to transform it as they continue to play.

On the courts of adolescence the game of childhood is revived. The old strokes and strategies are replayed, the old cues and conflicts rehashed in the hope that an interlude of mayhem will bring greater confidence and equanimity later. At fourteen, at fifteen, at sixteen I feel myself to be changing on the courts and elsewhere. One month I am slender and light on my feet. The next I have suddenly added tonnage and move as if through a far heavier substance than air. Some days I am pure energy, others all lethargy. One day my long hair waves behind me, proud, like a banner. The next I have restrained it in awkward pigtails and look like the child-woman that I am.

My father remains steady on his side of the net, puzzling out the situation. The same moves may provoke violently opposite response on alternate days. The old lines may provoke fury or complete vagueness. "You're dreaming," he says, when for the tenth time the ball sails by me, and I unleash my newfound power, my rediscovered aggression on the air. Just as he will say at the supper table, when my mind drifts after a pivotal question has been asked, "We're here. You're dreaming."

And he's right. At the supper table, on the tennis court, I am dreaming. I am lost in my own world, and it is a world of fantasy, a world of my own creation, where I make the rules and call the shots, where I am experimenting with my future. I still need to know that he is steadfast on the other side of the net, but in my mind's eye I am beginning the intricate and disorienting process of separation.

"You're dreaming," he says, and yes, in my fantasy he is no

longer my father, but now the perfect suitor, tall, dark, and handsome on a summer's afternoon. Back and forth, back and forth we hit the ball, and with the hypnotic hum I am laughing and talking with my phantom lover, who reads my every thought, understands my every move, adores me as I adore him. The face of my fantasy lover, my imaginary opponent, shifts with the wind, the day, my mood. Now he is a lifeguard I see on the beach, muscles rippling. Now again he is the hero of folksongs, poetic in faded denim. Then, just off a Harley-Davidson, black leather flashing in the sun, all thrills and hot energy.

"You're dreaming," says my father, a million miles away on the other side of the net. And he's right, for now my fantasies have once again shifted, and I am back at the center of my daydreams. Now it is match point at Wimbledon, pressure is mounting, the fans go wild. Then I am curtsying to the queen mother, raising the silver cup of victory over my head, throwing kisses to the crowd. Or then again I am off on a dangerous mission to trace a story, to the wilds of Africa, the mountains of Peru. Now it is the cover story of *Life*, the front page of *The New York Times*, a three-part serial in *The New Yorker*.

In my mind's eye I am no longer a sweaty-palmed schoolgirl, fighting with my mother, mooning at the dinner table. In my inner sagas I am no longer needing and resisting my parents' care, their concern and love. In my fantasies I am center stage. I am free and I am separate, tackling and transcending danger: a triumphant adult. It is hard to keep my eye on the ball.

On the other side of the net, the other side of the world, my father keeps the ball in play. He senses that I am not entirely with him, but permits me to withdraw while keeping up the pretense of the game. He allows the game to become the place where I can practice writing the script of my future. He remains steady: at once support and opponent, comrade and competitor. This is his gift to me, only one of many, but of course I cannot realize it at the time.

During adolescence the storms of the oedipal period, quiescent during latency, flash to the surface with renewed urgency. With the squalls of puberty, oedipal issues are recapitulated and for the most part resolved. The adolescent daughter struggles with separation and individuation, with the wish to know herself and be herself. Her psychic battles pit the urge for independence against the yearning for dependence, and this time she struggles against both of her parents, rather than one or the other. For the parent of the adolescent daughter the struggle lies between possessing and letting go, between knowing when to offer care and when to trust the daughter to care for herself. On either side of the generation gap the participants are walking a fine line. Without a necessary give-and-take, there may be painful repercussions later on. "Those parents will be most likely to 'lose' their children," comments Fritz Redl, "who cannot give up possessing them during adolescence."[15]

Early adolescence is often a time of increased erotic and aggressive drives—anger and black moods that emerge like beasts in the jungle, sexual stirrings that are both puzzling and titillating, fantasies that may have a stronger pull than reality itself. Later adolescence is typically concerned with mastering these drives, with experimentation and with fashioning new adult capacities, particularly the ability to love and forge a lasting relationship and the commitment to work.

In his classic psychoanalytic study of adolescence Peter Blos names the central issue of this period, "object relinquishment and object finding." That is, the child must learn to let go of the incestuous love objects (parents, siblings, parent substitutes) in order to form ties and commitments to people outside the family. The daughter's deep and complex ties to both mother and father are often loosened only with great difficulty, with sudden bursts of bravura, followed by setbacks and the need for continued nurturance. Often the first passionate attachments outside the family, amorous and engrossing as they may be, are still greatly influenced by the residue of the oedipal triangle. Child psychiatrist Samuel Ritvo suggests that "As the reactivated pre-oedipal tie to the mother is loosened, the girl's first heterosexual involvement during puberty may represent in reality an effort to replace the loss of her mother."[16] It is also possible that a girl's precocious affair during adolescence may be an attempt to stave off incestuous longings for her father and come to terms with his loss as well. Rushing into the arms of a young lover may also protect her from feelings of dependence on father and mother and reengulfment in the world of childhood.

The moodiness that characterizes the typical adolescent, the preoccupation of the "teenager in love," may indeed be a kind of mourning for the relinquished parent even in the heat of falling in love with someone her own age. Observes psychologist Alvin Winder, "The teen-ager's turning away from [her] parents leaves [her] with feelings of sadness, irritability, and lack of energy that normally constitute reactions to mourning the loss of a loved person. [She] is in fact mourning the loss of the internalized parental image. The parents, of course, are still present—with the result that the cause of the depression is obscure to both parents and adolescents. The parents, for want of a better word, label their child as moody."[17]

In any case adolescent love is often a reflection of the past and a mirror of the self as well as a reading into the future. For Erik Erikson, who labels the central struggle of adolescence "Identity versus Role Confusion," adolescent love is "to a considerable extent . . . an attempt to arrive at a definition of one's identity by projecting one's diffused ego image on another and by seeing it thus reflected and gradually clarified."[18] More than a search for a beloved, adolescent love is a search for the self, a self that is still ambivalently tied to mother and father but in the very process of loving another is becoming more and more separate and defined.

Just as adolescence can be the time when a capacity for lasting relationships is formed, so, too, can it be the time when a commitment to work is made. Again, in Erikson's scheme, the adolescent's increasing sureness of identity leads to a clearer focus on career:

> The growing and developing youths, faced with this physiological revolution within them, and with tangible adult tasks ahead of them, are now primarily concerned with what they appear to be in the eyes of others as compared with what they feel they are, and with the question of how to connect the roles and skills cultivated earlier with the occupational prototypes of the day. . . . The sense of ego identity, then, is the accrued confidence that the inner sameness and continuity prepared in the past are matched by the sameness and continuity of one's meaning for others, as evidenced in the tangible promise of a "career."[19]

In a later work, Erikson reviews his earlier theories on the developmental stages and summarizes adolescence this way:

> The specific strength emerging in adolescence—namely *fidelity*— maintains a strong relation both to infantile trust and to mature faith. As it transfers the need for guidance from parental figures to mentors and leaders, fidelity eagerly accepts their ideological mediatorship—whether the ideology is one implicit in a "way of life" or a militantly explicit one. . . . In summary, the process of identity formation emerges as an *evolving configuration*—a configuration that gradually integrates constitutional givens, idiosyncratic libidinal needs, favored capacities, significant identifications, effective defenses, successful sublimations, and consistent roles.[20]

For the adolescent daughter the father is now more than ever a powerful professional model, an inspiring representative from the world of work—again, particularly in families where he is the sole breadwinner. The daughter's increasingly sophisticated sense of her father as a worker—of what he does and how he feels about it, what power and prestige he wields or doesn't wield—may be a significant influence on choices she makes about her own work at this stage. Helen Tausend suggests that during adolescence "Many girls attempt to resolve their oedipal attachment to the father by identifying with his personal or professional traits, a mechanism that may be both advantageous and acceptable and not necessarily detrimental."[21]

With the resolution of oedipal desires typically accomplished in adolescence, there also comes a transformation of the erotic excitement and endeavor excitement of the childhood years into a more mature capacity for later commitments to love and work. As Lora Tessman explains:

> The experiencing and resolving of oedipal desires has a particular impact on the ego, in addition to affecting object relations. The necessary shift in object relations involves the familiar renunciation by the little girl of the father as her beloved, and the acceptance of the mother both as her primary identification figure and as a continued source of gratifying, supporting closeness.[22]

In addition, the resolution of oedipal desires means, at best, that the daughter finds her own way to transform the excitement of her relationship with her father into fuel for her future. The contribution of the father is, of course, pivotal, as Tessman describes:

> The contribution of the father in this process revolves around his simultaneous role as object of her excitement and model in its transformation. If the daughter internalizes the ego capacity for transforming excitement in a way that is not only tolerable . . . but is also pleasurable through a vibrant and tender affective engagement with her father, then her knowledge of that potential happiness may remain as a guiding force in her later work and loves.[23]

How the daughter disengages herself from her childhood love affair with her father, how she transforms her involvement with him, her erotic excitement and endeavor excitement, into a commitment to a love of her own and work of her own—these issues will be the central focus of the following chapters on five different kinds of father-daughter relationships.

On the courts of adulthood the game has become doubles: mother and father on one side of the net, my husband and I on the other. Back and forth in the unrelenting summer sun, back and forth in the shadows of late afternoon, first we rally to warm up, then compete. The competition is good-hearted, but intense, each side approving loudly of the other's shots but, nevertheless, playing to win. Tentatively at first, and then with more gusto, I try out my father's strategies, using the tips he has taught me to play against him.

With the addition of my own partner the dynamics of the game have, of course, shifted. Now that I am married, I am both more and less linked with my parents, my opponents. Mirroring them in the shared and comforting fact of being married, I have moved away from them in the necessary separation that marriage brings. Living on the other side of the country, my husband and I have our own world, our own new set of rules and mores. But still, this game is our common denominator, tying past with present, present with future.

Sometimes my mother and I sit on the sidelines and my father and husband compete. Watching them play, watching the two tall frames and similar gaits echoing each other on either side of the net, the long, deep strokes hit back and forth from the baseline or shrewdly volleyed from the net, I see how my choice was predestined from my past, part history, part chemistry, part mystery.

But watching them play, my heart is always in my throat. Do I root for my father, the strength of the past, the older and wiser, the deepest, earliest tie? Or do I root for my husband, the promise of the future, the younger and quicker, the unfolding and deepening bond? Back and forth goes the ball, back and forth the memories and fantasies, the lessons and dreams. There is no possibility of choosing. The only solution is that they might split sets.

2

THE PATRIARCH

My father is an Irish Catholic colonel who brought us up like privates. As a liberal arts, Jesuit-schooled Catholic he has great culture and morality. But I can never remember him ever holding me in his arms or letting me cry on his shoulders. He was quite stern in our upbringing and critical of our companions, particularly boyfriends, who had to call him "Colonel." He grunts from behind newspapers or books and never chitchats about personal or capricious subjects. After a few drinks he can be fun with company, but under most circumstances he provides critical commentary on all the ignorant, lazy people around him.

Molly,* *thirty-two*

My father is an authoritarian person; his ways are the only ways. Occasionally he sways to meet other people's

*All first names used alone are pseudonyms.

views, but generally speaking he argues tooth and nail to remain in the dominant position, even when he is clearly wrong. My father was not the sort of person one could sit and talk over problems with. He preferred to be the breadwinner, and that is pretty much what he did.

In the past my father and I were at opposite polarities. We fought terribly and painfully. There were days, sometimes weeks would go by, and we wouldn't look at each other. He always called me the rebel; to this day I don't understand why. Much of the struggle is most fortunately in the past, and today there are times I almost feel a sense of joy in him when he sees me.

Helen, *thirty-eight*

The Patriarch is the father with one foot still firmly entrenched in the nineteenth century. He is an authoritarian of the old school, believing father to be the undisputed head of the household, mother to be his solace and support, and daughter to do the bidding of both—no questions asked. In family matters he prefers his word to be law, a lesson undoubtedly learned from his father and his father's father in turn. His leadership, like his father's and grandfather's, may seem to be prompted more by duty than by love. And his sense of morality, on the surface as peerless as the family heirloom silver, may in fact be more tuned to please a public audience than to square with the private dictates of his heart. He wears his sense of propriety like black tie and tails at an informal dinner, daring someone to challenge him. And naturally his daughter does, for she is just as firmly entrenched in this century as her father is in the past. For every ultimatum he offers, she has an alternative. For every rigidity, she teases out the ambiguity. For every black and white, she counters with the gray. The daughter of the Patriarch often grows up with fists flying, her own sense of justice soon as finely tuned as his. The Patriarch is the father who often begets the feminist. Indeed, he fathered the Women's Movement.

The Patriarch has a stringent sense of right and wrong. He fathers by arming his daughter with a thick compendium of rules, which he may or may not follow himself. Do as I say, not as I do, is the message of the Patriarch. He may be the one to have a mistress and a love child while vehemently condemning premarital sex, or the one whose accounts are in total disarray while insisting on fastidious bookkeeping. His rules appear as intransigent as his backbone, as inviolable as the tomes that line the library his daughter is not supposed to enter. But even as she pays lip service to his rules, the daughter of the Patriarch knows in her gut that his rules no longer apply. She may struggle for a while to replace his rules with her own, and this effort may give her the patina of adulthood. But real maturity may come only with the frightening, then awesome, and ultimately liberating realization that there *are* no rules, that the ambiguities of the adult world must be met with an entirely different kind of flexibility and resourcefulness.

So as a model or guide in work and love the Patriarch often promises more than he can deliver. Although he appears to have all the answers about how to work, whom to love, his very arbitrariness may inhibit his daughter from figuring out the questions she needs to ask herself. Her early endeavor excitement and erotic excitement will provoke contradictory reactions in him, subtly determined by a network of conscious and unconscious motives. He will do his best to encourage his daughter's endeavor excitement—her early forays into projects and play—believing, as he does, that productive work is the cornerstone of happiness. But his strict standards may turn out to thwart her endeavors, damage her confidence, and dampen her experimentation for fear of failure or of incurring his displeasure. But however much he may consciously support her endeavor excitement, he may be disconcerted be-

ʋond response by her erotic excitement—those early flirta-
tions and tentative sexual sallies. Beneath his puritanical exterior and rigid moral code often lies a hotbed of intense and
unacknowledged sexual impulses, which his daughter's early
sexual stirrings may threaten to expose.

The Patriarch's posture as a moral arbiter is often used to
camouflage the irrepressible sexuality he makes every effort
to repress. So before she can be a free agent, the daughter of
the Patriarch must come to terms with both her father's repressed sexuality and her own burgeoning sexuality. Between
Patriarch father and daughter, adolescence is a particularly
highly charged time. Daughter's emerging sexuality provokes
a reckoning on both sides: Father must face the welter of his
own sexual feelings that have long been forced underground,
and daughter must examine the sexual strivings that are awakening with a vengeance. How father and daughter negotiate
this transition will not only color their future relationship but
will also influence daughter's future relationships with the
rest of the men in her life.

The category of Patriarch, like all the categories consid
ered, covers a range of fathering styles from well-meaning to
undermining and heavy-handed. A Patriarch father may use
a variety of approaches, depending on his situation and attitudes at different stages of his daughter's development. On
one end of the continuum is the Patriarch who is a wise and
kindly mentor, a *Father Knows Best*, dispensing wit and wisdom
from a position of inner strength and resolution, always with
his daughter's best interests at heart. At the other end is the
dictatorial authoritarian, an Archie Bunker without the
humor, possessive and punitive, binding his daughter in a
straitjacket of rules and prohibitions. The certitude and recti-
tude of his edicts betray an inner world that is full of fears and
uncertainties and needs a constant shoring up.

The voice of the mentor is heard in this revealing letter
written at the turn of the century by psychologist William

James to his thirteen-year-old daughter Margaret. James, whose own youth was beleaguered by phobic troubles, responds to his daughter's recent outpouring of woe with this comforting but straightforward portrait of the hills and valleys of life:

> Now, my dear little girl, you have come to an age when the inward life develops and when some people (and on the whole those who have most of a destiny) find that life is not a bed of roses. Among other things there will be waves of terrible sadness, which last sometimes for days; and dissatisfactions with oneself, and irritation at others, and anger at circumstances and stony insensibility, etc., etc., which taken together form melancholy. Now, painful as it is, this is sent to us for enlightenment. It always passes off, and we learn about life from it, and we ought to learn a great many good things if we react on it rightly. . . . And we must try to make it last as short a time as possible. The worst of it often is that, while we are in it, we don't *want* to get out of it. We hate it, and yet we prefer staying in it—that is part of the disease. If we find ourselves like that, we must make ourselves do something different, go with people, speak cheerfully, set ourselves to some kind of hard work, make ourselves sweat, etc.; and that is the good way of reacting that makes of us a valuable character.[1]

The mentor father knows the art of sharing life's hard-learned lessons while giving his daughter room to respond out of a place of strength. The authoritarian father, on the other hand, seems to know only how to impose his will while exposing his daughter's vulnerability. In *To the Lighthouse* Virginia Woolf takes her magnifying glass to this kind of a father, a tyrannical and unswerving Patriarch, modeled closely after her own stern father, Leslie Stephen, editor of the *Dictionary of National Biography.* As the novel begins, the eight Ramsay children are dancing around their parents, waiting for the verdict on whether, the next day, the family will make the expedition to the lighthouse. "Yes," says Mrs. Ramsay, the kindly, the permissive, the optimistic. "No," says Mr. Ramsay, the mean-spirited, the unrelenting, the pessimistic. "[The day] won't be fine," he swears,

> . . . standing . . . lean as a knife, narrow as the blade of one, grinning sarcastically, not only with the pleasure of disillusioning his son and casting ridicule upon his wife, who was ten thousand times better in every way than he was (James [his son] thought), but also with some secret conceit at his own accuracy of judgment. What he said was true. It was always true. He was incapable of untruth; never tampered with a fact; never altered a disagreeable word to suit the pleasure or convenience of any mortal being, least of all his own children, who, sprung from his loins, should be aware from childhood that life is difficult; facts uncompromising; and the passage to that fabled land where our brightest hopes are extinguished, our frail barks founder in darkness (here Mr. Ramsay would straighten his back and narrow his little blue eyes upon the horizon), one that needs, above all, courage, truth, and the power to endure.[2]

As the novel unfolds, the contrapuntal voices of mother and father clarify and intensify. "Yes," repeats Mrs. Ramsay, yes to the promise of tomorrow, to the lighthouse, to the adventure of life itself. "No," reminds Mr. Ramsay, no to the pleasure of the future, to the lighthouse, to the dazzle of the wide world. And the daughter of the Patriarch is, of course, trapped in the middle of this disagreement, this dialectic. Should she embrace life, as her mother urges, or retreat from it, as her father cautions?

For Virginia Woolf the dialogue was muffled—never silenced entirely—by her father's death. Brooding in her journal on what would have been her father's ninety-sixth birthday, she writes:

> Father's birthday. He would have been 96, 96, yes, today; and could have been 96, like other people one has known; but mercifully was not. His life would have entirely ended mine. What would have happened? No writing, no books—inconceivable.
> I used to think of him and mother daily; but writing the *Light-*

house laid them in my mind. And now he comes back sometimes, but differently. (I believe this to be true—that I was obsessed by them both, unhealthily; and writing of them was a necessary act.) He comes back now more as a contemporary. I must read him some day. I wonder if I can feel again, I hear his voice, I know this by heart.[3]

Though the daughter of the Patriarch may be the most openly rebellious of daughters, her separation from him may be particularly painful and protracted, often not even altogether eased by his death. The pull he exerts is often a confusing combination of the brute force of his tyrannical will with the undertow of his repressed needfulness and possessiveness. Even when she has wrenched herself from the overt sway of his will, his covert needs may continue to bind her, more insidious for being unnamed. When she can begin to identify the push and pull between them—deep and powerful as the changing current of river rapids—she has her first chance of altering the future course of their relationship, and beyond that, her relationships with other men.

On the surface at least, the portrait of the Patriarch presented in the interviews and autobiographies is as sharply delineated as a black on white silhouette. The rigidity, the fetish for rules, the preoccupation with appearances—these are the qualities enumerated by daughter after daughter, offered with a resignation that is not always a convincing mask for disappointment, fear, or frustration. When the Foundation for Child Development recently studied more than two thousand children and found that one out of ten said the person the child feared the *most* was the father, the Patriarch was the father that child must have had in mind.[4] The Patriarch often sits at the head of a larger family than the other fathers, often worries more about the daily pressures of sustaining his brood, often, perhaps in desperation, passes on lessons learned at his own father's knee without bothering to update them for his daughter's generation. His daughter may respond by feeling that she has to burrow beneath layers of bravura and defenses to find what may be a loving heart:

My father has been involved with the military nearly all his life, first as a marine for twenty-five years, then in the civil service, fixing war machines. This background has significantly affected his manner of speech and thought. He is ready to nuke any country into submission for any reason whatsoever. Underneath it all he is a loving and giving person, but he does his best to keep it hidden. He is a "family man" who works all day Thanksgiving and Christmas so he can make extra money.

"My father showed his love with his wallet" is the way another Patriarch's daughter made sense of the disparity between her father's keen sense of family duty and apparent absence of warmth. "If he loves you, he loans to you against the inheritance." But probing deeper, she acknowledges, "Money and investments do seem more important to my father than any other issue, which I know isn't true. I think that money is just something that he found he could talk about to his children. It's something he could advise and consent on." And finally she adds in a wry moment of self-awareness, "I guess money is the only thing he would start to talk to us about that we would actually listen to."

When asked to describe her father's messages about sex or money or work, the daughter of the Patriarch responds with the alacrity of a private answering a drill sergeant. For the Patriarch's family leadership depends on his steadfast conviction that behavior can be guided by rules spelled out in black and white. Among the various father types he is the one most likely to issue a family code as indisputable as the Ten Commandments. The twenty-four-year-old daughter of an Italian immigrant truck driver spells out her father's lessons this way:

Sex is wrong before marriage and shouldn't be discussed after you're married.

Money is everything, all-necessary, all-important.

Work is necessary and not usually something you should enjoy.

How much money and benefits are more important than satisfaction.

My *future* should include marriage and children and living closer to my parents.

However intractable the Patriarch's lessons, this does not deter his daughter's departure from them. The rigid moralist often begets the freewheeling daughter who lives with her lover without marriage; the archconservative begets the militant radical; the devout believer fathers the questioning agnostic. The Patriarch's daughter often meets her father's will head on with her own. When the truck driver wrote his daughter disapprovingly about her live-in lover and refused to come visit them, his daughter reported to me that she "pretty much disowned [her] parents." If her father could cut her off, she would return the favor first.

This twenty-eight-year-old financial planner similarly runs down her father's messages—"You can enjoy sex only with someone you are married to"; "You can find happiness only through Christ and His Church"; "You can find a husband only if you are slim and ladylike"—and similarly thumbs her nose at them:

I've found happiness as a fat feminist who goes to church only for the music. And before I was married I had wonderful sex with several men to whom I had no intention of getting married. And my husband loves me fat or thin!

Not every daughter rebels with this much verve and apparent confidence. For some, rebellion is a less clear-cut and straightforward process that moves in a pattern of feints and parries rather than in a frontal attack. A woman in her fifties looks back on the constraints of her lawyer father and her efforts to disentangle herself from them:

> Sex and money were to be expected, but *never* talked of. No more was religion or politics. My father expected accomplishments, not words. As a girl I simply did not have the investment potential he found in his son—I was sent to college, but more to find a husband than for my own direct benefit.

Her rebellion from her father's standards and expectations was accomplished in two distinct phases. The first phase was a sweeping opposition in which she took everything he stood for and turned it on its head:

> I rebelled against my father twice in my life. The first time was not conscious, but getting pregnant, dropping out of college, and getting married was surely part rebellion against his rigidity and his ambitions for me.

But the second phase was more deliberate, a series of conscious choices and experiments—"bisexuality, extramarital sorties, trying for nonpossessive love"—and now living with an older gentleman, bound together out of "affection, not love":

> The second rebellion was more gradual. It has come about in the last fifteen years as a gradual but quite definite distancing of my values and behavior from his conventional, conservative life-style. I am my own woman now and just as well.

Between Patriarch father and daughter there is rarely indifference. There is instead an inescapable intensity that may wax or wane during different phases of their relationship. The relationship is likely to be marked by a volatile advance and retreat of extreme closeness, bordering on possessiveness, and aggravated distance that may appear as punishment for some acutely felt betrayal. A thirty-two-year-old teacher, the daughter of a laborer, speaks for many Patriarchs' daughters as she sketches the sequence of stages this way:

> My relationship with my father was distant as a child and seemed to get closer as a young adult. During a period of time (late adolescence) as I was separating myself from my family (leaving home), he seemed angry with me, which created some antagonism. Once I was established as an "adult," however, we became very close (mid-twenties). We discussed everything openly and I even felt jealousy from my mother. He disowned me when I chose a man to marry —a person he would never even meet. I attempted to "make amends" five years ago at Christmastime, but he left the house before I arrived. Since that time I've mourned his death, mainly in the form of depression.

The relationship between Patriarch father and daughter derives much of its intensity from the secrecy and denial surrounding sex. The Patriarch's overt credo is typically that sex is neither to be discussed nor even acknowledged. But privately he may be absorbed, even obsessed, by his own powerful sexuality. When his daughter reaches puberty and becomes a daily reminder of the allure and tempestuousness of sexuality, he may find it more and more difficult and perilous to repress his own sexual feelings. Then, too, daughter's adolescence often coincides with father's midlife crisis, a time when he is questioning his virility and appeal and perhaps the satisfactions of his own marriage. For the daughter the upheavals of adolescent sexuality become all the more disturbing for being denied by her father. "I was raised to be the Virgin Mary, while the Sexual Revolution was going on" is the way one woman, now in her mid-thirties, recalls her adolescent bind.

So for this pair even more than for the others, daughter's

adolescence becomes a crisis during which the terms of their relationship become open for negotiation. Again and again the daughters of the Patriarch testify to this rupture, this exposure, this turning point. If the crisis is not faced and resolved, father and daughter may come to a wrenching parting of the ways that neither truly wants and that both grieve over. For the daughter of the laborer quoted above, her father's rejection felt as final and unalterable as death. Other daughters meet the transition of puberty with confusion, despair, and—for some, eventually—compromise.

For the twenty-seven-year-old daughter of the lifetime marine introduced earlier, the changes of puberty have still not been accepted by her father some fifteen years later:

> I was "Daddy's girl," the youngest and probably the one who could identify with him best when we were kids. But I made the disastrous mistake of growing up, and he can't handle it. My nonvirginal, unmarried state distresses him greatly.

Another woman in her early twenties, the daughter of a businessman who "looks like a bear, acts like a bear," is also still coping with the fallout of adolescent upheavals:

> Before my teen years my father was demonstrative and affectionate, but once I reached twelve or thirteen, his whole attitude changed. I have become aware of these things now and have tried to forgive him for any real or imagined damage, but it hasn't worked, try as I might to put the past behind.

She acknowledges how painful puberty must have been for both of them as the gulf between them widened with misunderstandings and misinterpretations on both sides:

> Puberty must have been as much of a trauma for him as it was for me. All the reassurance I needed because of the

disagreeable events that would happen to me on a daily basis was not there. I ran away at thirteen because I couldn't handle all the expression of negative emotions I was seeing. He thought it was because I didn't get to see a special TV show!

For a woman in her forties the aftermath of her adolescent rift with her father was serious enough to disrupt her father's relationship with her son—and has only recently begun to heal:

When I reached puberty, I think my father shied away from me, partly because of my physical development and partly because I became an adolescent smart-ass. He never seemed to approve of me regardless of what I did or tried. My father's animosity increased when I left home, married, and he found out that I had gotten pregnant before I was married. It took him years to recover. He would take it out on my son by treating him as though he were disgusting. In the last few years since my divorce he has begun to warm up to my son and me.

The Patriarch's possessive and jealous attitude toward his daughter at puberty only aggravates the very behavior he is trying to prohibit—not just the expression of sexuality, but what must seem to him the flaunting of it. The Patriarch's daughter is, of course, the one to date the "inappropriate" man, stay out till dawn, get pregnant before marriage. Were he to get some distance on this cycle of prohibition and rebellion, the Patriarch might be able to circumvent the inevitable breach between himself and his daughter. But often he is driven by unconscious fantasies beyond his awareness and control. Psychologist Marjorie Leonard speculates on what these fantasies might be:

It is not easy for a parent to give up an attitude founded on an unconscious reaction, in this instance the revival of counter-oedipal wishes. But why, in expressing [his] feelings of possessiveness and injury, [does the Patriarch] resort to a peremptory, authoritarian manner usually associated with the Victorian era? We can speculate that [he is] reverting to an attitude learned from [his] own father: by actively protecting his daughter from "evil-minded males" —not [himself]—[he is] able to deny [his] incestuous feelings, while projecting them onto others . . . he unconsciously equates his daughter's disregard for his authority with loss of control over his own impulses. The anxiety he then feels is betrayed by his unreasonable concern for his daughter's safety and his aversion toward the man of her choice.[5]

Beneath the controlled and controlling surface of the Patriarch lie the sexual fantasies, wishes, and impulses that from time to time burst unaccountably out into the open between father and daughter. The impact of these incidents becomes all the more traumatic for the daughter because of the force with which father tries to prevent them from happening. The interviews with these daughters and their autobiographies are pockmarked with pictures of the shadowside of the Patriarch, moments when his darkest impulses surge out of his control, moments of violence, terror, and abuse that are no doubt as frightening to father as to daughter.

A woman in her mid-thirties, the daughter of an accountant who prided himself on appearances, recalls this incident of adolescence when her needs and confusions collided head on with her father's:

When I was twelve, I was five foot eight, very leggy, had breasts and a pouty little mouth. One time I was practicing my wise mouth, as practice makes perfect, and intentionally goading him to the point that he would beat me. It was a power game for me. I knew how to get him mad enough to change his color, and then I knew how to get him even madder by not responding to his beatings. What a game. Anyway, one time when he was pissed enough to shit on the pope, he began to hit me and then to kiss me rather passionately. He threw me on the bed, and I was then very very confused. My mother came in at that time and screamed. I wasn't raped. My father was just too taken aback by having another woman in the house that he only knew how to handle in one way.

Such extremes of paternal emotion—attraction and punishment, affection and abuse—left this daughter with the feeling there was no safe ground in relation to men. Years later, married to an alcoholic who seems pitifully reminiscent of her father, she pins her poignant and pathetic hope for the future on her son. "In a way I'd like to have my son become a homosexual, rather than a limited heterosexual male," she writes at the end of her bitter life story. Perhaps secretly wishing she could renounce all men for the havoc they have wreaked in her life, she turns the fantasy around and imagines a future for her son in which he will reject women instead.

The daughter of the Patriarch struggles in her dreams with the sexual violence stashed beneath her father's propriety. At times she gives lip service to forgiving father for his excesses while her dreams expose her continuing vulnerability and fear. One wrenching example is a young college student whose conservative and rigid father served twenty years in the army, including a stint in Vietnam. Home on leave one weekend during his daughter's eighth-grade year, an incident occurred that ruptured all semblance of equanimity between them:

My father chased my sister and me around an empty apartment, trying to attack us. At this point I realized that Dad was disturbed (maybe from Vietnam?) and was very immature. I became less scared by his threats and began questioning his methods of discipline and his frequent outbursts. But not until much later did I actually challenge him as an adult equal.

But the voice of precocious maturity is belied by her dreams in which she sees her father "chasing me and raping me repeatedly." "I was frightened," she admits, "but not in pain." Having to cope with violence too early in life seems to have numbed her feelings in a way that may inhibit her chances for intimacy later on.

Yet another way in which the dreams of the Patriarch's daughter show her trying to cope with her father's shadow-side comes from a musician in her early thirties. Although her father had always been stern about sexual matters, nothing prepared her for his outburst one particular time when she stayed out all night with her friends. She was twenty-two and living at home after a "failure at college":

> I had stayed out all night with some friends and hadn't called home. I arrived the following noon and was immediately set upon by my brother and father. I mean, they really *beat* me (other than the usual spankings, physical violence was not in the family history). Later that day my brother and I made up, but Dad refused to speak about it. I realized later that he had completely wiped the incident from his memory.

But if father was able to wipe his memory clean, daughter's dreams remained tarnished and confounded by the incident:

> In one dream I was walking down a street in the opposite direction of our house. Dad came along, driving the car. I was terrified of him because I knew that (a) he shouldn't drive because of his poor eyesight and (b) he was going to punish me in some awful sexual way. I ran and ran to keep away from him. I woke up before the dream reached any conclusion (I have always had a sexual distaste about Dad, a slight revulsion and fear).

Between every father and daughter adolescence is a time of highly charged sexual feelings and fantasies. It is also the time when oedipal issues (daughter's desire for father and competition with mother) and counter-oedipal issues (father's desire for daughter and perhaps dissatisfactions with his own marriage) resurface and require resolution. When father conveys a strong sense of love within secure limits, daughter can test out her fantasies with the confidence they will not explode and damage her equilibrium with father and with the rest of the family. But the Patriarch's love is often conflicted and his limits so severe that they constantly threaten to break down, no longer restraining either daughter's or father's secret sexual fantasies. For the daughter of the Patriarch, adolescence can be a disconcerting time when her father's tight controls no longer protect her, and when her own sense of mastery is still too fragile to allow her to take care of herself.

When the crises of adolescence have been faced and weathered, there often follows a period of rapproachement between the Patriarch and his daughter. Often this period coincides with daughter's leaving home, gaining distance and maturity. Beyond her father's direct sphere of influence and the nagging dailiness of power struggles, this daughter may for the first time gain some perspective on her father's inner quandaries and pressures. Gradually she may replace fear with understanding, anger with compassion. As they grow up, many of these daughters grapple with their own dilemmas about authority and become more acutely aware of the painful division in their fathers' lives between appearances and feelings. They become more sensitive to the clash between their fathers' rigid beliefs about ideal paternal behavior and their troubling doubts and insecurities as mere human beings. And this awareness in turn helps to make more human and approachable the fathers who were the one-dimensional tyrants of their youth.

A woman in her late twenties, who has now left home and

set up married life on her own, puzzles about the man her father really is beneath his patriarchal pose:

> Though my father has mellowed somewhat in his behavior now that his children are grown, he is still judgmental and conservative in his mores and opinions. Still, I don't feel like I know the *real* Thomas. He seemed to have a picture of how a father should be and acted that role. I have seen him laugh, and I have heard him say affectionate things, yet I can't believe that he is really feeling these things. Yet I know that he is a very emotional person.

A woman in her mid-thirties examines the conflict between her father's public image and his private self with a newly felt affection born of distance and hindsight:

> My father is a large man who looks best in tweeds and wool sweaters, but he, like everyone else, wants to be smaller. And somehow or other he thinks that if he wears silk suits and Gucci shoes, someone will mistake him for Cesar Romero rather than Edmund Muskie. Appearances have always been very important to my father, especially the way his family looks. It would be too facile to explain it away as his being the only child of immigrants, but I'm sure that all of his life has been partially measured by how he thinks the whole world sees it. Anyway, he left home during World War Two and became a career officer, which among other reinforcements reaffirmed the value of a shined pair of boots.

She concludes her portrait on a more serious, contemplative note, acknowledging with new sympathy the poignancy of her father's inner life:

> My father is actually a very vulnerable man, in a very sad way. It is like he has no idea of what he really is, just what is always expected of him, how he is seen.

For another woman, also the daughter of an immigrant, it took a watershed trip together back to the old country to reveal the vulnerable man beneath the harsh Patriarchal exterior. As a child growing up, she saw her father as remote and formidable, "either discouraging or restricting." She yearned to reach out to him and make some contact, but she could think only of asking about his youth in Portugal. "Why do you want to know?" he would snarl but never answer, until once, he grunted, "There were no toilets in Portugal."

Finally, when he retired after forty years in the Postal Service, he invited her to accompany him to the little Portuguese town where he had grown up. "The people in this town," she remembers, "were still living in almost medieval conditions. They had a well for water, an open hearth for cooking, a single small bulb for electricity and indeed, no toilets." But it was there that she came to know a part of her father that in forty years in America he had never relaxed his guard enough to show:

> We had a joke in our family that if Father smiled once, it was a subject of conversation for months. But in Portugal he laughed all the time and was full of gentle communications. Our relatives there—almost everyone in town—were unbelievably sweet and sunny people. I began to see that to go from that warm world to the chill and tumult of Chicago without any preparation, my father had to become walled off. He needed support, but there was no one there to give it to him.

The trip, of course, became a turning point in their relationship. It was a chance for daughter to see the gentle, private person buried beneath the stone-faced public stance her father felt he needed to adapt to handle a world beyond his control. Coming to understand how her father became the person he was, demystified his power over her and realigned their relationship so that she began to enjoy his company rather than fear it.

In her search for self, in her struggle to find satisfying love and work, the daughter of the Patriarch is aided and abetted by her relationship with her mother. From these daughters' interviews and autobiographies a portrait of a relationship with mother emerges that is usually close, loving, and supportive, where the relationship with father is often conflicted, tumultuous, and critical. As in *To the Lighthouse*, mother provides the permissive yes that balances father's restrictive no. These daughters frequently describe a special identification with mother, a willingness to exchange opinions and a kind of interdependence that is not only missing between daughter and father but may also be missing between husband and wife. From a woman in her early twenties and then a woman in her early thirties, these descriptions convey how the daughters' sympathies ally with mother:

My mother has worked since I was two. I have always had a deep respect for her as she was so very different from my father. She has manners, gets along with everyone, is loving in a reserved way, and I never feared her.

My mother and I think and often feel deeply about the same things. I accepted her as a human being long before I did my father. This has made it much easier for me to communicate with her about my feelings, hopes, and dreams. I accepted her difference of opinion easier.

At times the interdependence between mother and daughter also necessitates a kind of role reversal, daughter bolstering mother as much as relying on her:

My mother is a pretty, educated, strong-minded woman. She has aged dramatically in the ten years that Dad has not been working, drinking just a little too much and developing hypertension. She and I have developed a very intimate, interdependent relationship. Advice, support, criticism, and love are freely and mutually given. I am the first person she calls in emergencies, and vice versa.

For many of these mothers and daughters the reciprocal openness and support in part compensates for what each lacks in her relationship with the Patriarch. But for others the meekness and submissiveness that husband expects of wife also makes mother a painfully limited model for daughter. Some of these daughters express disappointment and resentment over mother's apparent lack of backbone. They know firsthand the difficulties of standing up to father and fear if mother cannot do it, how possibly can they?

My mother's position in the family is subservient. She serves my father hand and foot and cared for all her five children. She had a tendency to overdo it a bit—almost a smotherer. She works very hard, in my opinion too hard, for it is almost a way of relieving her anxiety.

My relationship with my mother is not close but it is loving. I don't feel that I know her at all—she never expresses her own feelings and opinions. I asked her about this recently, and she said that she shuts up and lets my dad do the talking —twenty-nine years of that!

For the daughter of the Patriarch, whose apparently God-given certainties often make him loom larger than life, other family members become particularly important in keeping father's impact in perspective. Mother's quiet strength may often provide a hopeful balance, an encouraging sense of possibility. But her subservience may on the other hand only intensify her daughter's feeling of threat, her fear of fighting back.

Because he offers another male voice and yet a voice of her own generation, her brother often provides a powerful alternative to the Patriarch. Having him as another male model suggests that there may be different opportunities in work, different possibilities in love, not so rigidly circumscribed by father's rules and prohibitions. Seeing what her brother makes of his life, watching him test family limits and move beyond them, enables this daughter to believe she can do the same. The daughter of the Patriarch introduced earlier, the father who "looks and acts like a bear," finds in her brother a far less frightening kind of man who helps kindle the hope that she may be able to find someone outside the family capable of being a loving and equal partner:

> What I've learned from my brother that is different is that a man can be affectionate and giving, desiring, protective, and fully able to explain his reasons and actions.

The twenty-eight-year-old daughter of a Patriarch who was "unquestionably The Authority" finds in her brother a man who stands for flexibility instead of rigidity, humor instead of dead seriousness:

> From my brother I have learned that to be male doesn't mean to be The Boss, that to be occasionally zany is healthy, and that compassion within the family is very important. My father's zaniness I always took to be posing, and his compassion I took to be subtly scheming paternalism (a way to get out of me what he wants).

Another woman sees her brother as a charismatic romantic model:

> When I was young, I used to idolize my brother. I still do, I guess. I am constantly drawn to any man who slightly resembles my brother, even sort of walks like him. I've never been able to do anything but look at my shoes when talking to a man who reminds me of my brother, though.

Because the power relationship between sister and brother is more equalized and reciprocal than the hierarchical relationship between father and daughter, sister often feels freer to respond to brother's cues than daughter to father's dictates. So the possibility for intimacy and influence is increased —as is occasionally the opportunity for exploitation. The daughter of the lifetime marine quoted earlier sought refuge with her brother, but instead found additional skirmishes on the home front:

My brother was probably as big an influence on my life as my father, since he was around while Dad wasn't. He was always pretty radical and precocious, but he was very cruel to me, both emotionally and physically. He is a master of the "psych-out." I was totally psyched out by him and still am to some extent.

Within the strict confines of the Patriarchal family, daughter's behavior may be more sternly curtailed than her brother's. This inequity often understandably becomes a bone of contention:

I had to stay in on school nights (not even go to the library to study), and I was not allowed a job. I was an A student, by the way. My brother was allowed much more freedom and was a B/C student. I often smarted and fumed over the inequity of it.

But with the leeway of greater freedom, her brother was also more daring about challenging the family strictures. Thumbing his nose at the Patriarchal conventions, he became the rebel his sister did not have the nerve to be:

My brother is the "black sheep" sibling. I don't know him very well. He did not go to college, works at a blue-collar job, and parties on the weekends. He has never had a lengthy relationship with a woman, though he wants to get married. He drives a racy car and is very generous to others with his money. In contrast, my sisters and I all went though college and grad school and got married right out of college, after dating only one or two men steadily. My brother exhibits the rebelliousness that I wish I hadn't been too fearful to express.

For the daughter of the Patriarch, raised to believe there is only one right way to do things, the presence of other options in the family shakes up her own choices for the future. If mother is open or supportive, or simply steady in her loving, that helps counteract father's tightness, criticalness, or punitiveness and provides a more flexible model for moving forward into the world. If brother is affectionate or freewheeling or downright rebellious, that, too, suggests a style of greater adaptability for meeting the future. But for many of these daughters, father's voice is too overbearing to be muffled, and the path toward finding work and love is sharply narrowed by his stipulations and regulations. Psychotherapist Suzanne Gasner speculates that one stumbling block for these daughters is doubting the authenticity of their own inner experience. "The Patriarch father can't allow himself to be psychologically minded," she observes. "He has learned a way of living that keeps him from learning a lot of things about himself. If both parents are teamed up in this pattern, it would be hard for the daughter to know herself well. She will have little introspection and little comfort with the nature of subjective experience. Therefore, there will often be a greater disparity between what she consciously sets out to do and how things turn out. Of all the categories of daughters she may be the least able to do something creative, autonomous and spontaneous."

The daughter of the Patriarch faces the outside world and the world of work armed with a backlog of rules so extensive as to give the illusion of inviolability, yet so inflexible as to cloud all possibility for spontaneous response. As a result she may have little confidence to cope with the inevitable crises and complexities of the working world. The central task for the daughter of the Patriarch is to learn to listen to her own voice, follow her own instincts, her own dictates. This may involve a sifting through her father's messages, using what can apply but having the nerve to put aside the rest. This is a challenging and often circuitous process, and how each daughter handles it depends not only on her relationship with her father but also on her relationship with mother and siblings, teachers and friends.

When a subservient and capitulating mother pairs with a negative and restrictive father, the daughter's chances of developing her competence are most severely thwarted. A secretary in her mid-thirties testifies to the ways her parents dampened her self-esteem:

> I was led to believe that I was not capable of making my own way in the world. I was not able to take care of myself. Both my parents were very discouraging of my attempts to go out into the world on my own. Even the small things like crossing the street we lived on I couldn't do until my younger brother was allowed. This didn't make sense to me, considering the fact that I was older than he. I struggle constantly with low self-esteem. I feel I cannot do things before I have even tried, although I try regardless of the negative attitude I have and usually do very well. I have a hard time excelling beyond just doing well, because at this point I usually give up for the fear of success.

Her bind is further complicated by working for the same company where her father was unhappily employed. If she stays and is miserable, she corroborates his experience and gains the dubious security of proving him right. But if she moves forward and does well, she runs the risk not only of bettering him but also of proving his inhibitions and injunctions wrong. And if his rules turn out to be wrong, then she is faced with carving out her own guidelines for the adult world—and this she has a hard time trusting that she can do.

Certain daughters of Patriarchs go to great lengths trying

to mold their choices to meet their father's approval and reinforce his strictures. But occasionally even in the midst of excessive conformity, an independent will is forged, inspiring choices antithetical to father's wishes but nonetheless attuned to daughter's deepest hopes. Molly, the daughter of the Irish Catholic colonel who raised his children "like privates," took a tortuous route to find herself working for the leader of a rather different stripe:

> I tried to join the convent in high school, but the mother superior wouldn't let me, saying I was "too worldly." I also tried to join the army in college, but the recruiting officer said my security clearance hadn't cleared. Both of these are occupations my father would have approved of. He mocks my five years of commitment to Ralph Nader for its politics and financial sacrifice, whereas I should think he would be proud that I have reached a highly respected level of ethics and public acclaim. It is the main wedge between us at present. I feel that he is jealous of Ralph.

Every Patriarch's daughter must make her peace with her father's single-minded work ethic, his philosophy of work for work's sake often without much sense of vision, pleasure, or creativity. Some daughters manage to remain undaunted—the Irish Catholic colonel's Nader worker, for one—following their star without their father's blessing. Others allow their hopes to be daunted by father's kaibash. "When I told my father once that I wanted to be a writer," remembers a businesswoman in her thirties, "he merely said, 'What are you going to do for a living?' and never mentioned me writing." After her father's discounting and discouragement of her fragile literary dreams, the would-be writer sought refuge in business, trading the dreams she valued for the security her father valued.

But the thirty-year-old daughter of a geologist eventually sidestepped her father's double messages. "You will never be a geologist," he would say. "You spend all your time looking at the colors of the formation and the sunset." On the other hand, he indicated that geology—or another scientific field—was the only viable career choice. "Science or 'practical' jobs are more acceptable as a means of making money than having someone pay you for your 'hobby.' " But little by little she came to trust her own instincts about work rather than his. Gradually she came to accept, even appreciate, her sensitivity to "the colors of the formation and the sunset." She began to realize that pursuing her "hobby" gave her far more satisfaction than corseting her creativity to make it fit science. Now she works happily and quite successfully as an artist.

There are certainly some daughters of Patriarchs whose work energies are catalyzed by father's exhortations. A journalist in her late twenties sought the wisdom of a mentor like father and used it to motivate considerable achievement at an early age:

> My father's attitude toward work was that "if you aren't dead, you should be at work." That is exactly the way I feel now. He taught me to show up on time and do my job to the best of my ability. A half-assed effort was not acceptable. I can't help but believe (from my own experience) that very few people my age believe that—a job to them is simply something that must be done. My father taught me to enjoy my work, to do my best, and I would be successful. He also showed me that if I was not happy in my job, I should still give maximum effort and use the results to find a job that would make me happy.

Since there was no dissonance between her father's advice and her own instincts, the journalist could follow her father's credo without the agonizing sense of constraint that inhibits many of the other daughters of Patriarchs as they make their choices as working women.

A fervently dedicated young typesetter was similarly able to use her father as a mentor, even while acknowledging that their values and life goals diverged:

One thing my dad has said that has stuck with me concerns a worker's relationship with his/her boss: "If you earn a dollar, make sure your boss has made two." He is a super worker (although all my life he has been full of stories about what fools he works with). I have become a super worker myself, often staying late without pay to make sure the job gets done right and on time. Another message: "If you end up being a street sweeper, be the best damned street sweeper you can be." He thinks I'm "too good" to be a typesetter, but I'm sure he realizes that I'm the best damned typesetter in the West—and he's right.

While some Patriarchs' daughters find their fathers' adamant advice authoritarian and restrictive, for others—often in spite of themselves—their fathers' counsel provides a touchstone of security:

This is funny. My father's motto is "Everything happens for the best," and damned if I don't end up believing it. I hate that slogan, yet every setback that happens, I always think, "Oh well, everything happens for the . . ." It usually works out. But I hate anticipating it. I hate the thought of victory in defeat. It's a little alien to my skepticism.

At his best the Patriarch offers the steady leadership of a mentor and provides his daughter with a firm base from which she can develop the confidence to set out in the world on her own.

As unassailable an authority about the world of work, so difficult is the Patriarch as a model for love. Still, where the Patriarch's authority about the working world usually remains unchallenged in this family, his perspective about matters of the heart is often substantially offset by the mellowing presence of mother. When the daughter of the Patriarch looks to find herself a lover, she juggles two rather opposing models of intimacy: her father's strict authoritarianism and her mother's more conciliatory emotionalism. The yo-yoing of her love affairs often swings from one extreme of her parents' partnership to the other. If she chooses a man whose emotional temperament is more like mother's, she may feel more at ease in the romance but uncomfortable for betraying father. But if she chooses a man of harsher emotional mettle, like father's, she ends up loyal to father, disloyal to mother, and stifled in the relationship as she was stifled being her father's daughter. So the love lives of the daughters of Patriarchs are often pendulum swings of frustration and disappointment, which eventually inspire a search for compromise.

Two of these daughters describe the difficult push and pull between father's style and mother's style in their romantic attachments. The first is an unhappily married Chicana in her early twenties, whose father was negative and punitive, never abusing his wife physically, only "mentally with awful comments":

> My husband is in many respects like my father in that he has a bad temper and tries to pull macho, bullshit tricks on me. However, some of my other male friends have been more like my mother—mellow, witty, and good-natured.

The second is the thirty-eight-year-old Helen, introduced in the opening of this chapter, the daughter of a distant and authoritative father whose "ways are the only ways," and a subservient mother who played nurse to her daughter. Coming out of this no-win partnership, Helen now finds herself caught between two extremes of lovers, neither of whom makes her happy: "I usually choose men who want to smother me or reject me. I can barely tolerate either one at present." Either smothering like mother or rejecting like father, her lovers mirror the worst about each parent and snag her with the same hook by which each parent snagged the other. Bound to these lovers, she remains bound to her parents—and not yet free to find a compromise, a partner who will neither lord over her nor grovel at her feet, but join her on common ground as an equal.

At times the romantic tug-of-war for the daughter of the Patriarch seems to settle itself on a partner strongly reminiscent of one parent or the other. When the model is mother, the description of the relationship takes on a gentler, more satisfied tone:

> The men I have loved have been more motherlike, more gentle and less concerned about a macho image (my father would never admit to such a concern, but I'm sure he would never get caught exhibiting "too much" gentleness). My current love is not ashamed to cry with me. I can't imagine my dad letting anyone see him cry. The men I have loved have not been authoritarian or insensitive to my feelings. My dad is both.

When the model is father, the description of the relationship becomes charged with frustration and bitterness. A woman whose father was "unquestionably The Authority" until illness broke his reign repeats this familiar but destructive pattern with her lovers. In her love affairs she hopes to assuage her lovers' troubles as she could not assuage her father's—nor he hers:

> I usually choose men who are troubled in some way: closet homosexuals, men with mother problems, three who were truly mentally ill, alcoholics, etc. I thought I could "help" them. They only gave me headaches. I usually loved them more than they loved me.

Many daughters experience the unconscious urge to replay their relationships with father in their relationships with lovers—hoping that this time, or certainly next time, the relationship will come out right. They and their lovers will iron out the earlier disappointment, frustration, or rejection and finally achieve a wrinkle-free, happily-ever-after ending. For the daughter of the Patriarch this urge—and its built-in frustration—seem to be experienced most intensely. For her father has set himself up as the unassailable authority, and thus ensures that he will never be matched. If she tries anyway to find a lover to match him—and fails—she may feel she has bound herself to father all the more tightly and painfully. And if she succeeds in finding a partner in her father's image, she has served only to re-create a relationship in which she was unhappy to begin with. So in matters of both the heart and mind the task for the daughter of the Patriarch as she moves toward adulthood is to face and confront the long shadow of her father's authority and begin to replace it with a budding sense of her own authority, her own efficacy in making choices that are beneficial for her.

At fifty-six, *Ismene Judson*, born *Isabel*,* is still struggling with the shifting shadow of her father's Patriarchal will. The shadow is as menacing a specter in the imagination as the stentorian voice that responded to her childhood report card of A's, "Did anyone do better, and if so, why did you let that happen?" Ismene is an imposing woman herself, the kind it is difficult to imagine ever was a child. Like Pallas Athene, she, too, could have sprung full-bodied and fully armored from the forehead of Zeus. Even now there is a mythic quality about her. It is there in her stature, which is overbearing, larger than life; in her costume, which is often long velvet capes and turbans the color of coal; and, not the least, in her name. It is a name she gave herself after her father's death, partly a stage name and a pen name, partly an effort to re-create

---

*All full names are pseudonyms if italicized when they first appear. If not italicized, full names are the real names.

herself beyond her father's image. For the girl, Isabel, whose father read aloud from Greek mythology when she was seven, the name Ismene is heavy with meaning—for she was the younger and more faithful daughter of Oedipus Rex, who had unwittingly slain his father to marry his mother.

When Ismene speaks, it is Vesuvius erupting, fifty-six years of pent-up emotion spewing forth, stories and images and tangents, one fast upon the other, hot and incandescent, like lava. "My father is still the reference point, despite myself as a reference point, which I'm working on and which is so difficult." This is how she begins her story, leaning forward dramatically in her living room, high on a hill in San Francisco, windows taking in the full sweep of the city, its bay and bridges. "My father really had more going for him than either of my husbands. I still ask myself, what would my father think, say, approve? It surprises me that it's this emotionally loaded after recycling in my brain so many times." Beneath the majestic turban her brow furrows. Her gaze sweeps across the city to the bay, without even seeing it. "It was a case of unrequited love."

Ismene talks of her father the way a woman speaks of a difficult but adored lover. And the time she has spent unraveling his mystery and trying to disentangle from his grip is easily matched by the time other women might spend mooning and swooning, appraising and lamenting over the fatal attractions of a suitor who remains impossible to catch. Like the starstruck lover, Ismene places her father on a pedestal, inflating his importance out of all proportion, devaluing the worth of those who fall in his shadow, herself included. When she and I first meet, she introduces herself as "the daughter of a famous man." Later she adds with due solemnity that being her father's daughter was as awesome a responsibility as being the daughter of Freud. "Of all the famous men I have ever met, and I have shaken hands with many famous men," she confides, "my father was the most powerful."

But as it turns out, the magnitude of her father's fame is awesome mostly from the perspective of the child. A legislator, then a judge in a middle-size midwestern city, her father was a learned man, a distinguished man perhaps, but his impact does not parallel the colossal impact of Freud by any stretch of the imagination—except his daughter's. Indeed, in a more levelheaded moment, Ismeme concedes a closer picture of the truth, that in his judgeship her father "reached his perfect pond."

Just as her father's public persona was the archetypal Patriarch—commanding arbiter of right and wrong—so, too, was his private persona. Remote and intellectual, he spent his hours at home a million miles away, behind a newspaper, emerging only occasionally from his reverie to issue a pronouncement. "I never saw my father exercise in my life," Ismene remembers. "He sat and thought. He said he got his exercise pallbearing for his golf-playing friends." And just as he was detached from his body, he was cut off from his own feelings—and the subtle and sensitive needs of his growing daughter. And Isabel seemed more needful than most, understandably, since her mother had died only six days after she was born. Nor was her father ever adequately able to help his daughter understand or assimilate this loss. "Once I tried to ask him about my natural mother," recalls Ismene, "and he just sat there. Stone-faced. I retired, defeated." For a man who couldn't tolerate the disturbing welter of his own emotions, stonewalling was the only available response to his daughter's overpowering and confusing needs.

When Isabel was three and a half, her father remarried. The woman he chose was a kindly "spinster type, enormously grateful to my father for marrying her." Years later her stepmother would quote her father's proposal: "I think you are the right woman to raise Isabel." As it turned out, her stepmother did provide much of the warmth that her father, for all his stature, lacked. Family friends made no secret about the terms of the partnership. "People constantly came to me," says Ismene, "and said what a great man my father was and what a good woman my mother was." Nor was the contrast lost on Isabel. "Father was the one I admired and wanted to be like, but she was the one I would run to."

Not surprisingly, parents' expectations of daughter were equally contradictory. "My father's message was 'Excel.' And the only way I could get his attention was to be as overpoweringly intellectual as he was. My mother's message was 'Be very good and sweet and put everyone else first.' " With the advantage of hard-won adult hindsight, Ismene calls this "the primal conflict that spawned the Women's Movement." But as a little girl, grabbing for a thin reed of direction among the mixed messages, she describes herself as "swimming around in the soup." "My parents gave me so much," she realizes now, "but what I needed they didn't give me—like confidence in myself as a woman. It was a very rarefied, sexless world. And I was never acknowledged as a female." The one person from whom she craved that acknowledgment was never able to give it to her. Too Olympian and removed, too mired in his own doubts about sexuality, her father could never offer her that simple yet profound confirmation of her girlishness. Typically, she took the burden of her father's limitation on herself. "All my life I tried to reach him and I never did," she says now. Her father died when she was in her mid-twenties. "Had he lived," she adds, "maybe I could have resolved the enormous admiration and resentment I felt toward him." Instead she transferred that disproportionate admiration, that cavernous resentment, onto the men in her life.

"Let's take on the whole enemy tribe," she says, warming to the saga of her two marriages. Nor is the imagery of combat casually chosen. For both her husbands, as the story unfolds, were sparring partners in the battle of love. With each she fought to get the attention, the acknowledgment, and of course the love that had never been forthcoming from father.

But never knowing that love as a child and armed only with the backlog of contradictory parental messages, she sabotaged the chance of peace at every turn. "I wanted to find men who were unhappy and make them happy" is one of her appraisals now. "In fact, I did the opposite. I found men who were happy and made them unhappy. That's life." Or again: "I have always wanted to know how a man feels. But both my husbands have been nonlisteners. I've always been trying to tear down my father's paper."

Her first husband was her college professor of government. Ten years her senior, he was "very responsible and intellectually competent in a glacial way." He also had polio and walked "spiderlike" with two canes. To Ismene, the disability added to his glamor rather than detracting from it. "If anything, his polio was romanticizing. There had never been an emphasis on looks in our family. The polio was a plus, if anything."

When he proposed, he wrote one letter to her, one to her father. Her father went to the chairman of the government department to ascertain whether his future son-in-law was responsible and honorable. For Ismene the question was more elusive, the move from father's daughter to husband's wife threatening as well as exhilarating. "I wanted it and was afraid of it" is how she puts it now.

As it turned out, in the shadow of her husband who "was harsh in his judgments and found most people defective," she flowered little more than in the cool glare of her father's reflected prestige. "I thought he was marrying me for my brains," she observes, "but instead he wanted to stamp them out." She grimaces. "There is no lower form of life than being a nonprofessional faculty wife. I tried to see us as Beatrice and Sidney Webb, but my husband did not agree. He said, 'The movie *Sayonara* is the way a woman should be. I can get intellectuality at the office. From you I want serenity.' " After dinner he would go to his study and shut the door. Gradually it dawned on her with an all too familiar rage that she had re-created her childhood world, father's newspaper and all.

Just as once she had written her father finally venting her spleen only to get a raised eyebrow in response, now she filed a five-page letter of complaint with her husband—again provoking not more than a flicker of acknowledgment. But, she says, "He did modify his behavior. Things got better. There were high points, though I can't say they were emotional high points with him." They had three daughters together, traveled to Europe, hammered out a truce of sorts. Later he started drinking and again became more difficult to live with. Finally, swimming in their indoor pool—the one indulgence he sanctioned—he had a heart attack and died. He was forty-four, his wife thirty-four.

The years following her husband's death seem, in retrospect, the most satisfying of Ismene's life. Certainly they provided her with her first real taste of independence and her first chance to use the talents that atrophied as a faculty wife. "It was the first time I'd made decisions for myself," she says, "and I loved it." Relatively secure financially, she got a good teaching job at a private girls' school and began her whole social life again. This was also the time she first got involved in community theater and gave herself the stage name Ismene Judson. With her father's death and her husband's death, she hoped, too, she could put the girl Isabel to rest. Approaching forty, she wished desperately at last to be her own person.

But the man she chose to be her second husband—her director in the community theater—soon pulled her back to that painful childhood place where her needs were trivialized or ignored. "As the daughter of an authoritarian father," she realizes now, "I married my professor as a student and my director as an actress." At first her director, *David Stein*, this time twelve years her senior, did seem an improvement on her first choice. Gregarious and open to people, where her first husband was "more Olympian," David was, certainly on the surface, charming and witty. "I could be fairly natural with him," says Ismene, "and he wasn't intimidated by my intellect." Perhaps the best time of their marriage was the first nine months, when she commuted from her house in the suburbs to his apartment in the city. "It was like an assignation, even though we were married."

But proximity ironically revealed the gulf widening between them. "When we moved in together, the snake came out of the grass in the Garden of Eden." David's wit became a kind of chattering volubility—incessant talking about "everything but us, our problems." His charm turned out to be a kind of cover for a violent cache of anger, often unloaded on Ismene's daughters as well as on Ismene herself. Though he was more supportive about her talent than her first husband, David's ambivalence grew to jealousy as Ismene was offered more and more roles by other directors. Eventually, after his stormy urgings, she made her way out of acting and into poetry, taking on new territory, leaving him to guard his own.

"The first three or four years of our marriage," she admits now, "I felt like a hysterical child. I took his anger very seriously. I would dream of a man saying, 'Darling, tell me what you're feeling.' But David would shake his finger at me and say, 'Don't tell me that shit.'

"I went to a divorce attorney twice," she continues. "I would fantasize about freedom. When he was around, I felt I couldn't smoke, open the window, or talk on the phone. Then, both times, things got better after I threatened divorce." Once again she found herself under the jealous control of a judgmental guardian, sparring with him for attention, affection, and the gift of her own freedom.

Nevertheless, they have remained together, and a compromise, occasionally grudging, has been worked out. Ismene owns a small apartment building, and she lives in the apartment upstairs while David takes the one downstairs. They see each other often, but not all the time, cooking meals separately but usually eating them together, sharing a washing machine and the occasional evening out. The morning I meet with Ismene, David appears on the scene to tell her to turn off the washing machine because the noise is bothering him. He is a slight man who looks far younger than his almost seventy years, a Peter Pan to her Wagnerian Valkyrie. In the five minutes he remains in her apartment, she manages to make a slur against "little theater"—his life's work—while he reciprocates with a dig about writers who don't publish or earn money—her present vocational status. The sparring between them has escalated to brush fires, if not open warfare.

"David is such a loser," she confides to me after he has left. "My father was such a winner, because if he didn't have a four-flush hand, he wouldn't play." When she talks about her father, her eyes light up, then grow wistful. "I have had many things in life," she confesses, "but not the perfect man. Now I'm no longer looking for the impossible he." Like the virgin who remains attached to her first, chaste love, Ismene, despite marriages and children, despite vocations and talents, remains loyal and forever linked to father. Choosing first one partner, then a second who did not challenge her father's "greatness" but did manage to re-create the emotional chasm of childhood, she no longer needs search for the "impossible he." She has already enshrined him in her imagination. Days after we meet, she sends me a poem inspired by our recent conversation. She calls it "Electra Mourning," and I found no more fitting epitaph for her own story as daughter of a Patriarch:

Wafted, amphibious by limousine
from our domestic bog
back to the marble habitat
where you could shine
flanked by your fellow potentates
pot-bellied in a polished pond,
harumphing
and with gavel brandished high,
you were the frog-prince in my fairytale . . .

Small wonder now
that, tutored to refute
my every argument,
bound by opinions
other than my own,
and powerless to appeal
since never heard,
I worship angrily a god I never knew . . .

deep within my psychic center still—
scar tissue veils the niche
where, dozing on a pedestal, you sit
austere, contemplative, humane
and scented with the smoke of choice cigars
burning like joss sticks to perfume
in perpetuity
the shrine of an Ascended Master.

CHAPTER

3

THE PAL

GROWING UP, UNTIL I WAS SEVENTEEN, I PERCEIVED MYSELF as father's confidante, his right-hand child, his servant, his defender, his spiritual ally. I felt tremendously stimulated by the intellectual nature of our talks and also afraid if I did not earn this favor, he would oust me from his life.

Rachel, *twenty-eight*

Dad is intelligent, confident, loves to tease and play; he also tends to be selfish, domineering, and stubborn. He loves a good laugh and is also easily brought to tears. He's an intellectual who enjoys a healthy argument. I gave him a T-shirt with the following inscription: "Those of you who think you know everything are very annoying to those of us who do."

Monica, *thirty-four*

The Pal father uses the magical properties of fatherhood to turn his daughter from an ordinary girl into someone very special—his friend, his ally, his intellectual sparring partner. He closes the gap between parent and child and creates the illusion of comradely equality. By singling out his daughter for special favors, he bestows a double-edged gift. For his attentions fan her sense of self-worth and buck up her self-esteem, so that the daughter of the Pal has the widest sense of possibility, the most limitless potential for leaving her mark on the world. But the Pal's expectations may also become a heavy burden, psychological baggage that is part guilt (will she be punished because he loves her best?), part fear (will he desert her if she grows unworthy of his love?), part resentment (if he also needs her to parent him, will she ever be able to leave him?). The Pal's daughter has a privileged childhood but an anxious one, and may face adulthood expecting the moon—and doubting she'll ever reach it.

The daughter of the Pal is lucky in work, sometimes less lucky in love. Her father typically feels most comfortable with his daughter's intellectual strivings, more awkward with her emerging sexual ones. He is confident with her endeavor excitement, loving to teach her chess, take her to court with him, help her edit her papers. But her erotic excitement may put him ill at ease. Awkward about his own sexuality, he may feel even more awkward to be reminded of hers, preferring the fantasy of intimacy without sexuality that she, as a young girl, provides. So the Pal's daughter may grow up feeling more certain about her mind than her body, more confident choosing a career that will satisfy her than a mate who will do the same. The legacy of her father's mixed messages may be a conflict about integrating love and work as an independent adult, a struggle to balance these two important parts of her life and to feel entitled to both.

What sets the Pal apart from other fathers is his extraordinary involvement in his daughter's daily activities and his inclination to include her in his own. He is teacher and guide, adventurer and co-conspirator. He is con man Ryan O'Neal to scalliwag Tatum O'Neal in *Paper Moon,* loyal not to society, only to each other. Or he is criminal lawyer Carson Drew, guiding, encouraging, and inspiring his daughter, Nancy Drew, to take on her own cases, solve her own mysteries. Occasionally, their cases intertwine, as the plot thickens, and pursuing her own criminals, Nancy gets to save her father's life. The bond between Pals has come full circle.

On one end of the continuum is the Pal father who nurtures his daughter from a position of confidence and steadiness, offering but not smothering her with affection. On the opposite end is the Pal who, feeling a lack in his own life, turns to his daughter to be bolstered, depends on her as a companion, and tags his love with a price—to be nurtured in return. Any particular Pal father may move from one end of the continuum to the other, depending on his daughter's age and stage. But from either end of the spectrum what the Pal offers his daughter is tangible and lasting: He treats her seriously. He teaches her that her thoughts and feelings, her ideas and dreams matter and count. His interest in her gives her the first clue that she is interesting; his valuing her lets her appreciate her own value.

The autobiographies of the daughters of Pals stand out from the others in the richness of detail of time shared, activities pursued together. A common picture emerges of buoyant pleasure in each other's company and an ongoing discovery of the world that sharpens the daughter's skills and understanding and keeps the father's perceptions fresh and young. While her childhood lasts, the daughter and her Pal live a perpetual *Butch Cassidy and the Sundance Kid.* From one such daughter, who at twenty-four is a successful and hard-driving attorney:

> When I was a child, my father always took me to the movies. We saw a lot of westerns and killer movies. My father's favorite actor is Charles Bronson. My father also played games with me. We used to play Games of the States and Go to the Head of the Class. Educational games and a lot of cards: poker and gin. He also used to take me for rides and we would play Gas Station, where I had to read out the names of the gas stations.

But along with the pleasure of the closeness lurks an additional hint of pressure, of resentment when, in some relationships, the closeness becomes cloying, even claustrophobic. The memories of Rachel, the twenty-eight-year-old social worker quoted at the beginning of the chapter, are typical of the privileges and burdens of the daughter of a Pal:

> My father and I have gone to tremendous lengths with each other in terms of what we have shared and the kinds of responsibility we feel toward each other. He does not have any men friends his own age or within any sort of peer group. My father and I spent a tremendous amount of time together during the years in California. He would call me

to help him in the yard; this usually translated to literally standing by, handing him tools, and most importantly talking to him. We would talk about how to take care of plants, what it means to learn something, how to do research about how people learn, teaching, science, etc. We talked about everything intellectually; there has always been a lot of subliminal emotional content to our talks, but we did not talk about how we felt, particularly.

She continues, questioning her ambivalence at her father's favoring her in childhood, and the mark his favors left on her adulthood:

I remember these years as being a complex assortment of feelings and attitudes toward my father and, indirectly, the rest of my family. I vacillated between feeling special and "selected" for the honor of serving him in this way, and feeling resentment that no one else in my family was called upon to step-and-fetch for him. In many respects the pivotal points for this kind of vacillation remain the same in the present. I work very hard professionally (emotionally and intellectually) to live up to the standards he inculcated in me; I resent having to do things perfectly, because I fail; I am amazingly easily undone when I think/feel that he is angry or disappointed in response to what I have done, or who I am. The intellectual advice/comradeship is something I seek with him still, although I try to do it less than before, because my emotions get so bollixed up when we embark on a project together, or when he advises me that I'm doing something "all wrong."

For Rachel, like other daughters of Pals, her father's favors become a privilege that can be won or lost. To win guarantees the comfort of his protection and adoration. But if, to win, she feels she must "do things perfectly," then she necessarily sets herself up to fail. And to fail, to make a mistake means being ousted from his life. Her childhood becomes a balancing act as precarious as dancing on top of a flagpole.

Some Pal daughters describe a tone of emotional fragility between themselves and their fathers, but others report a kind of heartiness that comes from being treated as a surrogate son. These daughters are often only or oldest children, and many seem to stand in for the sons their fathers never had. A twenty-nine-year-old rabbi remembers the encouraging camaraderie of her childhood:

> As an only child I have been my father's son as well as his daughter; he encouraged me to be well rounded in my skills and curiosities and taught me many traditionally "male" things—carpentry and tool use, self-defense (twenty years ago!), how to drive and do basic auto repairs, interest in nature (hiking, wild plants and animals). He encouraged me to be physically active, strong, and coordinated.

Another woman, the eldest of five, recalls how the birth of a brother when she was thirteen disrupted the comradely relationship she had with her father:

> I resented my brother for two reasons: I was tired of Mom having kids, and Dad finally had a real son. Yet being thirteen, I was at an age when I started looking at other males besides Dad. So in a sense my brother's birth worked out all right, because Dad might have lost his "son" (me) soon anyway, due to the natural sequence of life. But looking back, Dad and I have never been as "palsy" since that time: when I discovered boys seriously.

For all fathers and daughters, adolescence is a difficult and highly charged time of transition, a time when oedipal issues reemerge and demand resolution, a time when the passage from childhood to adulthood is being negotiated with feverish intensity. For the Pal and his daughter, as for the Patriarch and his, this time may be especially problematic. What the Pal offers his daughter is a relationship that flatters and enriches her achieving side while often minimizing, overlooking, or even denying her sexual side. The causes of this disparity are complex and various. Perhaps this father turns to his daughter out of disappointment that he doesn't have a son, then denies her budding sexuality to keep the illusion intact. Or he may feel sexually insecure or disappointed in his own marriage and seek comfort in the nonthreatening, adulatory company of his daughter. Also possible is a deeper fear that he may care *too* much for his daughter, a counter-oedipal wish that he may cover with intellectualization or active pursuits rather than emotional ones. So puberty, when daughter's blossoming sexuality and womanhood can no longer be overlooked, often creates a crisis for both:

> Throughout my puberty, my father tried to exert control over me and make me into an intellectual. After school, when I desperately wanted to be out playing flirting games and basketball with the neighborhood teenagers, he kept me in and tutored me in foreign languages. I resented it very much but ultimately was docile about it.

Looking back as an adult in her forties, this woman still aches over the lack of emotional closeness that all the foreign-language lessons never filled. "I needed more basic physical fathering as a child. He was too intellectual and remote."

A thirty-year-old woman, whose scientist father had groomed her as his intellectual helpmate and successor, vividly remembers the pall puberty cast on their relationship:

> My father had taught me to relate to men in the most chaste way, only sublimated through the intellect. As I started to step out of line by having boyfriends, that was when our relationship ended. If I had dates, that would lead to days of coldness on my father's part.

Her confusion was doubled by mixed messages coming at once from mother and father. For mother was a great beauty who relied on her looks for power and prestige. Though he had clearly chosen mother for her ornamental value, father was nevertheless training daughter to rely solely on the power of her mind. The battlefield was all too typically teenage:

> Mother wanted me to be a majorette. Father was so grossed out by the outfit that he acted as if I'd become a porno star. I went down thousands of notches in my father's eyes.

In every Pal relationship, puberty becomes a crucial testing ground. Both father and daughter must confront the changes that the daughter's approaching womanhood provokes. Whether the daughter moves into adulthood with guilt or pleasure, anger or excitement, a sense of loss or one of expectation, depends in large part on the way she and father and mother manage this transition. How she sees herself balancing love and work is also first questioned at this time with her father's messages weighing heavily in the balance. Does she feel confident about her capacity to work, but more hesitant about the possibility of finding love? Does she feel entitled to happiness in both love and work or does she fear her birthright may be success in work alone? The changes of adolescence bring these issues up from underground, as daughter redefines not only her relationship with father, but also with mother and the rest of the family.

If the Pal has distinctive images and fantasies of his daughter, the daughter, too, has deeply lodged pictures of her father, her mother, and their marriage. Although many children protect themselves from envy or disappointment by denying their parents' sexuality—almost all the women I interviewed claimed their parents had an inactive sex life—the Pal's daughter needs to believe more than most that her parents' marriage is unfulfilled. Indeed, this daughter often fantasizes that she would be a more suitable, devoted, and understanding partner than her mother is. Helene Deutsch illuminates two powerful fantasies that have special meaning for the daughter of a Pal:

There are two very trivial and fully conscious fantasies of the normal young girl that relate to the father. In one he is a great man who deserves a better fate, a victim of the prosaic mother who has tied him to the gray business of earning a living. She, the little daughter, would be a more suitable object for him, though he must painfully renounce it. In a large number of instances, a psychologically sound woman may have as her first love object— an object to which she often remains attached for life—an unfree man, often a married man, who fans her love and responds to it but cannot break his old tie. . . . The other girlish fantasy that often exerts a great influence on woman's erotic life is based on the idea that the father loves the mother as a sexual object, but gives his better self, his ideal ego to his daughter. She is the one, she thinks, who understands him and possesses his soul.[1]

Both voiced and repressed, shared in interviews and hidden in dreams, these fantasies riddle the stories of the daughters of Pals. Often these daughters see their mothers as demanding and unappreciative, tyrannical and wild, while their fathers are kindly and long-suffering, needing from their daughters what their wives cannot provide. A professor in her early forties, for example, is still convinced her father married the wrong woman:

My father kept very much to himself in my earlier years. Then he looked to me more than to my mother (for good reason). He certainly could have had a wonderful marriage, but he married a very wrong woman. While they share certain values (crucial ones), they have no interests in common. . . . They've always argued a great deal—mostly about petty money and investments or how forgetful/lazy/stupid Dad is. Mother raises the accusations typically. Then after fifteen minutes of her ranting and raving, he'll tell her to shut up or that she's irrational.

Like many daughters of Pals, this woman polarizes the family into factions, pitting herself and her father in league against her mother:

I first started to like Dad when he invited me to help him make Sunday breakfasts when I was six or seven. But we really got to be friends when we could relate mentally about history, world events, and art (around age ten or earlier). At the same time my relationship with Mother was falling apart, and he hadn't related well to her for years. In other words, there was a shift from two-against-one against my dad to two-against-one against my mother.

This woman tries to control the disturbing inconsistences of mother's and father's behavior by using the rudimentary mechanism of "splitting." Rather than cope with the stressful uncertainty, however real, that each parent shares a shifting balance of "good" and "bad" traits, she polarizes the two into "good" father and "bad" mother. Father is a good companion; mother is a drag. Father is a good provider; mother is a nag. Father makes all the efforts; mother only undermines them. The daughter is not yet sophisticated enough to perceive the way her parents' troubles or neuroses may be interlocking. She makes her world more manageable by squaring off the good guy against the bad. The child's reasons for resorting to this defense are probed by John Munder Ross:

> . . . the child's representation of the father has to do with [her] experience of the mother, with needs to preserve, idealize, or devalue her by attributing her inconsistencies to someone else. Because of her, the father's psychic image may be reduced by splitting into all good or all bad, his strengths or deficiencies denied or buried for one reason or another, his being informed by projected aspects of the self or simplified by introjecting certain of his qualities as the child's own. The possibilities are manifold.[2]

The childhood memories of a twenty-five-year-old lawyer provide more evidence of this daughter's penchant for "splitting" the parental dyad. Her fantasies are fanned by freely-confessed-to oedipal fervor, rather startling in its bluntness:

My mother probably shouldn't have had children. She's too high-strung and self-involved. I have a lot of disdain for her. My father has always been more of a mother to me in the sense of being more attentive and involved.

When this woman was ten, an incident occurred that added more fuel to her oedipal fires:

When I was ten, my mother had her appendix out. I slept in the same bed with Father, and from then on that became a sexual fantasy. I have trouble sympathizing with Mother's complaints about Father, because I think he's a tremendous catch—generous and self-denying and in a material sense —goddamn. [She sighs.] You don't win if you are the daughter. The wife does. She gets the presents, goes to bed with Father. I tried to pretend Mother was the oldest of us four children—but she wasn't.

Sometimes these daughters' fantasies are not accessible to consciousness, but only admissible in dreams, and it is not unusual for the daughters of Pals to report dreams of making love to father, where this union accrues complicated levels of meaning beyond the sexual one:

The most vivid dream I ever had about my father was one in which I was walking down a street in what seemed to be a Mexican town that was having a festival. People were all out in the streets having fun and laughing, but I wanted to go somewhere quiet. Suddenly from nowhere my father appeared and began to walk with me. The next thing I knew we were in my apartment (although it was a place I was not familiar with). We began to talk and then began some very heavy petting, during which my father was the most active. I stopped the activity and told him he must never tell my mother what had happened (he had told me he wanted to divorce her and live with me) because she loved him so much it would kill her. Just about at that point I woke up.

On the surface, certainly, the fantasies of the Pal daughters are charged with a kind of unbridled enthusiasm for father and barely veiled scorn for mother. But what the daughter expresses on the surface—hostility, contempt, pity, anger, envy—may belie the deeper-seated need for mother's affection, in addition to father's. The daughter may have first turned to father because of disappointment in mother, because of fear that her mother's mothering was somehow inadequate. *My mother probably shouldn't have had children* is the way the lawyer put it. *My father has always been more of a mother to me.* But guilty at this transfer of affection, the daughter may also fear that her mother's continued withholding of love is her punishment for the provocative fantasies about her father. In the language of her dreams, the daughter remembers, *I told [my father] he must never tell my mother what had happened . . . because she loved him so much it would kill her.* Perhaps an even more deeply buried fear is that if mother knew her daughter's fantasies about her father, her mother would kill *her*.

The mother's attitude toward her daughter's relationship with the Pal father is a formidable influence on the daughter's later development and decisions. Does her mother allow, support, even encourage her daughter to be close to her father without feeling unduly threatened or jealous? Or does she try to intercept such a relationship or undermine it as it evolves, feeling left out or insulted, making her daughter feel guilty, a betrayer? Clearly the daughters whose mothers give them the leeway to be close to father without withholding their own love are the ones who grow up with the widest sense of possibility, the greatest confidence that they can accommodate a work life and a love life, without fear of punishment or recrimination. The daughters whose mothers punish them for proximity to father are often the ones who, as adults, fear that they cannot have it all. They fear dire consequences should they be happy in love and satisfied in work and therefore unconsciously make sure that conflicts snag their chances of contentment.

Like all daughters, the Pal's daughter must make her way between conflicting loyalties as she matures. As she begins to make independent choices as an adult, she is pulled between commitment to father and attachment to mother, between the power and allure of the wide world that father has introduced her to and the known confines of home and mother. For this daughter the choices may be further complicated by an internal dilemma between mind and body, between the flowering of her intellect and the nervousness about or denial of her sexuality. Many of the Pal daughters describe their twenties and thirties as continually disrupted by conflicts over work and love. Rachel, the twenty-eight-year-old social worker, looks back with painfully mixed feelings on an important college relationship, which she left to complete her education at a more rigorous institution—by no small coincidence her father's alma mater:

> My father has occasionally referred to that man as the one I should have married, and why didn't I? And it was not until fairly recently that I realized that my father does not even know that I chose to return to his alma mater over the relationship—in a sense chose my father. He naïvely seems to believe that I could have had both or maybe reneges on his assertion that my education was most important and so supersedes the long-term relationship I might have had. And maybe all of this analysis is only in my own head. My father has always told me what a wonderful wife and homemaker I would make; he also pushes me in my career. I do not see how to do both, feeling them to be incompatible, so I am often torn, painfully, in opposing directions.

For the twenty-nine-year-old rabbi whose father molded her into a surrogate son, the poles of the conflict are similar, but the tone is less desperate, the possibility for resolution seems more hopeful:

> My father and I are both workaholics. We share a strong sense of duty. Currently I have a job I very much enjoy and co-workers I care about deeply. My mother's strongest fear is that my career will prevent me from marrying happily and having a family (it is a clear and simple fear of mine as well). If I can't do both, *I* choose the career; if I can't do both, *she* chooses marriage and family. My father opines that I can do both. The truth may lie somewhere in between.

While both the social worker and the rabbi describe similarly tight-knit camaraderie with father, the pivotal difference may lie in their differing relationships with mother. The social worker reports a long-standing stormy and bitter relationship with her mother, whereas the rabbi's relationship with mother, though "mercurial," has something more of a "live and let live" quality ("My mother is, with some bewilderment, proud of me—perhaps because she does not know what else to make of me.") Even a degree more of security in her relationship with her mother—coupled with her father's faith in her—gives this daughter the added boost of confidence in making choices as an adult.

The daughter of the Pal may be conflicted as she takes on the task of assimilating work and love, but my interviews and the autobiographies suggest that in her work, she is most likely to be productive, ambitious, and successful. The day-to-day exposure to father and his world seems to widen her sense of possibility and scope, breaking down restrictive stereotypes that constrain other women from confronting a predominantly male professional preserve. Her father's expectant focus on her and unswerving faith in her build her confidence and competence. His gift of singling her out and making her someone special inspires her to prove her worth and motivates her to surmount the obstacles in her way. Certainly mother may contribute to this leavening of ambition as well. But in the generations of women I am studying, father is still the major representative of the world of work and the one with the most influential chance to help daughter decode its secrets.

In the autobiographies and interviews with daughters of Pals, the messages reported from father about work were unequivocal and unambiguous: Study hard, work hard, make something of yourself. Most important was the encouragement of limitless potential—often from mother as well as father—the sense that daughter could do or be anything she desired. A thirty-four-year-old professor remembers, for instance, "Dad always told me, 'You can be anything you want. You're smart, attractive, and healthy; but it won't come to you —you'll have to work on it.' " He mitigated this injunction with an "unspoken message" not untypical of the Pal: "Be independent—but not from me." Paradoxically, the Pal relationship generates its own internal dilemma. For the Pal father motivates his daughter to greatness by keeping her under his wing. As she gains competence and the first taste of success, he must necessarily let her go—or she must engineer the separation. He may one day gain a doctor or lawyer or rabbi —but he will also lose his Pal.

The Pal father may ease the pain of this separation by attaching his daughter's achievements as if they were his own property. And the daughter may encourage him to do this out of a protective kindness, a gnawing guilt, or perhaps a buried dependency that has not yet been broken. A twenty-four-year-old attorney, the daughter of a small-business man, explains:

My father is very enamored of diplomas, and kept my B.A. on his desk for years. My father's message was EDUCATION. I think it's fairly obvious that I have adopted that message without reservation. His subtle message was always that he lacked an education and thus many doors were closed to him. My father's message has made me feel proud about what I do, even when I think it's ridiculous. I still send my father copies of legal work I do, and he reads through them, although my mother doesn't. I sometimes think my father exaggerates my position, but I love it.

The sense of being someone special—first to father and en to the world—is a critical incentive for the daughters of ls. A thirty-five-year-old professor who grew up in the West dies remembers how her politician father chose her among his children to climb aboard the back of the truck when he ent speech-making in the country. Having been singled out him this way became a kind of magical cloak of protection, ving her a sense of personal power and destiny. Not until e came to this country at nineteen did she realize that she as black and might face barriers because of her race:

My father saw me as an *exception*. He thought I was not to fly off the handle, lose my temper, get disheveled, have a nervous breakdown—or if I did, no one would know about it. One was allowed to be aggressive, but that was an art in itself. My life has been unique, because for the first fifteen or sixteen years I did not have barriers. I did not realize that because I was black or a woman there were things I could not do. That changed when I came to this country. Many women I went to college with wanted to be dental hygienists—assistant roles. I couldn't believe that about America.

his woman's father had not raised her to be an assistant, but ather to run the show, even in the face of centuries of social onditioning that spoke to the contrary.

Although the literature on women and achievement is still volving and often contradictory, many significant studies onfirm the connection between the daughter's closeness to n involved father and her potential to leave her stamp on the world. Among the most provocative are Marjorie Lozoff's study of able college women at Stanford University, Ravenna Helson's examination of women mathematicians at the University of California at Berkeley, and Margaret Hennig and Anne Jardim's research on the country's top managerial women.

For "Fathers and Autonomy in Women," Marjorie Lozoff interviewed about fifty Stanford undergraduates, chosen from a larger random sample, after psychological tests and questionnaires showed evidence of potential for success—in the professions, personal relationships, or volunteer work. Lozoff eventually divided the sample into "Autonomous," "Moderately Autonomous," and "Least Autonomous" developers and found that the degree of autonomy and the amount of conflict students experienced seemed closely linked to their relationship with father. The Autonomous-Developers set far-reaching horizons for themselves and imagined lives combining "growth-producing marital relationships with personal development." Of the three groups, their relationships with fathers were also the most intense and involved:

> Most of [the] *Autonomous-Developers* had dynamic, ambitious brilliant fathers who married admiring and supportive wives. In many instances, the daughters were attractive women at the same time that they were energetic, ambitious, and vigorous like the fathers. . . . At the same time that these fathers encouraged the women students to develop competencies without linking any sex-role value, for example, to either traditionally feminine or masculine interests, they still treated their daughters in a way that conveyed to the students a sense of their value as women. . . . The fathers of the *Autonomous-Developers* perceived intelligence, energy, and talent in their daughters and pushed them to exploit these qualities.[3]

The fathers of the Moderately Autonomous, on the other hand, were "aloof and perfectionistic" and the fathers of the Least Autonomous were passive in the face of their wives' overemphasis on making "the right marriage."

Ravenna Helson's study, "Women Mathematicians and the Creative Personality," compared a control group of Ph.D. mathematicians with a "creative" group (those whose record of research and publication was outstanding and who were "highly flexible, original and rejecting of outside influence"). Searching for the ever elusive ingredients of the creative personality, she administered extensive personality tests and probed their personal history in interviews. Not only did she find that very few of the creative mathematicians came from families with a brother, but she also found a distinctive pattern of primary identification with father, not in this case an adoring "pal" of a father, but rather one whose affection had to be won by achievement:

> One forms the picture of a very intelligent child who was attracted by her father's intellectual status, felt alienated from her mother, adopted her father's attitudes toward work and achievement but received relatively little attention or affection from him. Isolated from both parents, she developed the strategy of making herself autonomous by nurturing, gratifying and "growing" herself in symbolic activity.[4]

In Margaret Hennig and Anne Jardim's important study, published as *The Managerial Woman*, the researchers interviewed twenty-five of the country's top one hundred corporate women executives. Here, too, the women's family patterns were striking in their similarity. *All* the women were either only children or eldest of an all-girl family, and all had had extremely close relationships with their quintessentially Pal-type fathers:

> Fathers and daughters shared interests and activities traditionally regarded as appropriate only for fathers and sons: physical activity, the acquisition of outdoor skills, an aggressive wish to achieve and finally a willingness to compete. Often her father's approval depended on the little girl's ability to succeed or to win.[5]

Hennig and Jardim appraised the impact of the father-daughter relationship on these women's potential for success:

> The father-daughter relationship provided an added dimension to these women's childhoods. From it they drew attention, approval, reward, and confirmation. It was an added source of early learning, a very early means of expanding their experience, and through it they gained a role model with which they could begin to identify. . . . To their fathers, they were girls. But they were girls who could do more than girls ordinarily did.[6]

Exposure to their father's world challenged these girls' stereotypes of male and female from a very young age. As adults they had an unconventional sense of what women could accomplish and the nerve to break through barriers into a formerly man's world.

Equally persuasive are the autobiographies of outstanding contemporary women whose early memories are testimony to the formative influence of the relationship with an involved and caring father on accomplishments in later life. Their stories speak both to the pleasures and perils of the daughters of Pals. From the autobiography of Margaret Mead, whose father, an economics professor, shared with her habits of mind that were pivotal to her development as an anthropologist:

> It was my father, even more than my mother, whose career was limited by the number of her children and her health, who defined for me my place in the world. Although I have acted on a wider stage than either my mother or my father, it is still the same stage—the same world, only with wider dimensions. . . . Father's vivid accounts of how a street railway in Massachusetts had failed and of the fate of a pretzel factory also gave me a sense of the way theory and practice must be related. And it was his knowledge both of the concrete sequences of activities necessary to carry out any process and of the men involved . . . that gave me a sense of how important it was to link together the concrete and the abstract.[7]

Shirley Chisholm's father was a bakery man who had a fifth-grade education, but from his expansive reading knew a bit about every subject. His messages about achievement were straightforward and nourishing as bread. "You've got to go to school," he would say, "and I'm not sending you to play either. . . . Remember, only the strong people survive in this world. God gave you a brain: use it." As many daughters of Pals find out, the special relationship between Chisholm and her father was both an incentive and a burden:

> Papa left a legacy of bad feeling in my family. Ever since I had been in grade school, we had always been the closest. We shared an interest in current events that Mother and my sisters did not have. He and I talked more than he did with the other girls. It sometimes seemed that it was the two of us against my mother and my three sisters. Papa left no will, but before his death he had set up a trust fund for me, with what had been left of his savings after he bought the house. There was no way I could change the arrangement, and the jealousy it naturally caused has been a barrier between me and my family ever since.[8]

A double-edged gift: a barrier between his daughter and the rest of the family, but a doorway into a world of achievement and contribution to others.

For Jane Fonda, being her father's daughter and following in his artistic footsteps also meant a contradictory journey— an enormous boon to the performing and public side of herself, but a detriment at times to the womanly and private side:

> Looking back, I realize that my only major influence was my father. He had power. Everything was done around his presence, even when he wasn't there. It wasn't an unusual way to grow up, but he was also famous and that increased everyone's sense of his power. . . .
>
> I became my father's "son," a tomboy, the one to bait our fishing hooks with bloodworms and pretend I didn't mind. I was going to be brave, to make him love me, to be tough and strong.
>
> My father was always attracted to strong women, and yet for him, women weren't where the action was. I thought women were to be scoffed at and scorned.

To please her father, Jane Fonda became a strong woman, which for her meant a male-identified woman, isolated from other women and from the deepest, most womanly part of herself:

> In fact, I never had a woman friend until after I had a child. I felt a lot of initial terror at being pregnant. It was irrevocable proof that I was a woman and therefore one of the people who were going to get wiped out.[9]

With a legacy of crossed messages—a mother who committed suicide, but a father who liked strong women—it is no wonder that her sense of herself as a woman becoming a mother was shaky. For Jane Fonda, having her own daughter and allowing herself to experience her connection with other women meant allowing another part of herself to blossom, a part that was not able to be nurtured by her father, close as they were.

For Susan Cheever, novelist daughter of the late novelist John Cheever, a close connection and identification with a literary father proved both an incentive and a hindrance to a literary career. Looking for work became the focal point of her life's journey—and not surprisingly the title of her first novel, published in 1980, when she was thirty-six. In an interview with her younger brother, Ben, shortly after the novel was published, she acknowledged how vehemently she both did and did not want to become a writer like her father:

> Because Daddy was a writer, I thought I wanted to be a writer when I was about twelve or thirteen. Then I decided that I was no good as a writer and that I definitely didn't want to be a writer. It was the last thing I wanted to be. So, when I graduated from Brown I got a job as an English teacher, because I didn't want to be a writer. Then I got married because I didn't want to be a writer. I learned to cook, because I didn't want to be a writer. We moved to England so my husband could write. I didn't want to be a writer. Then we moved back to New York and we moved to the suburbs and we didn't have a lot of money. I needed a job,

so I tried making macramé belts, but I didn't sell very many of them. . . . I got very desperate. . . . Finally I tried the Westchester-Rockland Newspaper chain and at first they wouldn't hire me either, but then they did. I got a job as a reporter on *The Tarrytown Daily News*. . . . Of course the minute I started I just loved it. I was about twenty-eight at the time. But I still didn't want to be a writer. When people called me a writer, I would say, "No, no, I'm a journalist."[10]

She found, as many daughters of Pals find, that her closeness to her father provided both blessings and drawbacks during her quest for work. She pondered both sides of his influence in a conversation with me a couple of years before her father died. Their relationship, she felt, taught her a verbal playfulness ("Talk was the coin of my childhood"), demystified the literary life ("I never had that much reverence for writing, because it was done in the house"), and exposed her to an influential network of other literary lights. But living up to, indeed competing with the Cheever name became its own burden and may, in part, explain the fits and starts of her twenties and thirties before getting her writing career off the ground.

A critical crisis in her father's life turned out to be a turning point in her own development as well. "I didn't start writing fiction until I was thirty-five," she realized. "Several years before that my father had had a heart attack, almost died, and came to terms with it. Soon after, I unplugged the whole inner mechanism and began writing fiction." In some subterranean way her father's reclamation of his life allowed her to come to terms with her own. And by the time her first novel, *Looking for Work*, appeared—to mixed reviews but a certain commercial splash—her father's fortunes were at their peak. Daughter and father could enjoy each other's success and their own. "Who knows what my father's reaction to my first novel would have been five years earlier," Susan Cheever speculated, "when he was broke, alcoholic and hadn't published in ten years. But by the time my first book came out, his fortunes were totally turned around. He had published *Falconer* and was in the flush of his success, making hundreds of thousands of dollars a year."

And if glossing a bit lightly over the struggles along the way, John Cheever boasted in the proudest Pal manner about the way their good fortunes turned out to intertwine: "When my daughter, the novelist, was tapped for the Literary Guild at about the same time that my Book-of-the-Month Club sales had peaked, we lunched happily together and it seemed to me perhaps that a career chosen through emulation can be less taxing than a career arrived at through ricochet."[11]

The same Pal qualities that are such an inspiration to achievement may also be an inhibition to falling in love and finding a sustaining and permanent relationship. Father's cultivation of his daughter's intellect and achievements may leave her sexual side less developed, more repressed. And her tight camaraderie with father may prevent a nurturing closeness with mother, from whom she may also have learned more about her needs and desires as a sexual woman. Then, too, she may find it difficult to match that all-encompassing attention from father, which made her every move special, her every activity a crowning glory. Becoming an equal partner in a relationship or marriage may take a different and more demanding struggle than the Pal daughter is used to.

Because of her intimate and supportive relationship with father, this daughter's separation from him may be particularly painful and prolonged. Often, to extend her attachment to father she chooses inappropriate or unavailable men—married, homosexual, or of a different, hence "forbidden" race or background. At times these relationships may repeat and reflect the very prohibitions or limitations that are part of her relationship with her father. These liaisons may be intellectual rather than sexual in tone; they may involve another woman in a hauntingly familiar evocation of the oedipal triangle. The daughter of the Pal often has the sense that she is looking for someone just like dear old Dad, who will love her as dearly as he does—but she simply cannot find someone who can fill her father's shoes, whose love measures up to his. She is torn between wanting and not wanting to leave father, between wanting to find his equal and proving to herself that this is impossible.

The ambitious twenty-four-year-old attorney introduced earlier attributes the failure of her marriage to her poor choice—a man she thought was like her father, but turned out not to be:

> I thought my husband was a lot like my father: a worker rather than an intellectual. On my last visit home, seeing the two of them together, I realized how wrong I was. I sometimes think I married my husband just because he wouldn't interfere in my career. It never struck me that maybe he didn't care.

Imagining a partner chosen in the image of her father, she has replaced the highly charged—perhaps overwhelming—intimacy between herself and her father with a cold and callous indifference. Instead of re-creating her relationship with her father, she fears she is re-creating her father's relationship with her mother—but with a disturbing and self-punishing twist:

> My marriage is becoming just like my parents'. Two people in the same house, but with little or no interest in each other. I sometimes feel as if I am my father and my husband is my mother. This is what I swore would never happen to me.

Pulled between wanting to stay Daddy's daughter and yet wishing to become another man's wife, her awkward compromise gives her the worst of both worlds.

Rachel, the twenty-eight-year-old social worker, chose another kind of compromise. Her love affair allowed her to prolong her relationship with father, both by repeating the old dynamics and also by preventing her having to make a permanent choice. The relationship turned out to be ego-enhancing, yet ultimately self-defeating:

> One man in particular, six years older than I, with whom I was involved for five years, was incredibly supportive and instrumental in helping me like myself better. He was consistently reinforcing of me: He would tell me what specific things he enjoyed about me, what he liked best about the work I was doing, and that I was very deserving of the very best. Over and over he would say such things; after five years, I started to be able to believe that what he said was true.

Like her father, he shored up her shaky image of herself as long as she continually proved herself to him. And also like her father, he was already married:

> He was married throughout our relationship; we broke up under duress about a year ago, but I can still conjure up his reassurances and praises as a reminder to myself not to act as though I am a pariah.

There are eerie reverberations of her relationship with her father in her description of her lover:

> Our relationship seemed in many ways a perfect blending of qualities for me. We had a very strong emotional attachment (although the commitment was severely limited by the fact of his being married), were compatible intellectually, and shared many romantic ideals. He was a professor of mine and so combined a variety of attributes: He was an intellectual equal but professionally stood "above" me; he was warm and enthusiastic and intense emotionally. He was a major point of stability in my life, and a driving force

behind my commitment to my career—encouraged me continually to go to grad school, to finish, to move forward in my job.

Strong emotional attachment . . . severely limited by his being married . . . an intellectual equal but professionally stood "above" me . . . driving force behind my commitment to my career—each observation about her professor lover could also be made about her Pal father, who was also a professor. Most symbolic, the guilt—on both sides—about prolonging the attachment rather than separating and becoming autonomous—was duplicated in a way that at first felt familiar and comfortable but eventually became a stranglehold:

> He also wanted me to have a stable, "marrying" relationship, and often told me that he felt guilty for continuing our relationship because he felt that it held me back from finding someone with whom I could develop a long-term commitment. I fantasized about remaining his lover into our old age; he was enamored of the same idea—it was something we looked forward to; seeing ourself at seventy-five, still making passionate love and teasing one another.

Her fantasy about her lover was most likely a copy of her unconscious childhood fantasy about her father and was still freighted with all its paradoxical power—she would never separate from him, yet would also never be completely involved with him. Even at seventy-five, with all the passion she envisioned, her lover would still be someone else's husband.

For five years Rachel cherished "the safety and limitedness" of the relationship, which provided "total freedom and independence," in addition to a "secret" lover to "bolster [her] through periods of loneliness." But little by little the sham of the affair began to dawn on her, how "deadly it was to [her] self-esteem." For the "total freedom and independence" of the love affair was, of course, illusory. Never having earned that freedom by first negotiating the gut-wrenching separation from father, she could not truly experience it with her lover. Finally she realized with a jolt what a lie she'd been living:

> Even when I was in the throes of mourning my loss of [my lover], I could not publicly decry my woe. Clamping down on myself this way is terrible practice for how I want to live and amputates my head from my heart. It exacerbates what has always been a difficulty for me: integrating my strong emotions and my rationalizations.

This split between the head and the heart, the rationalizations and the emotions, can be a painful holdover from the relationship between daughter and Pal father. Often her first forays into love are bungling attempts at resolving the head-and-heart conflict, and they may veer wildly off course in one direction or another. The happier matches seem to be the ones that allow for expression of both sides of the self. These are also the relationships that take longer to find and achieve —and usually require a delicate dance of disentanglement from father first.

For a nurse turning thirty who has just now managed to find such a harmonious marriage, a dream about her father shortly before the marriage took place may provide a clue to its success:

> My father was standing on the porch at home and he had a tie in his hands. He said he was going to drop the tie over the side of the porch, and if I caught it he would stay, and if I didn't he would leave. I caught the tie, and he started to disappear. I asked why, since I had caught the tie, and he said, "You won't see me, but I'll always be there."

In the pun of the dream language, father's tie is also the tie to father, and the dream is a touching evocation of the dance of separation between father and daughter. If the daughter marries, the dream is asking, will the tie be dropped and broken? Will she lose her father? In this dream the father answers that the tie may be altered and the father may disappear, but as the daughter moves to a new and more separate phase of life, the old familiar and supportive tie will still be there.

When the daughter of a Pal does work out the tricky business of separation from father and finds a lasting relationship, the new partner is nevertheless often chosen in the image of father—with variations appropriate to the younger generation. Often the mate is sketched as more of a "feminist" man than her father was, and the expectations and emotional life of her marriage are more reminiscent of her relationship with her father than of her father's relationship with her mother. The daughter of a Pal often chooses to marry another Pal, but this time negotiating the relationship on her own terms. The nurse describes the many comfortable ways her husband reminds her of her father:

> He is easygoing, he doesn't put his job over being a loving and feeling person, he supports my educational ventures and my career, he supported my decision to keep my own surname when we got married, and he accepts me as an independent person. He is a budding feminist. We have interests we share and interests we don't share, we believe in open communication and don't feel that a marriage isn't worth its salt without a few good fights. Our parents were not fighters and neither are we.

A thirty-one-year-old psychologist married to an economist provides another example of a contented marriage to a man similar in many ways to her father:

> My husband, Peter, is like Dad in that he's affectionate, romantic, kind, thoughtful, intellectual, unreligious, basically nonmaterialistic, fun-loving, ideological/philosoph-

ical, freedom-loving, travel-loving, easy to smile and laugh, rational, patient, nonargumentative, uncomplaining about life, easy to get along with, willing to play loose with sex roles and sex stereotypes (on this he's better than Dad).

Although she has chosen a partner who shares many of her father's cherished traits, she also feels that her marriage is a significant improvement on her parents' marriage, which was fraught with bitterness, tension, and disappointment:

Peter's and my marriage is almost nothing like my parents', thank God. We rarely argue or fight. When we do, Peter is more insulting to me than I am to him—the other way around from my parents. We have lots of fun together and get along. We have mutual respect. We discuss intellectual things as equals. We help each other in our work. We have a fine sex life. We go out drinking together like on dates. I believe our marriage is much like my father wishes his was, though I don't know this for a fact (Dad would have thought I was "fast" in his day).

For every daughter contemplating marriage, the past has a contradictory pull: luring her with the memory of safety and familiarity, yet pushing her away with the memory of pain and disappointment. Psychiatrist Philip Spielman explains, "The basic law is that you can't outlive your past. We all want to recapture the past, yet separate from it. Every girl wants to marry her father, and yet doesn't. She may choose a man who is too much like her father, which would be incestuous, or too much unlike him, which means she doesn't get what she wants. The people who become patients are usually those who married men too much or not enough like their fathers."

Marriage provides an opportunity to replay the relationship of the past with a new partner and confront the issues of the past with another hope at resolution. As family therapists Lily Pincus and Christopher Dare point out in *Secrets in the Family*,

"For most people the conscious decision to marry is an attempt to find happiness and comfort rather than to solve conflicts. Yet at some level of their minds most couples know that the latter is inseparable from the former."[12] For most daughters marriage provides a chance to heal some of the jarring discordancies of childhood and to accommodate some of the contradictions of parental differences in a relationship fashioned after parental scripts—but with a chance of improving on them as well. In the memory of the daughter of the Pal is a cherished relationship with father, but often a beleaguered bond with mother, and perhaps an image of a tense union between mother and father. Looking for a partner, this daughter's challenge may be to find a man reminiscent of father who will allow her the chance to play a different and more satisfying role in her own marriage than her mother played in hers. For many daughters of Pals, finding such a match turns into a long and sometimes taxing series of trial-and-error love affairs.

In an apartment in New York City a single woman lives alone with her two cats, her muted stereo and walls of books, her brass bed and closets full of caftans and leotards. At thirty-one, *Suzanne Sarton* has lived on her own for almost ten years, working to make it as an actress in a city that does not cushion the trek to success. But she has stayed with it and persevered, not caving in to self-doubt during endless deserts of dry spells, not losing her cool or popping pills during the frantic, hard-driving times when her reputation was at stake. And now, although her name is not a household word, her face is often recognized from television series and commercials. Lately she has been doing a Hollywood stint and starring in a new TV series. She says, characteristically, about life in L.A. that it is "too easy," that she "needs a kind of struggle to keep me up to par." Although she already doubts that the show will last, she knows it is a terrific break and she's ready for the chances that will follow. "I have needed to be on my own this long," she says, "so I could establish my acting career, being afraid I might otherwise have given it up for some man." But at her watershed thirtieth birthday, surrounded by friends and family and all her accomplishments, she stood back from her life, stared hard at what was missing, and realized how much she longed for "a committed partnership," a man to live with and eventually start a family with.

Like many daughters of Pals, Suzanne's success and her longings are inextricably linked to her relationship with her father, whom she calls "the most influential person in my life." He is a surgeon and a workaholic who suffered a debilitating bout with polio in his twenties and still walks with a limp. Introspective and slightly depression-prone, he loves good talk, good food, and more than anything, his daughter. Her mother is small and determined, self-sufficient, self-enclosed emotionally, a civic servant, perhaps more capable of doing good works for humanity than of lavishing warmth upon her family. There are two older brothers, one more like mother ("You don't know how they feel, you have to extrapolate"), one more like father. This one, she says, is iconoclastic and "can be a little strange." During the drug-hazed days of the sixties he once said he "wanted an incestuous relationship with me." Baffled and shocked, she turned him down and estranged herself from him for years. But the request suggests the lack of boundaries in this family, the overlap of roles that can be unnerving and threatening.

Theatrical in manner and attitude, Suzanne has woven an elaborate mythology about the family, in which she and her father are the soul mates and she is the only person in the family whom her father can feel close to. A recent psychic reading fanned the fires of her imagination. "In my last life," she was told, "I was a music-hall actress and the mistress of a nobleman who had family elsewhere. My purpose in this life is to integrate those things, my independence and career, with a family life. When I asked about my father, the psychic said we had known each other in many past lives, but this was the first time as father and daughter. He said that in at least one past relationship my father had had a Svengali-like influence on me and that the purpose of our relationship in this life was for me to develop my emotional independence from him."

This scenario—the intense attachment to a nobleman who has family elsewhere, the push toward and pull away from his Svengali-like influence—meshes perfectly with the script of earliest childhood. "I was always Daddy's favorite little girl," Suzanne remembers. "I rarely saw him during the week, but on Sundays he and I went down to get the ice cream for dessert. And whenever I bought clothes, I gave him a fashion show and he oohed and ahed."

But thrilling as this romance might be, there was also an element of danger—and of guilt. "One night during the week my parents were eating after I had been put to bed. I came downstairs giggling, and my mother sent me back. My father was glad to see me but didn't want to challenge my mother, so let her take care of it. I could see he was not behind it. I came down twice more before my mother slapped my bottom, very angry with me. It is the only time I remember her spanking me. I got the message and did not return."

As a little girl intent on spiriting her father away from her mother, her reaction was foot-stomping rage. But looking back on the incident as an adult, her appraisal is considerably more complex. "Because my mother was emotionally distant, I always felt that I was providing that part of the relationship with my father. Instead of fighting for him, she gave him over to me, Electra, at a very young age. How does a little girl deal with feeling that she is responsible, as a wife would be, for a grown man? The spanking incident is the only time I remember her defining the limitations on my relationship with Dad. And I appreciated it." Her relationship with her father was tantalizing, but it was also an awesome burden. Shocked and guilty as a child at the power of her passion for her father, she needed her mother—and her father—to set limits for her, to show her that they did indeed love each other and could include her in the circle of their love without allowing her to disrupt it.

With this contradictory childhood history—pleasure and guilt, triumph and burden—Suzanne's romantic liaisons as an adult have, not surprisingly, followed a rocky path, also riddled with contradictions and crossfire. With each successive lover, she attempted a different strategy at breaking free of her family circle, and particularly of her father's tight emotional hold. First, at eighteen, she chose the most obvious line of attack, a lover who seemed utterly unlike her father: "Both my parents were extremely permissive, and I had little sense of what limitations there were on me or my behavior. My first lover knew exactly what he wanted me to be, how he wanted me to behave. I was happy to have a strong structure for my life, even though it was often counter to my own desires."

The limits on her childish fantasies and wishes that she needed from father and mother were provided by this young man. But within that framework their emotional life took on a distressingly familiar tone. "He turned out be very *like* my father in that he depended entirely on me. I was his rock, he couldn't do anything without me. I was the only person he allowed himself to be close to." In spite of herself, she had recreated the very bond with father she was trying to avoid.

So the next time, two years later, she upped the ante for her efforts and chose a boyfriend who was downright belligerent to her father. "I chose him, unconsciously I think, because he expressed so much hostility to my father and the way he had chosen to live his life. He was a radical and berated my father for making so much money, confrontations that began before I started going out with him and usually went on in my absence. I felt badly about it, but secretly wished I could see how my father dealt with being forced to defend himself." This lover expressed for her the anger and frustration that Suzanne felt too inhibited or ambivalent to express directly. She chose him because she hoped that his crude attacks on her father would somehow hasten the painful process of separation she was still unwilling to negotiate herself.

Years passed, during which she showed every sign of moving away from home and leaving her Pal behind her. Outwardly she was on her own, living in her own apartment, establishing a career. But inwardly the old ties were still constraining her. Having discarded the two men who were very unlike her father, now, in her late twenties, she chose—and almost married—a man "who indeed was Daddy." He attended her father's medical school, chose the same specialty, provided "an incredible psychic connection, just like with my father." Old pictures even showed an uncanny physical similarity. But despite these haunting resonances of her father, the dynamics of the relationship took an unexpected turn. Her lover "ended up more like those negative aspects of my mother—somewhat critical and aloof, extremely nonexpressive of his feelings toward me. In an argument once he said, 'I'm not going to be your indulgent daddy,' and I said, 'No, you're going to be the strict daddy I should have had.'" After all, her lover seemed to combine the positive qualities of her father with the more negative qualities of her mother, and she felt as trapped in this union as she had felt in the cocoon of her family.

Looking back on her lovers, she sees a parade of men who "are either unavailable to love me back—usually because of involvement in work and themselves and sometimes other 'steady' girlfriends—or so unresponsive emotionally that I don't know how they feel." She sees herself choosing these emotionally reserved partners the way her father chose her mother, so that "his emotions could be the important ones." But her father may have also picked her mother to avoid a certain scary depth of intimacy and commitment—a depth that he then tried to reach with his daughter, with loving intentions but nevertheless inappropriately.

The high charge of the Pal relationship may sustain the father but backfires for the daughter, later, when she searches for a love of her own. "When I was a kid," Suzanne realizes, "Dad was the good guy and Mom the bad guy. As I grew, however, and began to feel suffocated and not merely loved by my father, their roles switched, and I relished the autonomy I was able to experience with my Mom. With men, however, autonomy still needed to be enforced by their lack of involvement. This has changed considerably since my last love affair broke up, but there is still a residue of fear that emotional closeness will result in getting stuck in a quagmire that I can't get out of." In matters of the heart, the Pal relationship often leaves a residue of fear—fear of being unfaithful to father by loving someone else, fear of never finding another man who will be as adoring as father, fear of having to become as distant as mother to attract a man like father, and—most damning—fear that emotional closeness inevitably leads to suffocation.

Suzanne's dreams voice the shadowy shape of her fears: "I am lying on my back in a room with blue light coming through the curtains. A man is making love to me. His weight is very heavy on me. It is my father. I cannot breathe and feel I am suffocating, must push him away." Her father's love is a paradoxical presence, buoying her ambitions, but weighing heavily on her emotions. Before she can love another man, she must free herself of this burden. She must learn to make her father's love manageable enough to share while standing on her own two feet, then learn to share another man's love with give-and-take, while retaining her own balance.

The last time we speak she sounds buoyant at first about her future. She is riding high on the adventure of starring in the new series, and there is also a special new man in her life. This time, she assures me, the relationship feels different. Looking ack, she believes her last love affair with the doctor she lmost married purged a lot of residual feelings about her ather and other men. "That was a very analyzed relationship, vhere he represented my father to me and I represented his nother to him. After that, a whole lot of stuff dropped off. I elt more able to relate to men as they are, less in terms of how ey can save me."

She has been seeing her new lover for two months. She eels "more generous toward him, more accepting." Still— she admits this sheepishly—he is twenty years older than she. 'I finally found a man," she says, "whom my father couldn't overpower." She sighs and pauses, as if her thoughts drift elsewhere, back to the room with the blue light coming through the curtains where the presence of her father is not the easygoing Pal but a troublesome weight she has still not lifted.

4

THE BYSTANDER

My father is a complex man. He can be very charming —he has the "twinkle in the eye" charm when he wants to use it. But there is also a dark side of him. He has tremendous anger inside of him that he is unable to express. He withdraws, without any apparent reason, into a stony silence that can last for two to four months. He then becomes unapproachable.

Laurel, *twenty-eight*

My relationship with my father is zero, that is, it barely exists. My father is a very reserved person, and when I was growing up, he was usually at sea, so I barely remember him as a part of my childhood. In fact, I remember once when we were going to meet his ship, which had been gone for some months, I asked my mother what he looked like, because I couldn't remember. Now I feel some acceptance from my father of my life-style, which is somewhat different from his, and we seem to have arrived at some sort of peaceful coexistence. I would like it if we could communicate more openly. I would also like it if both of us felt less pathological attachment to the other.

Cynthia, *thirty-seven*

The Bystander is father in word, but often not in deed. He is at once alluring and frustrating, for he offers proximity without closeness, tangibility without intimacy. Unlike the Absent Father, who may be an elusive support but is certifiably physically removed, the Bystander is a physical presence but not an emotional one. His withdrawal may be the result of repressed feelings or his own difficult psychological history, illness or alcoholism. But to his daughter his emotional absence may be more painful and inexplicable than a literal absence or loss would be. Trying again and again to elicit his attention and involvement, she is bound to feel a misplaced and unaccountable responsibility for his moodiness or apathy that may eventually lead her to rage. What is there about me, she may anguish, or what have I done that is so terrible to warrant this chilling vacuum of response? Only with great effort, insight, or guidance does she come to realize she is neither cause nor effect of his yawning and frightening silence.

The Bystander can be both benign and malevolent. On the one hand he can be the mild and unassuming onlooker, passive in the face of the world's demands and limited in response to his daughter's, but well-meaning and well-intentioned. On the other hand he can be the remote and inaccessible father, withdrawn into his private nightmare and oblivious to his daughter's dreams. His passivity is a none too convincing cover for deep feelings of rage and despair, and to his daughter he may seem a threatening and aggressive presence. In between are many variations, which this chapter will document.

The daughter of the Bystander is always haunted by the hidden, by what is held back, stashed between the lines. With or without being fully aware of it, this daughter spends a great deal of psychic energy trying to ferret out and decipher the secrets her father appears to be keeping from her. Perhaps the secret is the low murmur of disappointment, an aching sense that life has let her father down, left him hopeless and despondent. Perhaps it is the nervous rustle of fear, a pervasive sense of anxiety, of not being able to cope with the world, of feeling at its mercy. Or more likely it is the churning and pounding of suppressed anger, a boiling rage that life has mistreated him, a rage that all too easily, the daughter fears, may be redirected against her. Now every daughter, of course, sees her father feeling disappointed, fearful, and angry. But the Bystander can be excessively tormented by these troubled feelings, while refusing to acknowledge them, so they fester within the family and may become an unspoken burden weighing upon the daughter as she moves forward into the world.

In Alice Hoffman's haunting novel, *The Drowning Season,* the image of a father's recurrent wish to drown himself—an image of lure as well as terror—inspires a kind of cautionary fable about the tenuous but powerful bond between the Bystander and his daughter. Phillip is the father, a strange and remote and eerily singleminded character who, every summer since his sixteenth, has tried to walk deep into the sea off his family's Long Island compound and drown himself. Obsessed with his own demons (among them the memory of a child-hood nursemaid who disciplined him by submerging his head in a sinkful of water), he has long since opted out of his role as a father. "Dear," he answers his wife when she voices a worry for their daughter, "what would you like me to do? I'm an invalid." This is the lament of the Bystander at its most unadulterated.

Esther the Black is the daughter, caught on the brink of womanhood in the net of her father's obsessions, caught between the oppressive borders of the family compound and her own growing need to break out. Sitting on the shore and watching her father make his annual attempt at drowning, Esther ponders the troubling connections between her father's patterns and her own:

> Esther the Black rocked back and forth in her chair; Drowning Season had become a part of her internal clock. She wondered if she would even exist in another place, if her plans of escape [from the compound] were worthless. She stared at the stone beach, where the gills and tails of bluefish and flounders the fishermen had caught moved without power. . . . Esther rocked back and forth; she had watched a drowning every summer of her life; and she watched again now. . . .[1]

Though the momentum of the novel leads inexorably to her father's successful drowning attempt, it also leads to Esther's gradual disentangling from her father's myth, a gradual drawing on her own resources, which enables her to move forward in the world on her own. Like many daughters of Bystanders, Esther seems to garner her own strength to persevere from the very sea, the very circumstances which consume her father.

In work and love the Bystander presents a frustrating kind of anti-image to his daughter. Too limited to respond to her endeavor excitement and too frightened to respond to her erotic excitement, he may leave her stranded as a child, providing neither outlet nor channel for her girlish enthusiasms, offering neither help nor focus on her journey to adulthood. This daughter may be aware, at least subliminally, of her father's hesitation as a worker and his limitations as her mother's partner and lover (perhaps delineated in no uncertain terms by her long-suffering mother). She may still find herself struggling to avoid her father's mistakes without really knowing how not to repeat them. As she grows up, he may come to define what she may be by what he is not. His limits provide a framework against which she must struggle to move beyond. But to better one's parent can be a dubious and unsettling achievement, so this daughter may battle guilt and her own inner demons as she becomes an adult. Certain she does not wish to tread in his footsteps, but uncertain about the unknown, untrodden path, she may feel mired in a place that feels uncomfortably similar to her father's passivity and lack of direction. And when she does motivate herself to move forward, she may need to keep up a heady momentum, as if fearing that any interruption to her progress might stall her in a standstill like her father's.

The autobiographies of the Bystanders' daughters are haunting with their images of secrecy and containment, of withheld and repressed feeling. The relationship with father is rarely experienced openly and directly, but rather as if father and daughter are separated by a long corridor, a darkened room, an obscuring haze. A Chicana recalls an immigrant father who was either bellowing with anger or sitting in a chair, sucking his teeth, lost and forlorn. A Jewish woman sketches a father who was famous for one-liners, but "they might be years in coming." A forty-year-old woman describes the distance that was imperceptible, but always there:

> I see my father through a haze as somewhat amorphous, the soft, "loving," round person (as opposed to my mother's distinctness in mannerisms, actions, words). He was con-

cerned that his family reflect himself well. He noticed his kids when they had a problem he could help with. I sought his attention by being the good girl he said he wanted.

Early on, the effort of being "the good girl," with no leeway or permission for venting the darker feelings of childhood, became too much to bear:

I developed migraine headaches at about age eight. My mother had no use for headaches, she felt they showed weakness. My father ignored them (ignored my pain).

Only years later was this woman able to unearth her feelings of rage against her father, because he could neither reach, nor assuage, nor even recognize her pain:

Through therapy I got in touch with my anger at him for not loving the real me but for loving me only as his daughter. I did not feel visible to him. Because I needed this for the development of my self-esteem and because I didn't get it from him, I sought identification and self-definition through my husbands.

I did not feel visible to him—again and again the daughters of the Bystander voice this grievance. Raised by a shadowy father who is too self-absorbed to see beyond his own turmoil, this daughter often feels like a specter herself. Her aches and confusions are mystifying to her and invisible to her father. But if and when her inner pain finally becomes accessible, she may experience an anger against her parent startling in its intensity, disturbing, yet eventually clarifying and cleansing. So for both father and daughter of this pair, visibility and anger are pivotal and connected issues.

A woman in her mid-thirties and the mother of two children remembers, for example, how unnerving it was when her father, who had been an active and involved companion during her early childhood, gradually turned off and withdrew:

> I wish I could convey how strange it was as a teenager to have a father who would go into his room and lie in the dark after dinner. Mother and Father would be angry at each other for years. Father would sit around the house in his undershirt and underpants and it would drive my mother wild. She would say to me, "Your father is a very intelligent, honest man and I don't know what happened to him."

Nor did this daughter ever find out what provoked the disturbing transformation in her father. By lying in his room in the dark, he also kept his family in the dark about what was plaguing him, driving him away. Lying in the dark, he could neither see his daughter nor be seen by her.

A twenty-five-year-old daughter of a factory worker describes a relationship with her father that suffers from what is withheld on either side. Rather than lying in his room in the dark, this father keeps his family at a distance by joking about or ignoring what is really going on:

> My father has a twinkle in his eyes, but there is also something sad about him. He has a proverb or joke for everything. In fact, it's very hard to get him to say something serious. He steers clear of stating his opinions, but at the same time complains that no one takes him seriously or that we think he's an idiot. I love him very much and always want to talk with him in a real way, but it's very hard. In a lot of ways he has always been outside the family circle, working nights when I was young, then days with a lot of overtime.

She sums up his central credo this way: "Keep it to yourself. If anything threatening gets too close, make a joke or pretend it's not happening."

Often a father becomes removed or withdrawn not only from the distortions of inner turmoil but also from the force of circumstances, the pressures of class. In *Worlds of Pain*, her study of life in the working-class family, sociologist Lillian

Rubin explores the anger, pain, and frustration experienced daily by the working-class father. Again and again he is forced to confront the limits of achievement, not from lack of talent or capability but from the accident and outrage of class. Rubin's description of the ensuing psychological bind could also portray the dilemma of the Bystander:

> . . . in their effort to bind their wounds—to restore dignity and affirm self—they redefine self so that it is more compatible with their modest accomplishments, and they accumulate possessions as the visible symbols of their achievement and status. Often, however, it's not enough; it doesn't work. Some find the respite they need in angry explosions, some in deep withdrawals. Again and again, the men and women I met recall parents, especially fathers, who were taciturn and unresponsive.[2]

In her research Rubin differentiates between the "preoccupied" father of the middle class and the "withdrawn" father of the working class:

> It's true that fathers in the professional middle-class home may also be recalled as silent, as not "part of the family." But none of the adults who grew up in those homes recalls the kind of brooding, withdrawn quality that so often describes the experience in a working-class home. The child of a professional father may recall that he was "always working even when he was home"; that he was "preoccupied" a lot; or that he "always seemed to have something on his mind." But that same person also is much more likely than his working-class counterpart to remember some ways in which fathers participated in family life, even if only to recall the dinner hour as a time for family conversation. Preoccupation, then, would seem to be the most remembered quality about fathers in professional families; withdrawal, the most vivid memory in working-class families.[3]

My own research does not emphasize this class difference so emphatically. My interviews do reveal that the pain inflicted and damage done by the Bystander correlates with the intensity of what he withholds. The "preoccupied" father who appears to have something else on his mind can be tolerated, even indulged by his daughter. But the brooding and seething "withdrawn" father who is obviously fuming yet incapable of outright emotion is perceived—justifiably—as a far more dangerous threat. Nowhere is this threat explored more openly than in the unfettered language of dreams. Just as the daughter of the Patriarch struggles in her dreams with the sexual violence hidden beneath her father's propriety, the daughter of the Bystander grapples in her dreams with the anger buried beneath her father's detachment. A social worker in her late twenties confronts in her dreams her father's frightening impassivity:

> I was standing in front of my father crying and screaming and pounding on his chest. He was like a stone wall—no reaction or movement.

And a newspaper reporter in her thirties explores her nightmare image of rage at last unleashed:

> This sounds awful. But the only dream about my father I really remember is one I had two years ago in which he was trying to murder me. It was terrifying. He calmly told me he would "have to" kill me and then kept trying to do it. My mother, in the dream, agreed it would have to be done. It happened when I just graduated from college and moved back home.

These two dreams bracket and sum up the extremes of psychic struggles faced by the daughter of the Bystander. Both are images of rage and impotence, first the daughter's, then the father's. At one extreme, shown in the first dream, her father is as immutable and inviolable as a stone wall. His fury is utterly contained and self-protective, so that her fury is powerless to reach him or change his grim reality. At the other extreme, shown in the second dream, her father's anger has finally burst its contours and been unleashed in all its murderous intensity. Here she is powerless in the face of his onslaught. Just at the point of breaking away from her family, she fears her father and mother will pounce on her and punish her for her attempt. This daughter may experience her father's rage as his means of controlling her, but before she can circumvent it, she must come to terms with her own.

Most daughters of Bystanders do not live their daily lives at either extreme of intensity, not demolished by their father's anger, nor fearing that they will demolish him with their own pent-up rage. One crucial mitigating influence is, naturally, the daughter's relationship with her mother, who often provides a counterpoint to her father's style, for both better and worse. The passive or withdrawn Bystander typically pairs himself, indeed is drawn with the irresistible pull of a magnet, to a woman who complements or compensates for what he is lacking. She is active and outgoing where he is passive and remote. Or she is gregarious and flamboyant where he is reclusive and self-effacing. Or he appears modest and mellow, and she seems shrill and manipulative. The daughter of this pair, like the daughter of the Pal, may grow up rigidly classifying father as "good guy," mother as "bad guy." Only with maturity and hindsight will she begin to have an inkling that their positions interlocked, that father's passivity may have driven mother to further manipulations, that mother's manipulations may have sent father further into his own cloister. Novelist Gail Godwin muses with the raised eyebrow of irony about the typical marriage of this pair:

Oh God, the polarizations, the trade-offs, the assignment of family "roles." ("Let's see, what have we got here? One calm man, one excitable woman. Put them together as 'husband and wife' and look how *well* they complement each other. The wife's passionate nature is kept in check by the husband's prudence—

or vice versa, depending on which marriage we're discussing—and the husband's passiveness seems more attractive when given shape by the agitating molecules of his wife's surrounding energies. He may even become known in that marriage as 'the Rock,' or 'the Anchor,' or 'the Grounding Force,'—pick your favorite metaphor. . . .")[4]

For the daughter of this marriage, mother's more outgoing style may provide a relief to the frustrations of father's withdrawals. Or mother's dominant, demanding energy may become yet another pressure. In either case this daughter grows up jockeying her way between contradictory parental messages, modeling after one parent or the other, feeling the push and pull of divided loyalties, searching for the middle ground. Psychotherapist Suzanne Gasner explains, "In this family, the daughter has a model of opposites—the father is passive and the mother is dominant. Her parents have very different values, since their partnership is based on the complementarity of opposites. This increases both the daughter's options and her conflicts. She has difficulty identifying with either parent. On the one hand she feels guilty being strident like her mother, because she remembers how father was berated by mother. On the other hand she feels guilty being passive like father, because she remembers how irritating he was to mother. Her struggle to find a middle ground can be either productive or anxiety-provoking."

The newspaperwoman in her thirties, mentioned earlier, speaks of this struggle, which for her was both productive *and* anxiety-provoking:

My mother and I are very close. She is young for her age and, unlike my father, full of life. She returned to college in middle age, began a long-hoped-for newspaper career recently, and takes dancing, acting lessons, etc. Because my father is a stick-at-home, she must go with women friends or by herself. But my father never tries to stop her and she does not seem to mind. She wants my approval and considers me the feminist catalyst in her life who keeps her going.

She goes on to describe her contradictory points of identification with mother and father:

> I am like my mother in that I cannot sit still. I take violin lessons. I am into photography. I often take short vacations with women friends from college, even though my husband loves travel and enjoys doing things with me. I am like my father in that I am timid and neurotic about this activity. Even though I vacation and fly on planes often, I am generally scared that something awful will happen to me while I am away from home. This is a message I believe I get from my father. I am also like him in that I have nervous stomach problems and get easily cranky and irritable.

For this daughter, mother's high-spiritedness and sense of adventure provide a welcome alternative to father's stagnation and apprehension. Yet fired up with her mother's energy and ready to dazzle the world, she still cannot shake the constraints of her father's doubts. Itching to move forward in the world, she must again and again rebuff her father's whispers that the world is a dangerous place, that she should not dare to outwit it if he cannot.

Still other daughters of Bystanders do not even have this much encouragement or relief from mother. Instead they find that mother's complementarity to father only compounds his problematic messages, rather than offering an alternative to them. Laurel, the twenty-eight-year-old teacher introduced at the beginning of this chapter, whose father withdrew into stony, months-long silences, faced another kind of bombardment from her mother:

> My mother is as social as my father is antisocial. She tends to be hysterical and melodramatic, rather overbearing, narcissistic, totally needing to be the center of everyone's life,

to have love and devotion and uncritical adulation from everyone. She is a dominating and controlling woman. Also very frustrated. My parents have the classic marriage relationship—the silent, obsessive-compulsive husband and the hysterical woman—pure archetype.

Antagonistic opposites, like Laurel's parents, were perhaps initially attracted to each other by the strong lure of compensating for what they missed on their own. But their merger proved a wedge rather than a synthesis, each driving the other farther and farther into remote and warring corners. Laurel was left isolated in the middle, butt of her mother's frustrations and her father's chilling silences. With neither parent's choice providing a satisfactory option for adulthood, Laurel was faced with turbulent feelings of disappointment, outrage, and frustration. But out of this maelstrom of emotion the strength to find the middle path began to emerge. She was also nurtured by the help of therapy and the serendipitous guidance of her father's best friend, a "bolder" man than her father who encouraged her to pursue her dreams. Over the years a plucky and passionate person developed, with a fierce and independent will:

I see myself as a very strong person, willing to try for what I want, to take risks, to demand the best from myself and not to let others dictate the way I should do things. I am enthusiastic—very quick and energetic—with a good mind and a strong body (despite its small size—five feet, ninety-three pounds). I am competent in a lot of areas I never had training in from my parents. And I feel that I have developed in ways that had little to do with them.

In a curious and indirect way her father's passivity provided an impetus to her own ingenuity and activity. His limitations became an imaginary line she pushed against and eventually moved beyond:

My father's messages about work were nonexciting—that one had to earn a living but not necessarily like it. He never took a vacation—there was always something to do —and I think I work in a similar way. He is a hard worker, and I may have picked up that style from him. I do remember at one time I got a summer job at a firm he was with, and I wanted a raise, and he told me not to ask for it because one was never indispensable. I asked anyway —and they were willing to pay my price. I remember thinking that he never went very far because there was a timidity in him and a lack of self-confidence. I don't think I'm like him in that way.

Like many Bystanders, Laurel's father became a kind of anti-image for his daughter in matters of work. A hard and steady worker but a conservative and cautious one ("trapped," as his daughter saw it, "by the War, marriage, children right away"), he nevertheless managed to pass on to his daughter permission—and the gift—to move beyond him. Other of these daughters' autobiographies describe a similar pattern, a father whose own work life has been curtailed in some way, a daughter who nonetheless uncovers her own reserves of competence and drive and blusters ahead, perhaps ahead of him. The newspaperwoman introduced earlier is a striking example:

> My father has been sickly for the past decade. As a result he cannot work but is not bedridden. This is the most important aspect of my relationship with him, for I am a workaholic, am not happy unless I am working, and have somehow always blamed him for not working, even though he had a good pension and we were always comfortable.

Her father's illness had a kind of catalytic affect on her work life. Disappointed in him, even ashamed that he was not strong enough to support the family, she translated these feelings—as well as her own guilt about them—into a feverish and defensive workaholism that said, in effect, I will not allow what happened to him to happen to me. She was further buoyed and supported by her mother, whose barely veiled disappointment in her husband found an outlet in her daughter's energy and accomplishments. But with the growing distance of adulthood, the ambitious journalist is beginning to acknowledge the connections, the similarities between her father and herself, the ways in which he in fact enabled her to become the person she is:

> I never used to think my father made any real impression on my life. I see I am wrong. I resemble him. I share his fears and I am the realization of at least those dreams that he has verbalized to me. It is almost as though he purposefully educated me to be beyond him.

In *Don't Fall Off the Mountain* actress Shirley MacLaine tells a painful but poignant story of the way her father, who was afraid to dare, paradoxically inspired her to dance beyond him:

> An incident occurred when I was about sixteen that still blazes in my memory. I came home from a dancing-school rehearsal distraught because they had taken the role of Cinderella away from me for our Christmas production. Miss Day and Miss Gardiner said I had simply grown too tall, and that I looked clumsy.
>
> I remember blurting it out in tears as I climbed the stairs to go to my room to be alone. Dad was coming down the stairs. He stopped, and with finger wagging told me that should teach me to stop trying to do things I wasn't capable of. Wasn't this episode proof enough for me that, if I attempted to go beyond my range, I would only be crushed? Hadn't he told me many times during my life? When would I believe him? When would I understand that if I tried I would only be hurt?

For the actress who would one day kick her heels to heaven in *Can Can*, the image of herself falling on the stairs must have a haunting irony:

I fell on the stairs, that December evening after rehearsal, with my father over me, berating me not only for trying to perform, but for thinking that I could dance Cinderella, and for making a conspicuous ass out of myself as a result. And I cried hard—I cried so hard that I vomited. But the vomit on the stairs didn't stop him; he went right on driving home his point, that I would only be hurt if I dared to dare. I couldn't move. I looked over at Mother in the living room. Warren wasn't home. Mother sat quietly until finally she said, "All right, Ira, that's enough." But Ira knew that wasn't going to be the end of it. He could see, even though I had dissolved into a little pile of protoplasm, that I would never stop daring. And he seemed to understand that ironically he, in effect, was teaching me to dare, because I saw that he was such a spectacular disappointment to himself for having never tried it. A strange clear look of understanding came into his eyes as he realized I didn't want to be like him. He stepped over the vomit and went to the kitchen to fix himself a drink. It was then that I determined to make the most of whatever equipment I had been born with, and part of that equipment was to dare. But mostly I didn't want to be a disappointment to myself.[5]

And meanwhile, waiting in the wings, Shirley MacLaine's mother was rooting for her to make it. A frustrated woman whose independent spirit had long ago been crushed, she nevertheless saw the chance to kindle for her daughter the flame that had been snuffed out in her own life. When Shirley confesses to her mother her restlessness with ballet and her desire to go to New York and study acting, her mother responds with unequivocal support:

All her years of frustration came alive in one moment. The sad sparkle vanished from her eyes. She answered with unflinching certainty. "Yes, it's time. Your father won't like the idea, he'll think you'll get hurt or taken, but then isn't that always the risk? I think you're prepared."[6]

So for Shirley MacLaine the combination of a withdrawn, discouraging father and a disappointed, encouraging mother became a heady spur to ambition.

But there are other daughters of Bystanders who are never able to burst beyond their fathers' limits. Their sense of competence, their view of themselves in the world, and their image of themselves as workers are forever circumscribed by the fences around their fathers' world. Their fathers' timidity or negativity, hesitation or passivity become constraints beyond which they see no solution or alternative—nor in these cases are their mothers sufficient counterbalances. The factory worker's daughter quoted earlier remembers, for instance, watching her father compose himself for ten minutes before making a phone call. That disturbing image was hard to erase, and it cautioned that the world was a scary and unmanageable place. Neither to question nor to dare too much was her father's lesson that sadly impeded her progress and pleasure in the world:

> About work—my father's philosophy was just to do it. He was definitely a rank-and-file worker and had no aspirations to management or anything like that. And that's the same way I feel about it.

To a secretary in her late twenties whose father was a shadowy figure away at sea for large chunks of her childhood, work and life have become disengaged:

> To me, work is what you do to pay the bills while you get on with your life. I have only just come to grips with my own lack of career interest, and with my many and scattered other interests—studying Sanskrit and astrology, riding my bicycle across the country, writing my grandmother's biography.

Without a guiding image of a father working and achieving in the world, this woman does not have a conventional sense of ambition or a driving urge toward achievement. But instead she has discovered an adventurous spirit about the world, a spirit that suggests that on one level she remains undaunted by her father's lack of guidance, or that on another level she remains susceptible to his unspoken, subliminal message. Off at sea for mysterious and open-ended stretches of her youth, he—at least in her idealized portrait—was the grand adventurer she now is striving to become.

The Bystander is disappointing as a model for work and even more frustrating as a model for love. His lack of spontaneity and warmth, his secrecy and evasiveness, and, most damaging, his bottled-up rage not only deprive his daughter of an early fantasy partner with whom to try out the first wings of romance, but also cause her to wonder whether such a partner exists outside the family. Lacking the practice and lacking the faith, this daughter may find her early disappointment becoming a self-fulfilling prophecy. The search for a mate may often lead her through a shadowy thicket of lovers who do not really love her, who serve only to confirm her miserable image of men. "The men I love and have loved," writes the bitter daughter of an alcoholic, for instance, "have either been the disapproving, put-down sarcastic type or the passive, calm type. The passive men are just as dangerous as the negative men in that their passivity can be used to control my life."

Through the autobiographies of these daughters runs a painful strain of contempt and scorn for men, a defensive buffer against the disappointment inflicted by the first man in their lives. Often this contempt and scorn—and disappointment—have been picked up from mother and confused with her needs. Explains Suzanne Gasner, "The daughter sees that her mother has both need and contempt for passive and withdrawn men like her father. The daughter then has to struggle with her own contempt for men. Even though the outside world defines men as more powerful, these daughters know better. But they still might defer to men because men are weak and need shoring up."

Such scorn is written in boldface by the ambitious newspaper reporter whose father's incapacitating illness must have felt like a desertion. Her need is more deeply buried between the lines:

> I have never particularly looked up to men. In fact, when I was dating in college and after, I usually found them somewhat repulsively weak, obnoxious, and sexist. I still do not trust men. I compete with them in life for jobs and professional success and never feel comfortable with them.

The anger she must have felt at her father for failing her because of his illness she then translates into anger at men. Scorning herself for the intensity of her need, she turns instead to scorn for "weak and obnoxious" men.

For the daughter of the Bystander, anger is a recurring theme in the story of her search for love—anger at her father for the myriad ways he has let her down, anger at her lover for being unable to compensate for the abyss of her original loss, anger at herself for the depth of her need and her inability to fill it. Whether she can acknowledge, examine, and eventually come to terms with this anger—or whether she must strangle it the way her father strangled his rage—has everything to do with her chance of finding contentment with a partner. For the forty-year-old woman introduced earlier in this chapter whose childhood was scarred by migraine headaches, buried anger was at first a painful obstacle to finding a loving and enduring relationship with a man:

> We knew virtually nothing [in my family] about expressions of anger. My pattern in my marriages was to withhold sexually when I was angry for that was the core of me. That couldn't be forced from me.

As her father withheld love from her, she withheld sexual love from her husbands, punishing them but punishing herself as well:

I feel now that I have never really loved a man. Married twice, in both cases I was looking for the man who would appreciate and love me just the way I was. Instead I married insecure men who needed me and my strength. I never felt the support that would enable me to find out who I really was.

For this woman the difficult task of finding out "who I really was" began as a succession of disappointing liaisons with men but ultimately became a turning inward. As she sifted and sorted through the layers of the self, she gradually uncovered the anger that for all its protective coverings was still hot and painful to the touch—and yet, when at last unearthed, proved miraculously revitalizing. At the time she wrote, she was living on her own and working on the challenging process of learning to take care of herself. The release of ancient anger had been the fuel of change, and now, although she was alone, she seemed genuinely optimistic that her next relationship would be freer of distorting fantasies and more likely to bring contentment.

My interviews also suggest that certain daughters who suffered growing up with the more withdrawn Bystander fathers eventually turn away from men and seek the company of women for companionship and love. For some this transition is made with upheaval and rage. For others it is made with a certainty that must feel at last as if the contradictory messages from mother and father have been resolved.

For Laurel, introduced in the opening of this chapter, whose father withdrew into months-long silences, disappointment in her father and then in a lackluster first marriage, prompted her eventually to choose relationships with women. With her present lover she believes she is compensating for the appalling lack of nurturing from both father and mother:

My relationship with this woman is different (from my relationship with my father) in a very important way—my father never says, "I love you" or kisses or hugs. He is a hard man to get physically close to, even casually. I think my marriage was like that—but since then I choose people who can express affection, love, sex very easily.

Asked to describe her fantasy of an ideal man, she defines instead her ideal woman, and perhaps her image of her ideal self:

The ideal man would be more like the best women I've known—strong, assertive, gentle, achievement-oriented, but with a priority that was clearly one's relationships—able to express the full gamut of emotions, to go to the absurd and the rational as easily, to not be as linear as the white man's world of business and science demands, but to take the creative leaps. Nontraditional women often combine the best of both worlds—and so would my ideal man.

But even safely ensconced in a relationship with a woman, thinking that she has completely redefined the terms and driven out the specter of her father's buried rage, still it comes back to haunt her:

I think in some ways I play out my father when I'm angry —I withdraw, ignore my partner. It never goes on for long, but I do feel like my father at those moments.

What the father withholds from the daughter—whether anger or affection, approval or dismissal—the daughter must face in herself, grapple with in her work, and struggle to resolve in her relationships. What cannot be spoken or shared between father and daughter becomes the puzzle to be sorted out between daughter and the world.

Judith Stern and *Maggie Peale* are strong and outspoken daughters of a mild and passive father, a strong and controlling mother. Sharing the same parents, they made different sense of their parents' contradictory words and images. Sharing the same father—a staid city doctor with a hidden, inner life as an artist—they interpreted his model in different ways. Each registered his submerged anger, lamented his lack of visibility to her—and hers to him—and set out on a path guided by her own conclusions. Their divergent paths reflect some of the conflicts and options of the eighties.

At forty, Judith Stern lives alone in the stucco bungalow her mother bought after her father died. A professor of anthropology, she is an active and opinionated presence in the university town where she lives. Married, miserable, and divorced in her twenties, she has not had a lover in almost ten years. "I hate men in a pure way," she says, with neither a flinch nor an ironic smile. Her trademark is to offer the outrageous as if it were the matter-of-fact. Large-boned and heavyset, her own presence adds considerably to the weight of her opinions, as if to defy her listener's disagreement.

As withdrawn from the world of men as Judith is, so immersed in it is her sister, Maggie Stern Schwartz Peale. At thirty-seven, Maggie is married to her second husband and the ebullient matriarch of a household of children, a son from her first marriage and four stepchildren, most of them boys. "I love men," she says, "I always wanted lots of sons. Throughout my childhood I thought I didn't want daughters. I thought girls were sucky, dependent, insecure." She speaks quickly, with lots of gestures and energy, her comments a blend of confidence and vulnerability. It was that confidence that propelled her to apply to medical school at thirty-five, when her kids were cutting loose, when her own life needed definition. But it was that vulnerability that made her first year a tentative gamble: "I gave myself permission to hate it and flunk out." By the time we meet, she has admirably weathered the first two difficult years of medical school and is gradually beginning to define herself as a doctor, once only her father's remote and mysterious province, soon enough to be her own.

So if anger and visibility are two braided themes for daughters of the Bystander, then Judith's choices have been woven with the strand of anger, of showing her anger to the world, and Maggie's with the strand of visibility, of making herself visible to the world. These choices are, of course, influenced by a complex and interwoven skein of factors: by both order and temperament, by teachers and friends, by luck and circumstances. But mother and father are naturally the original influences, and this story begins with the subtle variations in each daughter's portrait of her father, negligent or mild, cowardly or cozy.

"My father sort of melts into the background," remembers Judith, settling herself deep in an armchair. "I don't really think I knew him." At first her tone is wistful, almost remorseful, but soon takes on an edge of criticism. "He was a very benign presence and he did always love me, but it didn't matter much. His love wasn't helpful. It wasn't very nurturing. I never saw his office, and he never talked to me about work or money or the outside world. He was a bit wimpy, I must confess." She sighs, looks uncomfortably around the room, still decorated with some of her mother's artifacts, her mother's opinions. "I was never afraid of him. He was an object of affection and a certain mild contempt, which I retain for males to this day."

For Judith her father's passivity, "wimpy" and unassuming on the surface, was nevertheless experienced as a personal blow—disappointing, even punitive. Now, many years after his death, she still catalogues, with exasperation and pain, the ways in which he let her down—the way, despite their sometime allegiance ("father and me against mother and sister"), he was unable to defend her against her mother's cruelty; the way, despite his avowed liberalism, he forbade her, at eighteen, to go out with a black man ("I never loved him as uncritically afterward"). The debilitating asthma attacks that scarred her childhood and threw a monkey wrench into family life were a crude and unconscious attempt to deal with the anger that could not be expressed elsewhere.

Now to her own list of grievances she adds one of her mother's, adding her mother's anger to her own. "Early in their marriage my mother got pregnant and had to have an abortion. My father felt he couldn't support the child as well as his own family, who still relied on him for money. I believe that poisoned their relationship from then on."

This story has long been one of the cornerstones of Judith's mythology about her family, adding pathos and weight to her own brief against her father. It is never mentioned in her sister's saga of the family. In Maggie's portrait her father is again a mild and unassuming character, but in her eyes more well-intentioned and considerably more involved. Instead of her sister's sense of deprivation, which she camouflaged with a veneer of scorn, Maggie paints a rather lovable and nurturing person who made his affection clear. She remembers him putting on an apron and baking pies for the family or bringing home Sunday-morning brunch of bagels and lox. "He wasn't active," is her memory, "but you could wheedle onto his lap. He loved it when I got dressed up and went to his office in the city. He would show me off to his friends and take me out to lunch. When I got older, we would have heart-to-heart talks. 'I'm not going to tell you what to do,' he would say. 'I'll just tell you what I think.' He was a uniquely nonjudgmental person. He had trouble holding his own in a household of three loquacious women."

But the gentleness, Maggie also realized, covered up the turmoil beneath the surface. "There were very few times I remember him angry. It was hard for him to get anger out. Now I'd say he did a lot of denial." Though cause and effect can only be speculation, when Maggie was in the fourth grade, her father "had a mind-blowing, whopper of a heart attack. The cure was immobility for months. From then on I lived with the constant fear that he would die." From her vantage point as an adult, she considers, "I knew he had a lot of pain. Maybe if he could have unloaded it, he wouldn't have had the heart attack. He didn't get much off his chest."

As a rambunctious teenager, beginning to be interested in boys and the thrills of the outside world, Maggie often felt she was walking on eggshells around her father. When she was twenty, an incident occurred that snapped the peace between them and catapulted Maggie out into the world. "One night mother and father had been at the opera. They came home early and caught me in bed with my boyfriend. That night father had a stroke. He might have had it anyway. But, boom. It was the classic guilt trip." She laughs nervously at the proximity of comedy and tragedy. "We had a huge confrontation where they told me what they would tolerate and what they wouldn't. By definition, anyone who touched me, slept with me, or loved me was loathsome. They told me to shape up or move out, so I moved out."

Moving out ruptured the bond with father and began a search, a somewhat frantic search, for a bond with a young man. Her first "real, alive, true love" was a crazy and charismatic figure, an artist—"the reincarnation of Leonardo, I believe to this day"—as flashy and temperamental as her father, at least on the surface, was placid and staid. "There was an unbelievable magnetism that went on for years," she says, her eyes still blazing for his memory. "But I knew he was irresponsible and wouldn't be an equal sharer."

Instead she married a man seventeen years older and the father of two kids. "I was a hot twenty-one," she recalls, "and itching to get married. I hated college and was more concerned with my emotional life. I wanted to get married and be validated and be an adult." Now, years after her divorce and remarriage, she still looks back on that early marriage with bitterness that the distance has not assuaged. "He was not a generous person. He was emotionally stingy. He wanted a mommy for his kids. It was my responsibility to extricate us both from whatever problems came up. He was entirely passive. I can think of millions of ways he was *not* like my father, though they both walk to an internal drummer. He was more like my mother—verbal, aggressive, and witty. But I felt depersoned by him."

The day after she left her husband and their three-year marriage, she called her old artist lover. All her efforts at playing the "good wife" had not managed to snuff out the torch she still carried for her first love. They reconciled, had a "brief honeymoon," but then, as before, the relationship soon burned itself out with its own high-voltage energy.

Sorely disappointed, perplexed, and grieving over her losses, Maggie finally decided to seek a psychiatrist's help. For months she and he sorted through the rubble of past relationships, looking for clues, linking past and present, clearing the path toward the future. Gradually she began to feel herself freed of her old baggage, readier to make choices, to take care of her needs. The day she had chosen to terminate therapy, her psychiatrist met her good-bye with his usual steady and penetrating gaze. "Guess what?" he said. Then he told her that he had fallen in love with her.

"I didn't see this coming at all," realizes Maggie, who, flattered and intrigued, rose to the occasion. "Three days later he moved in. We spent those three days talking nonstop about *him*. He was fourteen years older than me and had four kids. When I told my mother about him, she shrieked, 'You've fallen in love with your shrink. Just what you need, another middle-aged man with two children.'" "Four" was Maggie's cool retort.

About her second husband, to whom she has now been married for more than ten years, Maggie says, "He's like my father in many ways. He's the quiet man. He thinks before he speaks. He does have a temper. But usually he's even-tempered, fair, and considerate of everyone's needs. He's generous of spirit and not passive—just stubborn as hell. In some ways I suppose he's my resident shrink, though I don't feel in conflict or chaos, but I am secure." For Maggie the path toward a contented marriage involved a reckoning and resolving of the contradictory images of early family life. Her youthful passion for the wild artist was a flirtation with the demonic side, an experimentation with the taboo and forbidden, with everything hidden by her father's tight lid on the turbulent inner life, that must have seemed both creative and destructive. Her first marriage forced her up against a personality akin to her mother's—intense and demanding—and breaking free of that marriage was another chance at resolving conflicts that allowed greater separation from her mother as well. Finally her marriage to her erstwhile psychiatrist was a merger with a partner evocative of her father yet able to give her the gift her father could not: visibility, her own and his own. Quiet and fair as her father was at his best, her husband was also easy enough with himself to recognize and validate her emotionality as well as his own.

For Judith relationships with men corroborated her worst fears and impressions from early family life, rather than healing or resolving them. She married at twenty-one, as her sister did, and the man she married was a wild and irresponsible artist, as her sister's first love was. "Maybe I married my father's alter ego," she speculates now, "the wild artist inside my father who could never get out." But on the surface, at least, Judith's husband, like Maggie's, resembled their mother and subjected her to an exaggerated and intensified version of her mother's harsh criticism and merciless harping on inadequacy. Now Judith labels her former husband in no uncertain terms "a psychopathic loony." But as a young woman struggling to settle her own identity and make sense of the contradictions still fresh from her family, she realizes, "I thought of my husband as some sort of god who could rescue me from family life. I looked at him with a mixture of awe and contempt. Men were irretrievably other. They could get you stuff you couldn't get for yourself, so I thought—status, security, sex, children, a family, adulthood. Our collective imagination didn't imagine otherwise.

"At the time of my marriage," she continues, "I wanted someone to look up to, and I tried. For four and a half years. Then I 'came home.'" At twenty-six she began to make her own life. Her father died soon after, and she had "nine years to be with my mother as two single women. That was wonderful. Much healed. My mother seemed to be much happier without my father."

As she found herself knitting her life back together with her mother and other women friends, she was also withdrawing more and more from relationships with men. After her marriage broke up, she had a brief flurry of lovers. The last try produced a pregnancy that ended in abortion. She does not draw the connection, but the experience seems an unconscious echo of her mother's unwanted abortion decades earlier, the act for which husband and father were never entirely forgiven. Whatever its remote and complex resonances, Judith's abortion prompted the curtain to be drawn on liaisons with men. The fears and scorn and disappointment of childhood were at last confirmed, calcified by a series of condemning events, rather than healed, as in her sister's case, by a series of restorative ones.

"Since that abortion," explains Judith, eminently reasonable, not apologetic, "men have been extraneous to my life. The whole idea of the male seems superfluous. No man looks better than the life I have alone." She looks around the living room that once belonged to her mother, her mother's possessions mixed in with her own, the space she has so conscientiously marked out for her own still influenced and determined by choices out of conscious control. "I'm in a very enigmatic position," she confesses. "I'm a sexual anomaly. I have no female lovers. I still consider myself heterosexual, but I hate men. I hate them for their assumption of power and irresponsible use of it. I hate them for their misogyny. I hate men for fearing women and not facing it." She seems unperturbed by her own circularity, her rationale armoring her against doubt. Then she smiles, as if at length willing to admit that she may be too harsh. "I do have a nice brother-in-law," she says.

5

THE CHARMER

I DON'T THINK YOU'RE EVER TOO OLD TO SIT IN YOUR
daddy's lap.

Holly Heston, *nineteen,* daughter of Charlton Heston.

My father was dogmatic, charming, furious, generous,
flashy, paunchy, semidrunk, and sad. A theater director
who once seemed about to make "the big time," he relished any really good show. Pageantry, not people,
brought easy tears to his eyes. He lived his shows while
they were in rehearsal—any dinner conversation could
call forth entire speeches from the script—and promptly
forgot them as the next tryouts began. My father seemed
to live his life as he produced his shows—appearing fully
involved with people and places while he was around
them, quickly pushing them out of the spotlight when he,
or they, moved on. He acquired many drinking buddies
but few friends. And he usually managed to avoid examining any of his own questions.

Christine, *thirty-four*

The Charmer is the Peter Pan father whose perpetual youth is his allure and his snare. By the sheer force of his charisma he can convince his daughter that he can fly, that she can fly, that together they might lift off to never-never land. Often the romantic appeal of his fantasies may seem more attractive than the real world. The Charmer is a master magician and performer, teller of tales and poseur. He is often lavish in his display of affection, almost childlike in the outpouring of his attentions—and also his demands. But with all his posing, his daughter may need to question the certainty of his love. Like the Pal, the Charmer is ambivalent about the parental role, and that ambivalence may make him narrow the gap between himself and his daughter, jockeying for her to meet his needs rather than conscientiously caring for hers.

But where the Charmer's needs may be similar to the Pal's, his mode of operations is not. While the Pal fans his daughter's endeavor excitement but is abashed by her erotic excitement, the Charmer takes the opposite course. The Charmer enthusiastically engages with his daughter's budding sexual self. He approves of and abets his daughter's erotic excitement, encouraging flirting and playfulness, teasing and displays of femininity. But with her endeavor excitement he is far more ill at ease. He may even be threatened by too early shows of intellectual muscle. So this daughter's active or creative side may be woefully undernourished. Therefore, the daughter of the Pal is likely to become the performer or achiever; the daughter of the Charmer more likely to become the pleaser or placator. The Pal grooms his daughter for professional success; the Charmer grooms his for social triumph. The Pal's daughter goes for the brass ring; the Charmer's daughter wants to get her man.

The category of the Charmer, like the other categories, includes a wide range of fathering types, from the pleasing to the hurtful, and any one father may show a variety of styles throughout his daughter's development. On one end of the spectrum is the Charmer who manages to impart a genuine *joie de vivre* to his daughter. He is the one who fathers by playful and spirited involvement, but also has enough self-awareness and confidence to set limits to the play. He knows how to guide his daughter to transform the high-spiritedness into an opportunity for learning. At the opposite end is the Charmer who is really the seducer, either figuratively or literally. This is the father whose own needs are so overpowering and whose own sense of boundaries so fragile that he uses his daughter to serve his own ends. There is often a sexualized quality to his affection, an inappropriate flirtatiousness or seductiveness that may begin when the daughter is small and sometimes continue, ever more damaging as she becomes a woman.

These daughters may unconsciously adopt the seductive pose they come to believe is necessary to hold their father's love. Psychotherapist Suzanne Gasner comments on this phenomenon: "All daughters want a seductive and coy relationship with their fathers. That's normative. That the daughter of a Charmer father wants love from her father doesn't separate her from other daughters. But the parent is supposed to be the one to create the climate for the family. If the daughter appears seductive, the father has obviously promoted her seduction." At the most extreme end of the continuum is the father who commits incest with his daughter, violating all protective boundaries between them. More the exploiter than the Charmer, this father uses his fatherly prerogative to manipulate his daughter for his own gratification. His daughter is left defenseless to face a lifetime of consequences, as the last section of this chapter will explore.

Jack Bouvier, father of Jacqueline Bouvier Kennedy Onassis, was a classic Charmer father who sired a classic Charmer daughter. Charismatic and debonair, Black Jack—as he was called—was a member of the New York Stock Exchange and handsome enough to be summoned to Hollywood to read for the part of Rhett Butler in *Gone with the Wind*. He was also a gambler, a drinker, and a womanizer. His taste was only for the best, both for himself (custom-made clothes and a Stutz car, built to his own specifications), and for his eldest daughter, Jacqueline, on whom he doted and who doted on him. When Black Jack was too drunk to give Jackie away in marriage to Senator John F. Kennedy, Jackie nevertheless forgave him. On her honeymoon she wrote him a loving and understanding letter that mended the incipient rift between father and daughter.

The Bouvier story briefly illustrates both the seduction and the betrayal of the daughter by the Charmer. For the Charmer sets out to expose his daughter to the best life can offer. He will wine her and dine her and introduce her to the temptations of the world. But beneath the patina of his charms may hide another personality entirely. Just as the shadowside of the innocent Bystander may be a furiously angry man, and the shadowside of the proper Patriarch may be an irrepressibly sexual man, so the shadowside of the Charmer may be a frightened child, using his bravura to camouflage his deep vulnerability and self-doubt. The Charmer is often given to wildly inconsistent behavior, sometimes exacerbated by alcohol. So the daughter of the Charmer faces the difficult and confusing task of trying to accommodate both extremes of his personality: the father who amuses and enthralls her with the father who disappoints and undermines her, the father who dotes on her with the one who ignores her or, worse, abuses her. At times this task may seem—justifiably—insurmountable, and its resolution may be maddeningly beyond her reach. The daughter of the Charmer may be raised to be a winsome social butterfly, but she often must develop a fierce will to survive. She may be trained to retain the perpetual charms of a little girl, but she may be forced to become a young woman, wise and mature beyond her years.

In her stunning novel *Imaginary Crimes*, Sheila Ballantyne documents the painful and profound coming of age of a daughter of a Charmer. Ray Weiler is the Charmer father, a con man confident and smooth. He is perpetually waiting for his ship to come in, his invention to score, his gold mine to make him a millionaire, so he can move his wife and two daughters out of their one-room basement apartment and into the house of his dreams. Sonya Weiler is the older daughter who wants desperately to believe in the efficacy of her father's charms.

"Bucking the wind" was Daddy's term for what he did on his way to the store to buy another bottle. The wind would blow in from the south and he would hold his collar around his neck, lower his head, and charge. I came of age when he let me go with him. I was his "buckaroo." . . .

He used these walks to the grocery store to draw parallels between our bucking the wind and what people had to do in order to get through life: you bucked. I remember the wind in my face, being scarcely able to breathe, and my hand in his. When we reached the store, he would let me have a ball gum while he played the pinball machines. Mother waited back in the apartment for her loaf of Wonderbread which, she knew, would come home disguised as a bottle of bourbon.[1]

When mother dies of undiagnosed and untreated cancer, Sonya and her sister, still young girls, are left to the erratic care of their father. Buffeted and unprotected, they are exposed to the wild and skittish and ultimately well-meaning spectrum of his charms. Fumbling through parenthood, he remains a dreamer and a schemer, the lothario who romances each of the ladies hired to help with the girls, the drunkard who comes home smashed, shouting that he "should have left you two rotters to shift for yourselves," the ne'er-do-well who neglects to pay Sonya's college tuition until it becomes an embarrassment. And Sonya, meanwhile, often lost and desperately at loose ends herself, gradually plumbs her own resilience and finds the ironic humor that becomes her salvation and later the scaffolding of the novel. She works her way through college, raising and supporting her younger sister as well. She discovers her gift as a writer. She marries, has two children, goes into analysis. She begins, in her own way, to learn to buck the wind.

At the end of the novel Ray is mysteriously dead, lost in a hunting trip in the mountains. Sonya will never learn exactly what happened, whether his death was accident or foul play. But wanting to put the past to rest, she returns to the place where she grew up, impelled toward an inner reckoning, driven to complete unfinished business. She walks through the doors of the railroad station and, as if entering another realm of consciousness, begins a conversation that is as much an inner dialogue as a conversation with her father's ghost:

> *Did you really love me? Or was that a con job, too?*
> He is still. It's hard to tell if he is stunned, or thinking fast. I don't let him get the upper hand, I hurl every doubt I've ever had at him; they echo for miles across the filthy station floor.
> *Larcenous! Fraudulent! False! Trick! Device! Bunco!*

He doesn't even blink. I try a different angle. This is hard.

When I was sick and you sat with me all night, when you stroked my face, when we bucked the wind, was it real?

No response. He really means to have it his way this time. The train is about to leave.

Where is my proof? I scream at him.

It's inside you! he finally shouts. A trick.

Why weren't you a better parent? I cry.

Why aren't you? he yells back.

I do my best!

Yes, well, that's the way it goes. So did I.

And then I see. And then I forgive.[2]

And forgiving him his crimes, whether real or imaginary, she forgives herself for the same and allows herself to move forward. Sonya's journey, both real and symbolic, sums up the central task for the daughter of a Charmer. That task is the arduous and often thwarted effort to dig beneath the layers of father's charm, his hype, his shuck, and ferret out the inner core beneath, which for Sonya was at last revealed as a bed-rock of love and concern. And finding and believing in father's core may also be a prerequisite to finding and trusting one's own inner self.

The interviews with the daughters of Charmers and their autobiographies testify to the success of their fathers' socialization. These women are often the living proof of their fathers' training: artful and pleasing, loquacious and effervescent. Schooled from earliest childhood to be Daddy's girl— pleaser, placator, and often plaything—these daughters have learned their lessons well. But the interviews show evidence of another side as well—a searching, perplexed, often troubled quality that is as much their fathers' legacy as their charm. These daughters have been raised in a kind of fantasy world, cushioned with games and jokes. But the price of this fantasy world has often been their own maturity. Craving companionship in a make-believe haven, their fathers have kept them little girls longer than age would warrant. So when they become women, these daughters of Charmers are painfully unprepared to face the challenges, dilemmas, and disappointments of the real world.

The thirty-eight-year-old daughter of a scientist who had died a month before we met shares memories of a father who was indulgent as well as neglectful, doting as well as insecure. Only the year before had she fought back against father's implicit and explicit prohibitions against growing up and taken the risk to enter medical school:

My father was more comfortable with women the younger they were, preferably under five. I had trouble being his kind of woman, the kind of woman who makes a man feel good, a compliant and feminine woman. I don't think I felt comfortable with him until my late twenties. I was in therapy for three years and realized I was never going to get all I wanted from him. I got more relaxed and more appreciative of him. He didn't really have friends of his own. He couldn't take criticism. He had a need for approval and for the relationship to be on his own terms.

This father's charms were often displayed in a sexual manner, in his relationships both with his daughter and with other women. More than many other fathers the Charmer is often physical in his affections and open with his sexuality. The response he provokes in his daughter may range from pleasurable fascination to disturbing dismay. Sitting on Daddy's lap is a magnetic memory for these daughters, still charged with associations, both real and symbolic, long after Daddy is gone. The Jungian psychologist Katherine Whiteside Taylor carried the memory well into her seventies, as if it were a private talisman. Sitting by her desk with its photographs of Jung, Buber, and her father, she recalled, "Some of the happiest times of my childhood were spent sitting on my father's knee. My father was the Ideal. He was King Arthur, Lancelot, and Galahad." Her idealization of him had only intensified with the years.

But for the thirty-eight-year-old medical student, the memory of father's manliness, of his sexuality and her connection to it, is more ambivalent, more fraught with doubts:

> It is touching that Father gave me the message that affection was nice. I would sit on his lap after dinner for years. He always kept his bedroom door open. I would climb into bed with Mother and him, but only on his side because Mother didn't approve.

"There was a real seductive part to Father," she admits. "He wanted me to remain a young girl." As she got older and achieved a measure of separation from her father, she became more aware and more critical of his "seductive part." She began to acknowledge the other women in his life, whom he had chosen and cherished for their dependence on him: "Women he would meet in his travels around the world, whom he'd help, send money to, advise about where to go to school. There was probably some sex, but it was pretty minor." His sexiness with other women she does her best to brush off, but his sexiness with her became more difficult to dismiss:

> My father would have two or three drinks every night. When he would kiss me good night, he would have his mouth open. There was something seductive about it. Also, he wanted me to make much of him, showing me off to his colleagues. Maybe he even wanted people to think I was not his daughter. Perhaps the reason was that he couldn't express his sense of fun with Mother. I didn't confront him or make things difficult for him. I was his young plaything, in a funny sense.

For this daughter, as for many daughters of Charmers, father's sexuality, intoxicating at first, soon becomes a dangerous and disturbing burden. And father's inappropriate behavior, his crossing the fine line between the loving and the leering, will reverberate on daughter's sexuality for years to come. The fear, guilt, and anger initially provoked by father can create an inhibiting barrier between this daughter and the later men in her life.

Often the daughter will blame herself for father's provocative behavior, which she may learn to reciprocate if only to hold his love. In one of her early diaries Anaïs Nin remembers how her father used to photograph her naked when she was a child. Many years later, performing a concert of Spanish dances, she hallucinates his face in the crowd. Her analyst, Dr. René Allendy, draws the connection between her father's early seductiveness and her guilt about her own:

> You may have wanted to dance for him, to charm him, to seduce him, unconsciously, and when you became aware that the dancing was an act of seduction, you felt guilt. . . . Dancing became synonymous with seducing the father. You must have felt guilt for his admiration of you as a child, his admiration may have awakened your feminine desire to please your father, to hold him away from his mistresses.[3]

Provocative about sex, the Charmer is also provocative about money. Indeed, for many of these fathers the two may be intertwined, powerful currency of the adult world with which his relationship may be ambivalent. Both sex and money may be used, rarely consciously, to charm, seduce, even manipulate his daughter. One daughter remembers a childhood routine in which her father would appear from the bathroom wrapped only in his towel. Then he would make her hide her eyes while he got dressed, and with the gusto of a magician he would empty all the change from his pockets and give it to her. Another woman recalls the drawerful of money her father kept in his dresser. "Whenever you need it, you know where it is," he would say, while her mother struggled to educate her about money and its reasoned getting and spending. Both these memories show the Charmer's playful and indulgent side but also suggest his difficulty with setting limits, his resistance to assuming parental responsibility in both sexual and money matters. For the Charmer often insulates himself from the adult world, swaddles himself in a cocoon of his own uncertainty or his own narcissism, and blunders forward, moody and self-involved, as if not parent but child. His need to remain a child may deprive his daughter of her childhood; his refusal to grow up may sabotage his daughter's chances of maturity as well.

Now in her late twenties and struggling to find her way in love and work, the daughter of a Chicano salesman describes the self-absorption and volatility that prevented her father from giving her steady parental guidance:

> My father has had various changes in his career. He doesn't have a high tolerance for having a bad time. He has done well and badly for fifteen years. He's a real charming man, at least to people outside the family. He's good at selling things. He enjoys good food and wine. He's very conscious of the way he looks. He wears tons of aftershave and has rows upon rows of suits. It takes him an hour to get ready for work.

There was also a darker and more dangerous side behind the charming façade, coiffed and suited for the world:

> My father has a tendency to drink, and then he gets ornery. He has a really bad temper. My memories of childhood were that my parents didn't get along. I remember waking one night and hearing silver being thrown. I don't recall liking my father very much. I was afraid he would hurt me, my mother, or my grandmother, who lived with us.

Coping with father's inconsistencies, trying to reconcile the dazzling façade with the stormy interior is a puzzling and often painful process for the Charmer's daughter. An artist in her late twenties paints a contradictory portrait of a magician-like father whose magic flipped violently from white to black. On the one hand she is captivated by his charms and he in turn by hers:

> To meet my father, you would think he was the most wonderful man in the world. He thought I was a brainchild, too, the world's wonder. I thought he was magical.

But beneath the white magic lurks a black magic that erupts uncontrollably:

> The flip side of my father is that he is a wife beater. He has an outburst about every three months. He will remember something that happened fifteen years ago and all of a sudden get furious about it. Once when my parents were arguing, I said "Fuck off" to my father, and he threatened to kill me. The cops were called. Later he brought it up and said "I'll chop you in little pieces if you ever do that again."

For the young girl growing up, such wildly erratic behavior may be disturbing beyond comprehension, forever undermining her faith in father, her trust in others, her confidence in the world. The grown woman will struggle to provide an explanation. This woman knows that her father's father beat him, too, "whether he needed it or not," and feels that her own father "is much improved over that." The daughter of the Chicano salesman quoted above also knows that her father's mother had him when she was fifteen, that he had a hard time because he was illegitimate, that he "had a lot of difficulty with his self-image because of his background." Such explanations generate understanding and forgiveness that may begin to heal the cavernous breach of trust between father and daughter. But the process of building a bridge of trust with the rest of the world may be a lifetime's work for this daughter. Whether she finds other supportive and dependable relationships along the way will greatly influence the pleasures of the journey.

Her relationship with her mother, and particularly her mother's relationship with her father, tends unfortunately to present a source of tension rather than support. Many Charmers seem to flaunt their charms to everyone but their wives, and their marriages are often frayed by strain and disappointment on both sides. The thirty-eight-year-old medical student, whose father was seductive with her, describes how at the same time he withheld affection from his wife:

> I don't remember any kind of sexual relationship ever between my parents. Father didn't satisfy a lot of emotional needs of Mother. Mother needed more demonstrative affection. He would pat her on the back. If she ever said, "Oh, give me a hug," he'd be passive resistant.

Another daughter in her early thirties contrasts her mother with her father's longtime mistress, whom she inadvertently stumbled on years after the affair began. The portrait of the mistress is of an artistic bohemian; the portrait of her mother is of a proper Victorian—who nonetheless showed great promise of spunk:

> My mother is a Victorian. That's an easy out, but I think she would *like* to be a proper Victorian. A head-of-the-class student with a master's in mathematics, a 1950s mother, a retired teacher. . . . She was also an aspiring off-Broadway actress, a children's drama teacher when none of her female acquaintances worked. A complicated woman. Two steps sideways for every one step forward. A master of evasive action. My sister and I, for once, argue in cold, loud voices. My mother hovers nervously and brightly asks, "Now who wants orange juice?" It works, actually; we have to laugh. She can't stand visible, audible strife. She'd rather eat Gelusil forever.

Of the women who choose to stay married to these Charmers, it is the luckier ones who suffer only from neglect. The unluckier ones must often bear the brunt of the violence lurking beneath the polished charms. The artist whose father was "magical"—as well as abusive—describes the outrages perpetrated by her father on both his wives, first her mother, then her stepmother:

> My mother was seventeen when she had me. She left when I was four and my sister was two. No one has ever said why. I think she flipped out—being beaten and with two small kids. My father will only say, "Your mother was a whore."

When she was eight, her father remarried, and the patterns begun in his disastrous first marriage were painfully repeated:

> My sister and I were not allowed to come to the wedding. Life turned to shit after that for ten years. My stepmother was twenty-five. She was pregnant within a month. She knew the marriage was ridiculous soon after, and she took out her anger on my sister and me from the beginning. My father may be very charming, but he lets out his other side on the family. If we complained about my stepmother, he would beat up on her and then she'd take it out on us.

Although the warfare within this family triangle is more acute than most, still it dramatically illustrates the bind trapping many Charmers' daughters. The daughter of the Charmer is lured to father's side by the considerable sway of his charms (even the abusive father is called "magical" by his daughter). Meanwhile she observes that father neglects or rejects or in the extreme case abuses her mother. His behavior only intensifies those early oedipal fantasies that she would be a far more exciting and satisfying partner for her father than her mother is. She shares the intensity of these oedipal longings with the daughter of the Pal. But the difference is that in the Pal daughter's fantasies the Pal is won through intellectual companionship and achievement, while in the Charmer daughter's fantasies the Charmer is won through flirtatious femininity and doting service. For both daughters the apparent oedipal victory is won at a terrible price. Superseding mother in fantasy or, in the case of incest, in reality, arouses agonizing feelings of guilt. And the loss of mother's love—real or imagined—deprives her of a crucial alternative to her father, undermines her feminine identification, and robs her of the support she desperately needs.

So in affairs of the heart this daughter is often confounded by contradictory cues. On the one hand she is schooled by her father in the arts of attracting and pleasing a man. She is taught by him that this is the path toward happiness and fulfillment as a woman. But success in the pursuit of a man is a conflicted victory, and her guilt about "stealing" her father from her mother may undermine her pleasure in finding a man of her own to love. Her fragile or fragmentary bond with her mother also hinders the crucial feminine identification that would enable her to feel worthy of a mature and happy relationship of her own. So the daughter of the Charmer often finds herself snared in the web of her father's charms, and then struggling out of it with a kind of precocious sexuality that may win her father's approval but is inappropriate beyond adolescence. Believing that the search for a mate is life's major quest, this daughter may end up running in circles to find one. At times the quest takes on the tone of an obsession, a repetition of an old script that eludes the happy ending.

For the thirty-eight-year-old medical student whose seductive father preferred his girls under five, the search for a contented relationship has involved recognizing her prolonged period of girlishness and making the risky and oblique moves to maturity. Her husband was a man she met at fourteen, a friendship that deepened into romance and then pregnancy. Because abortion was "inconceivable," they married after high school. Although they stayed together through three children, their marriage, like that of her parents, was never satisfying:

> My husband is a really strong man. It was hard to be with him. I couldn't overcome the feeling he was stronger, better, more powerful. I see that as a task for the rest of my life. Sexually, I had a lot of problems with him. I couldn't ask for what I wanted. It was safer to remain presexual. I was looking to him for the part of father I didn't have—someone who would help me grow and show me the way in the adult world.

But gradually, with therapy and a strengthened sense of her own goals in the world, she felt a more adult self emerging. The decision to leave her family and go to medical school in another town gave her a heady feeling of independence. It was not surprising—but also not easy—that she fell in love with a different man:

> My lover was the other side of the moon from my husband. He's very sensitive and into his feelings. He's very quiet. He doesn't take over every situation. That gave me the opportunity to shine some, to be more assertive. He appreciated me for my softness, my sense of humor, my sexiness. I felt like a natural woman with him.

With her husband—the man she met in the first blush of adolescence—she was never able to outgrow the little-girl pose her father so encouraged. That kept their relationship unequal and presexual, as if she were waiting for permission, either from husband or father, to grow up. As she slowly learned to bestow that permission on herself, she also met another man who could appreciate her as a mature and sexual woman. That proved intoxicating enough to break apart her marriage and her family. But after four difficult years of yo-yoing between the two men, she has recently severed ties with them both. Nearing forty, she wants to give herself time to finish her medical education and take her life into her own hands.

The artist daughter of the "magical" yet abusive father also finds herself in love triangles that obsessively replay the early oedipal fantasies of the original family triangle. Her first affair was with her high school teacher. She was eighteen, he, an "older man" of thirty-four. She grimaces as she recalls:

> I propositioned him. We didn't date but would meet and go to bed. Meanwhile he was involved with other women. Although we slept together, he didn't care about me at all. The first time we did it, I just did it so I wouldn't be a virgin. I asked, "How did I do?" He said, "Fine, I'd give you an A."

She married at twenty. Her husband was her cousin's friend, a man she went to bed with the first night they met, with whom she "laughed a lot and felt very much at ease." Their relationship turned out to be more intense, full of conflict as well as laughter:

> He's a very warm, physical person, open with his emotions. He's more like having a girlfriend around than anyone I know. He's also passive and very subtle in his manipulations.

Early in their marriage the old issue of other women reappeared with the disturbing intensity of a recurrent dream, the kind of dream in which the characters are mysterious but the parts are familiar as family:

> He got a letter from an old lover who wanted to resume with him. That was a thorn in my side for six months. Finally I had it out with her. Meanwhile the women surrounding him—his sister and cousin—wanted to do me in. They were unhappy to see him married because it denied their accessibility to him.

Gradually their relationship got more and more strained and their sex life deteriorated. Finally, at a restaurant where she often went to read the Sunday paper, she met a woman she became enthralled with. Dancing around one another at first, like shy kids, soon they became lovers:

> I was convinced I was gay for a year. I didn't have any background or old systems with this woman. Everything seemed new and easy.

For three months she lived apart from her husband and nestled in the snug harbor of her relationship with this woman. But as the comfort of the "new and easy" faded, she became restless, eager, in spite of herself, to resolve the struggles with her husband. Reunited with him, they were seeking counseling to work things out between them.

The problem that had a stranglehold on her sexual life was the aftermath of the unresolved oedipal triangle of childhood. The seductive father, the absent mother, and then the punitive stepmother—they all collaborated in depriving her of the kind of family life in which healthy girlish fantasies could be expressed and worked through. Instead she found herself replaying the old triangular scene, each time hoping for the happy ending, first with the older teacher, who was also involved with other women; then with her husband, surrounded by women "who wanted to do [her] in"; and finally turning the triangle on its side and making "the other woman" her own lover.

At the time we spoke she was struggling with awareness around the edges of this pattern, beginning to question her own complicity in the wearing repetitions that had yet to bring her peace of mind:

> I think that some of the early problems in our marriage happened because of my inability to trust the relationship. I had doubts that my husband really loved me, that he wouldn't screw me over emotionally, and because of this, I kept myself at a distance, even going so far as to create certain situations as "proof" that we weren't possible. Inti-

macy is hard, and we have both had to work at it; in the meantime, we set ourselves up some.

For the daughter of the Charmer the question of trust is the essential issue in falling in love and seeking a mate. With all the dazzle and flamboyance of the Charmer's affections, his daughter may still be driven to question the deepest core of his love. And if she is also exposed to the perilous shadowside of his charms, like this daughter of the charming yet abusive father, then she becomes all the more uncertain of the reliability of his love, or of the possibility of love with any man. *Did you really love me?* the woman Sonya asks the ghost of her father in *Imaginary Crimes. Or was that a con job, too?* The daughter of the Charmer is forever sifting pretense from feeling, fantasy from reality, theater from life. And finding that core of father's love that is real and enduring, that can truly be trusted, is often the first step toward trusting the offer of love from another man and trusting herself to be able to respond to it.

"I know I have my father wrapped around my finger, but he has me wrapped around his." Holly Heston, daughter of Charlton Heston, smiles the smile of the Charmer's daughter pleased with herself for naming the game so neatly. At nineteen she hovers between teenager and woman. Round and eager, talkative and effervescent, she's dressed in a purple sweater and skirt, which she hikes above her knees when she sits down to show off her smokey blue stockings and very high heels. Her fluffy brown hair is cut in a bubble, and she pushes back the wisps of bangs from her forehead as she talks, widening the eyes behind the blue plastic sunglasses. The words "fabulous" and "fantastic" drip from her speech like candycanes from a Christmas tree. At times it is wearing to sound out the complexities beneath her unceasing buoyancy, her relentless jargon, as in, "My father always has these fantastic lines, and he's got a fantastic sense of humor, and we get along fantastically." But it is also hard not to be touched by her infectious spirits, by her gracious efforts to please—in short, by her charm.

Like many daughters of Charmers, she takes advantage of her charm while also pushing against it. "I kind of got the label of being a very happy child," she says, "the little girl who never had any problems, and who was always happy and laughing and giggling." ("The outstanding characteristic of Holly's personality," her father will say later, "is a remarkable sanguinity.") But Holly also chafes at her image. "I found that even when I was unhappy or in a bad mood, people wouldn't notice, because I never let it show. I was always very, very inside—I didn't want to subject people to that. And when I couldn't help but let it out, it was 'What's the matter with her? What's her problem?' And finally I said, 'Hey, listen, I'm a human being, I'm going to be in a bad mood every once in a while. I'm not perfect. I'm not a paper doll. I have emotions, too.' "

We are sitting in her father's living room several days before Christmas, her season. Holly boughs hang in the entry of the house, set deep in the canyon lapping the Hollywood hills. Huge pine wreaths deck the fireplace, and the grand piano is blanketed in Christmas gifts and cards. A Chinese mural of dancing horses, proud and golden, presides over the room. A horse's head, carved boldly out of stone, sits sentry-like outside. And indeed, Charlton Heston, when he joins the conversation later in the day, looks like a tall, proud stallion himself: strong chiseled features, reddish blond hair, blue eyes, cool as a racehorse, steady as a jockey. Even dressed for tennis, he is regal in his bearing, and the room is designed to enhance this bearing. Everywhere there are lordly touches: the massive gold chandelier, the king's portrait on the wall, and the muted gold sun in the center of the royal blue rug with its rays emanating around the room as if to remind all visitors that royalty presides. For the actor who has been Moses and Ben Hur there is a palpable sense of *noblesse oblige*.

Ever since she was adopted by Charlton and Lydia Heston at five days old, Holly Heston has had to grapple with this legend. Even now at nineteen, her relationship to it is ambiguous, to this family myth that is regal, inflated, larger than life. "I want to talk about my father as a man, as a person," she insists. "He goes to the bathroom, gets up at seven-thirty, plays tennis. He's not just an actor, he's not a god." She pauses as if on second thought not entirely convinced. "He's a god to me, of course." Or again, "I look upon my parents as kind of immortal. I look at them as Greek gods to a certain extent. Growing up, I never had to look in a dictionary. I'd always go to one of them and they had the answers. I put them both on pedestals. Mostly my father."

Like many daughters of Charmers, Holly found her relationship with her mother more problematic than the bond she shares with her father. A thin, dark-haired, intense woman whose talent for photography has flowered in the past few years, Lydia Heston seems as different from her daughter as an iris is from a daisy. From the time Holly was about eleven until about fourteen, Lydia Heston suffered desperately from migraines that incapacitated her for many things, not the least of them mothering. Still a child, but awkwardly moving toward womanhood, Holly understandably resented this apparent abandonment and turned the full force of her love and the brunt of her needs to her father. "I didn't really get the kind of output from my mother that I really needed" is how she puts it now, "and that's why I became very close to my father. There was a time when she was very sick and I found that it was my responsibility to take care of things, to run parties and take care of my father. You know, little odds and ends like that." The offhand phrasing doesn't entirely hide the hurt beneath, like the flowered chintz slipcover that doesn't altogether camouflage the old couch's history, the spots, the tears, the pawprints of the dog.

Lately mother and daughter have begun to heal the breach between them, sitting down for long talks to untie the tangles of the past, smooth the skeins of the present. "I think it makes my mother feel better that I take the time out to talk, because I never really did," Holly confesses now. "I automatically went to my father. It was just a real easy thing for me to do. And he always had the time. He really didn't have the free time, but he made it. And that's what made it so special to me."

When she talks about her father, her tone takes on the sweet indulgence of romantic love. And yet describing their romance, she so lacks self-consciousness that the listener feels almost like a voyeur. "My fondest and earliest memory of my father is being able to get in his lap and sit. I still to this day sit in his lap, and he loves it, and I love it. I feel some sort of vibration, some kind of warmth. I think it's fantastic. I don't think you're ever too old to sit in your daddy's lap."

Behind the blue-tinted shades her eyes widen in childlike delight as she describes the protective cloak of her father's love. "One of the most important things he's always done for me is to just always impress on me that no matter what I did in my life, whether I killed someone or did something horrible to anybody, he would always love me. And through my whole life he would say, 'I love you with all my heart.' I always felt special because I was an adopted child. He would say, 'You're the most important thing to me. You're my chosen baby. You're my munchkin.' And my whole life he's called me munchkin. I don't like anybody else to call me that. It's so special to me. And he said, 'Don't you get tired of me calling you munchkin and darling and sweetheart?' And I said, 'No, it means so much to me and I wouldn't want you to stop.'"

The father declares his passion as ardently as the daughter. In resonant, honey-smooth tones perfected for the screen, but here no acting job, he describes the depth of his affection for his daughter. "Holly came to us when she was only five days old, and from the instant I held her she was my daughter,

I fell in love at first sight with her. I fear sometimes that my love for her is so total that it prevents me from being as good a father as I might have been. You want to feel that you have a certain responsibility as a father to provide shaping examples and controls. I hope I have not failed to do that entirely, but it requires an enormous effort of will."

He settles into the black leather Eames chair, resting on one ray of the sun blazing in the carpet, and waxes philosophical. "I think another problem for a father of a daughter is that from the time a girl is very young, very tiny, she is a woman. And there is to a man a mystery about a woman, an impenetrable mystery. And every so often I would look at her at five or seven or nine and say, 'There's a woman back there and there's country I don't understand.' And now when I call her up or have lunch with her, as she grows more fully each month into a fully mature young woman, the mystery of woman is there and is enchanting."

Even allowing for a dash of theatricality on both sides, there is an intensity to their relationship, a fascination and absorption that suggests romance rather than kinship, flirtation rather than family. For the father the relationship is a respite from the pressures of a competitive and hard-driving career. For the daughter it is a magical entrée into a world she cannot yet navigate by herself.

When I ask Holly to describe the most special time father and daughter have ever spent together, she at first demurs. Because their actual time together is limited by her father's demanding schedule, because "every five minutes was an hour to me," every moment they spend together is special, she insists. But finally one recent evening comes to mind, an evening when her brother and mother were both away and just father and daughter were together. She is not at all aware that the evening she chooses symbolically sums up both the pleasures and the pitfalls for the daughter of the Charmer. "I went up to the house, and we were eating dinner together and the lights went out. So my father got down all the candles in the house, and he sat down and started reading to me from Ray Bradbury stories. And it was fantastic. And then the lights were turned on, and we put *Breakfast at Tiffany's* on the Betamax. And I totally related to her character, maybe because her name was Holly—Holly Golightly—and to her whole attitude about things. She just wanted to mingle with the elite, and she really wasn't one of them herself, but she was having fun. She was playing games not only with herself but with them, you know. And I just really identified with that."

Here in the house where the lights went out with all the candles lit is the shimmering world of the Charmer. But when the lights come on, it can also be a place of high expectation and doubt, a place where perhaps, she is not entirely sure she belongs.

When I ask her whether there have been stormy times with her father, she shakes her head immediately and insists, "No, not with him. Never. Because he meant too much to me." And then, with only a slight loss of the usual exuberance with which she greets the world, holds the world at bay, she adds another answer, "I was always too afraid of maybe losing him, I think." And that, of course, is the price of the candlelit dinners, the mystique of specialness and theatricality. Somewhere hidden beneath the swinging skirts of "sanguinity" is the secret fear that someday the lights may come on to show everybody, everything gone. And the daughter of the Charmer is raised to believe that by the sheer force of personality she must, at all costs, prevent this loss.

And again when I ask her whether she's ever been in love, she admits that her expectations are very high, perhaps too high, and she doubts that she will ever find a man who matches her father. And she confesses that she never brings home her boyfriends, not the casual ones and certainly not the most serious one, the man fifteen years her senior with whom she spent eight months during her last year of high school. "It started out as sheer infatuation and then I fell madly in love with him. And I'm still in love with him, even though we're not together, because he was such an important part of my life. It was kind of a transition from spending a lot of time at home to spending a lot of time outside of home. It was the first time I really started doing things, trying new things, like eating sushi or squid or grasshoppers. And that was really a big deal. But my parents never met him. They knew about him and said they'd like to meet him. But there was also a problem, because he was traveling and so were they, in Europe and the Midwest. So it was a year when I spent very little time with my parents and quite a bit of time alone. Still, it was a great growing period, a great growing period."

For Holly Heston, at nineteen, this is a time of transition. She is poised between the enticing world of her father, the world of the theater and private school and the marble statues of stallions, and the lesser-known but increasingly seductive pull of the world beyond, the world of boyfriends and sushi and making her own way, her own *faux pas,* her own attempts at vision. She is about to leave for Europe, to live and study art in Paris, to dream about how she will make her mark. And on this journey she is luckier than many daughters of Charmers, because she takes with her her father's faith that she may do more than merely charm the world. She may engage with it, take it seriously. " 'Never give up, never give up, never give up.' That has to be one of the most important things my father ever said to me. 'Stick with it. If you've got your heart in it, you can do it.' " And as she remembers his words, they carry with them the echo of Ben Hur, the tenacity of the warrior and underdog. "Stay in the chariot. Stay on the horse. Don't get out. Try your hardest. Keep your promises. The most important thing is to keep your promises."

Most Charmer fathers place far more emphasis on success in the social world than on competence in the work world.

With loving attention and involvement they may train their daughters to be gracious partners to the men who will one day supersede them. But their attention may well stop short at training or encouraging talents useful for productive and creative work. These fathers favor looks and charm over brains and sweat. "If you're pretty enough, you can get anything you want" is the message many daughters of Charmers have been bamboozled by. But as these daughters begin to reach adulthood, they often fight back against their early indoctrination and begin the long struggle to be taken seriously.

The woman who embarked on her medical-school career late in her thirties was raised by her seductive and infantilizing father to be a very different kind of woman, the kind of woman her mother was—the proper companion to an important man:

> When I was growing up, I thought I'd marry, have children, probably never work. I'd be an "interesting" woman, a suitable companion to an "interesting" husband. I was never given permission to express feelings, do hard things. I was given strokes for being entertaining and pleasant. I'm the one who wants to make the party succeed.

But after fifteen years of making the party succeed as wife and mother, she ached to put her considerable energies to more constructive uses. Her experience at medical school has involved, in part, a gradual peeling away of layers of social veneer to search for the person of substance beneath. Sometimes the old brainwashing is so strong that she loses track of which layer is the real one:

> When I was a third-year medical student, I would give a case presentation as if I were a person of authority. Sometimes I can't believe I'm a person with something to say without cracking a joke, being charming, being nice. At times I feel I have to pretend I'm a person of authority, and maybe I will be.

Still, she feels satisfied with her choice and not the least with its opportunities to undo the lessons of her early training:

> My career has endless possibilities. Even without a man I have something interesting and broad. It is an opportunity to grow in a personal sense—to become an authority, to be adult.

The Charmer's lack of vision for his daughter's possibilities as a working adult often reflects his own fragile sense of his own capabilities. Unstable and given to erratic shifts of fortune, the Charmer cannot usually transcend his own limitations and impart to his daughter a self-respect he has not achieved. At times he may ensnare his daughter in his own fantasies, which may be alternately too constricting or too grandiose. A disappointed musician father of an aspiring painter projected his own fear of risk-taking onto his daughter, limiting in advance her options for achievement the way he had muzzled his own:

> In trying to remember my father's actual advice, I come up with mixed messages. When my college acceptance letters arrived and I was opting for the larger, more competitive school, he asked, "Don't you want to be a big fish in a small pond?" Well, no. What I really wanted was to be a big fish in a BIG pond, but open competition was not encouraged in our family, and I never acknowledged my closet competitive spirit, even to myself. Only last year, at thirty-three, did I realize that limited success in my field means almost nothing to me. What I think I want is, simply, national recognition. As did my father, without ever entering into open, aggressive competition.

A variation of this script is that father's fantasies for his daughter become inhibiting by their very grandiosity and unreality. This woman in her early twenties describes how her father's narcissism found an outlet in fantasies of wild and extravagant success for her. Yet his childishness prevented him from offering her the kind of concrete support that would allow these dreams the glimmer of reality:

> My father thought I was brilliant and encouraged me to be precocious. I grew up with the idea fostered by him and his mother that I could go to any college in the world when the time came. But the converse of that is that I became a "girl" at some point, probably after father's second marriage. He also abdicated responsibility for me to my stepmother, and this seems to have leaked over to education. When I was ready to go to college, I was also ready to leave home, and suddenly there was no money. I was verbally encouraged to become "something" (my father wanted me to be a brain surgeon or president of the United States at the very least), but the back-up support was not there.

The daughter of the Charmer often approaches the working world shouldering a backpack of dreams—her father's and her own—but without a sure sense of direction. Along with her backpack she takes her savvy, her talents, and her finely honed instinct to please. But without either a strong parental model or even a steady hand of guidance, she may flounder. Lacking a sense of purpose, she may veer wildly toward one titillation or another while searching for the balance that suits her needs.

From the back *Tiffany Green* looks like a very pretty, very average all-American girl. She has a trim, lithe body dressed in jeans and a T-shirt, and a mane of strawberry-blond hair cascading to her waist, thick as wheat, shiny as coins. From the back she looks about sixteen. From the front her looks become more enigmatic, her age less decipherable. There are the expected freckles and crooked smile. But there is also a certain wariness around the eyes that says, I have seen more than you might assume, and a certain toughness to the stance that says, Don't mess with me for I have withstood more than you might imagine. So it is difficult, but not impossible, to picture Tiffany Green—daughter of a charming father and a churchgoing mother—working the streets and raking in the bucks for her pimp. And it is troubling but not incomprehensible to imagine her masterminding a dope ring. Nor, finally, is it unbelievable that this year, at thirty-five, she has closed a chapter on her past and enrolled in law school.

"I was always a Daddy's girl as a child," she begins, tucking her feet beneath her and tossing her hair over her shoulders like a fanfare of punctuation. "I would wake up very early when I was a little girl, and then I would wake up Daddy. Mother couldn't. I would massage him. Then I would give him a hundred kisses." She laughs with unconcealed delight as if, even in remembering, the ritual is still tangible. "I would put out his underwear, his pants, his shoes and tie, so that they all matched. Then I would get out the towels. My first ambition was to be a valet! I would massage him some more, and he would scratch my back. My tactile needs were met by him."

To the entire world—and to his baby girl—her father was demonstrative, charming, and suave. Professionally he was a performer whose fortune varied according to his gig, "first a musician, then public television, then public school teaching, then TV again. Also summer stock and singing, in the church choir and in synagogue." But at home—and especially to his wife—he was erratic and temperamental. Tiffany remembers the marriage as shaky, nights her father would return home late and without explanation, harsh words, bowls being hurled. His relationship with her two older brothers—and theirs with each other—was also ragged with conflict. So, under the cover of her role as "baby," Tiffany became the family peacemaker and go-between. "I felt I had to settle all the family trouble. I got very good at assuaging everybody and stroking their egos. That became my role. I felt otherwise

I would be left alone and everyone else would be taken away. I made it my profession to rub egos."

For a long time this rubbing egos in the family seemed to fill her emotional needs, even her sexual ones. In high school and later in college she siphoned off her extra sexual energy and poured it into dancing, often rehearsing and performing around the clock with little sleep in between. "I danced off my sexuality," she says now. "I used my sexuality to be a fierce dancer, to give me that extra spark. I loved the Martha Graham technique. I would practically have orgasms on the floor." Like her father, she, too, had become a performer, creative, obsessed, the two in the family "who probably couldn't balance a checkbook."

The one serious relationship she indulged during college was an affair with a friend of her brother whom she met at sixteen and reconnected with years later. "He was dark and hairy and snarling. Because I grew up with blond, smooth, slender men, I have always been attracted to dark, chunky men." He was in law school in another town. She would pack a chuck roast in her weekend suitcase, arrive at his house, take off her clothes, "and have an orgy of sex and eating." Food and sex, caretaking and femininity, service and pleasure, were as interwoven as the strands of her braid when she danced. But serving and satisfying his needs grew stale quickly when he did little but neglect her in return. "I had nothing but my dancing and him fucking with my head. He thought I was a good cook and a good fuck, but not a mind. He lorded over me. He thought he was trying to make me be smarter." Fed up, she finally summoned the nerve and left him. "He fell to pieces," but, she adds, with characteristic bravura in the face of calamity, "it took me about five minutes to get back together."

Still, she returned to college for her senior year with an unnerving sense of incompleteness. She had her dancing, she had her trim, lithe body and her mane of gold. But Tiffany

Green had been raised to believe that unless she was serving someone, her life was empty; unless she was buffing someone else's ego, her own was worthless. "I felt I needed something" is how she explains it. "And I decided it was a man." She met the man at a friend's house on the day he got out of jail. He was a black man who called himself Prince, and he was to change the course of her life.

When she speaks of him, her voice gets very quiet, eerily quiet, as if the words are coming through her rather than from her. "He was beautiful," she says. "He was also a junkie, which I didn't know at first. Once he took drugs he lost interest in sex. We fucked three times in six months. I had no energy either, because he turned me out in the streets." She is totally matter-of-fact about this, but as she talks, the girlishness seems to give way to the other, tougher stance. "I had no experience with street life. I was strictly milk and cookies and dance. But it was a big challenge for me. He wanted money, and I wanted to please him. I like to please men."

In a perverse way prostitution became the payoff of her early training. "He was very proud to have a white girl, a college girl, not a junkie. I would work in the worst part of town, but I'd always wear a little gray suit with a bow, like a schoolmarm. The first night I was kidnapped and gang-raped. So Prince told me not to do certain things, like back alleys. He would come to pick up the money, and then I wouldn't see him. I don't think he ever knew my name. He called me 'Precious.'"

Still, she projected her fantasties on him, for they were charged with unfired ammunition from the past. "I was helping. I wanted a man. I admire moderation, but I've never achieved it. I thought if I made enough money we could go away together. Also, I felt I could change him. I thought I was powerful enough to pull that off." Powerful enough to change him, but too powerless to leave him—this was her legacy as a Charmer's daughter.

One day Prince brought her with him to show her off at the prison where he'd put in time. There she met another man, named Sam, who eclipsed even Prince in her fantasies. "It was a flash, like in the comic books. I saw him running across the African veldt. We never said anything, but he said, 'I'm going to get that little white girl.'"

"It was inevitable," she goes on. "He came to get me when he got out of jail, and he got me. He bought me from Prince for half a piece of dope." To begin their life together Tiffany naturally wanted to do something for Sam. When she asked him what he wanted, he answered "Ten thousand dollars." So she set out to get it for him the fastest way she now knew—back on the streets. At twenty dollars a trick she had no time to lose.

"I fucked a lot less than you would think," she says, giving a soft swoosh of her mane to offset the crudeness of her words. "I gave a lot of head. A lot of men want warmth, touching. I'm good at that. It was business. You tried to do it as fast as possible. I made a lot of money on the streets, but I also got robbed a lot. Sam decided I'd do better in Nevada. Someone told him they were wearing leotards that year." She smiles her crooked smile, distance making a joke out of the incongruity.

So leaving her man behind, she went to Nevada, where prostitution was legal, and continued her mission at the Starry Night Ranch. There, although the house took half her earnings, life was considerably easier. "It's a jail. You are not allowed to go outside. The windows are covered with aluminum foil. It's a plastic world with red lights. New clothes, the wig man, the false eyelash person all come to you. Psychologically it was easy. Just stand in line and get fucked. By and large it was a great improvement over the streets.

"You're not supposed to have a pimp, though everyone does. We never talked about our men. We were all there as independent women. I was very proud of myself. I had baskets of money. Then my productivity, as it were, began to decline."

Isolated on the ranch with the windows sheathed in aluminum foil, she began to feel lonesome and restless. Finally she made her way back to the city, back to Sam, and back to what had become, in her absence, a big-time drug business. "Gradually I took over his dope business. Dealing was very scary. But I ran the business with an iron hand. I was what was known as a cold bitch. Sam was respected, because I was a strong, good woman who was running his game so well. I brought in a million dollars' worth of dope. We were very rich. We had suitcases of money. We would get two to three Cadillacs a year. We had more cars than anyone could possibly drive."

The talents of the Charmer's daughter—the smarts, the savvy, and the drive—were channeled into their clandestine operation. Tiffany became obsessed with making the business the biggest and most secure possible, as if preserving the business were the only way to maintain the ever-threatened bond with Sam. To the outside world she was "a cold bitch." Inside she felt like Scheherazade, magically, manically spinning one more story for her prince to defer her fate another night.

"I gave up everything for Sam," she admits now, "my opinions, my morality. The more I did, the more I needed Sam." And the more she did and the more the business flourished and the more she needed Sam, the less Sam could tolerate. "He had moved up from painted velvet to Marimekko," she says with a bloodless laugh. "You get the picture?" The picture was also that he took on more women, more obligations. Finally success unleashed his crazy, paranoid side. "He would turn his paranoid smile on me—beat me up, hold a knife to me. I would take care of him and after eighteen hours he'd go to sleep." She pauses for breath, as if even in memory that feeling of him taking possession of her is still suffocating.

"When Sam began to doubt that I loved him, it meant I didn't exist, because loving him was all I had."

For a long time, however tenuous she felt, she remained Sam's one link with reality. But, she says, "somewhere along the line he knew he was going to die." When it happened—at thirty-seven—it was as ambiguous as the rest of his life. Driving home from his father's funeral, he got into a fender accident, and checking his car by the side of the road, he was smashed by a truck and killed. The law concluded accident, not foul play. Tiffany had her suspicions, but she was too numb to pursue them.

"It took me years to realize that Sam was dead," she says now, letting her hair enshroud her like a shawl. "He had had about three hundred suits. When he was alive, I would put all his clothes out for him. One day I spent eight hours cleaning up his clothes after he dressed. After he died I would go to the storage place and stand around in his suits. I would space out. I realized it was not a good sign." Perhaps it was there, among the suits of her dead lover, that she could finally put to rest her childhood ambition to be a valet. Perhaps it was there, in that storage place, that she came to terms with her own deep storehouse of memories and freed herself for a task that would equal her present need.

It took a long time for her energy to return, but when it did, a new ambition unfolded. "Sam told me to go to law school because we needed a lawyer in the family. It was set up to do, so I did it." At first she defined law school as part of her commitment to Sam, part of the way she would continue to please him, even beyond the grave. But in truth she was doing it to please herself. She liked to envision herself in court, passionately arguing a motion before the judge. She would be wearing an elegant gray suit and a beautiful silk blouse with a bow, but this time the incongruity would not smart as it did on the streets. This time she would not be lurking in the shadows, shuffling and toadying, while inside anger buried too deep for consciousness corroded her self-esteem. This time if she met competition, betrayal, manipulation, she would know how to fight them. In her mind's eye she was arguing for justice as ardently as she had once accepted injustice as her rightful fate.

This chapter on the Charmer would not be complete without a discussion of the incestuous father. For the father who commits incest with his daughter is often an extreme exaggeration of the Charmer type. He shares certain personality traits with the Charmer, yet finally is unable to draw the line between appropriate and inappropriate behavior, between playful and loving affection and cruel and injurious exploitation. Like certain of the Charmers, the incestuous father may keep up a smooth and polished public front but turns violent and abusive at home. Disappointment in his wife and often her sexual rejection as well make him turn to his daughter for comfort and approval. But where the Charmer will usually be satisfied with ego stroking, the incestuous father demands physical affection from his daughter to satisfy his overwhelming needs. He is utterly unable to assume the responsibilities of being a father. Instead he is forever stuck in the needy, demanding, adolescent phase or, worse, emotionally remains a child, needing to be sustained and nurtured by his own daughter. Psychologists Lora Heims Tessman and Irving Kaufman suggest that when incest occurs in a family, both parents agree unconsciously that it should happen:

> The father who overtly acts out incest with a child, rather than being sexually involved with an adult, appears to wish to be a child himself. The mother who unconsciously fosters the incest is also seeking mothering, and is threatened by the adult sexual relationship. . . . The daughter was often prematurely pushed into a mothering role, including the incestuous relationship with her father. . . . The girl who has experienced incest with her father tends to see herself as the adult in the family and feels responsible for providing the mother and father with care.[4]

Since the time of Freud, controversy has surrounded the question of incest and incestuous fantasies. Freud heard so many reports of incest from troubled Victorian daughters that he ultimately discounted them. He offered instead his "seduction theory": The daughters' reports were only fantasies of what they *wished* had occurred with father, more evidence of the lingering power of the unresolved oedipal crisis. As late as 1970 American health professionals generally agreed that actual incest was rare: one case in a million people. The number of cases has always been elusive, both because little research has been done and because the subject has been cloaked in shame and silence.

But recently the subject of incest, like many other sexual issues, has come out of the closet. Revisionist scholars of Freud are now suggesting that those Victorian daughters may indeed have reported the very prevalent reality of incest—and not merely oedipal fantasy. In a recent article called "An Epidemic of Incest," *Newsweek* cites revised estimates in this country that "one out of every one hundred women was sexually molested as a child by her father—an astonishing figure in itself and one that many experts think is far too low."[5]

Coping with the searing aftermath of incest is the work of several landmark programs, including the Santa Clara County Child Abuse Treatment Program, for several years the only national training center for the treatment of incest (and recently curtailed after budget cutbacks). Its director, Hank Giaretto, maintains sympathy for each participant in the painful drama. "Sexual abuse of children is self-abuse," he says. "You can't avoid the hangover of guilt and self-hate. A normal father's greatest fulfillment comes from knowing he has contributed positively to his child's growth. But if, say, he himself came from an abused or emotionally deprived childhood, he feels in his bones that life has dealt him a rotten deal and that no one can possibly love him. Imagine that at some point he senses a separation widening between himself and his wife; that his job is going poorly; that his carefully patched-up life is falling apart. He turns to his daughter, feeling she is the only one he can trust, the only one who might really care for him. Parents who molest their children are like neglected children who destroy a favorite toy."[6]

For the molested daughter, the damage runs far deeper than the sexual abuse alone. Worse than their fathers' sexual attacks, many daughters feel, was missing out on childhood because of them. "I feel my childhood was stolen" is the way many girls describe the loss. In addition, many experience a debilitating sense of responsibility for the tragedy. Their fathers' guilt becomes their own culpability. "I felt I was the cause of everything that went wrong in my family" is a typical response and a hint at the global burden these daughters carry with them into adulthood.

The opportunity to indulge in oedipal fantasies is vital to healthy female development. As Tessman and Kaufman explain, the flowering of the adult personality depends in large part on the utilization of these fantasies:

> The ego utilizes libidinal energy at this stage to reorganize the pre-Oedipal and Oedipal wishes. In this process, [girls] enrich their inner experiences in such familiar ways as intellectualization, creativity, self-discovery, and the establishment of new ego interests around a philosophy of life or political or social issues. Frequently . . . the fantasies also have a quality of psychic "nest-feathering" for [their] future libidinal life.[7]

But when these fantasies are acted out in incestuous relationships, the repercussions are severe on every facet of the personality: on self-esteem and competence, on love and sexuality, on work and success. Psychologist Patricia Straus, who has studied incest victims and specializes in their treatment, describes the impact of the incest experience on the girl as she reaches maturity: "She primarily sees herself as a sexual creature, and this interferes with taking herself seriously. Often she sees only two roads available to her. Either she can become the mini-seductress, evolving a kind of pseudosexuality, looking very interested in sex, but really afraid of it. Or she can deny her sexuality, gaining weight as an adolescent, feeling guilty about her mother, phony, and isolated from friends."

The girl's process of healing after the trauma of incest often begins with the chance to unburden herself of her weighty secret. This revelation may occur in a group of other girls who have shared the experience or if and when she finds a man to trust and love. "Being relieved of the feeling of guilt that she was seductive is tremendously healing," suggests Patricia Straus. "It is relieving to learn that father was an adult and could have stopped the incest."

Susan Caldwell is a victim of childhood incest whose healing did not begin until she was nearly thirty. Her father was opinionated and authoritarian. He was also an alcoholic who frequently lashed out at the family with violent verbal abuse. Mother slept with daughter rather than husband, except for two hours every Saturday night. "My father's sexual abuse of me began when I was around eight or nine and continued until I was fifteen. It consisted of his fondling my genitals and breasts and stroking me—never intercourse. I hated going to his bedroom at night to kiss him good night."

Her childhood was made bearable by the nurturing presence of three other men—her grandfather, her uncle, and her brother. But during adolescence her problems with her father intensified. "I recall my father saying often to me, 'If you had only stayed three years old.' When I reached sixteen and was the last child at home, my father's drinking and verbal abuse and accusations concerning my sexual permissiveness (untrue) became worse. I was not allowed to go to school functions, dances, or parties because of religious beliefs. It was quite difficult being away from my peer group."

At eighteen, the legal age in her state, she moved away from home. "I was discouraged from attending college and encouraged to marry—which I did, at twenty." She sought relief in this early marriage, but her husband was unable to provide it, and they divorced sixteen months later. Then followed a number of painful and self-destructive years of drugs and sexual experimentation, including a "doomed love affair with a married, older man."

Finally, nearing the end of her twenties, she met a man, a black army officer—"headstrong as I am"—with whom she began to hammer out a "workable" relationship, then marriage. For the first time she was able to confide in her husband about the sexual abuse, and their own sexual relationship blossomed. Recently they have adopted a little boy, and both she and her husband are determined to create the kind of family life this time that she never knew. She is more detached from her father, and more forgiving. She recalls the trauma he suffered at five when he lost his mother and three brothers to a flu epidemic. She sees that he has recovered from alcoholism and is making another attempt at his marriage. So, encouraged by her husband, she has begun to close the gap with her parents. But living on the other side of the country from them, she also maintains a necessary separation. As a mature woman with a family of her own to raise and protect, she has used geography to make indisputably clear the boundaries that her father was unable for so many years to respect.

The attentions of the Charmer and the abuses of the incestuous father fall on opposite sides of the boundary separating appropriate from inappropriate involvement. Wishes, fantasies, and fears on the part of both father and daughter may obscure this boundary, but careful and loving attention on the father's part is necessary to maintain it. Knowing when physical bonds are crucial and when to let them go is the gift father must present daughter to enable her to grow up healthy and whole. Psychotherapists Lily Pincus and Christopher Dare describe this delicate balance:

In infancy and early childhood, close physical bonds of love with parents are vitally important, but we need to recognize that the child's healthy development involves growing free of these bonds. If the difficulty in attaining this freedom, both for the children and for the parents, can be acknowledged, then their secret longings can be more clearly understood, and the acting out of incestuous fantasies stemming from the infant's earliest feelings is much less likely to occur. Loving relationships between family members can then be enjoyed, despite their erotic components, without inappropriate anxiety and guilt.[8]

For the daughter to flower under her father's charms, she must have the security of knowing that he can control these charms, that they will remain benevolent, not intrusive, not malevolent. If she has this security, she is free to enjoy his company, to thrive on it until she is ready to let it go. But without this security from father, finding security and fulfillment in love and work later on will be a profoundly more difficult task.

6

THE ABSENT FATHER

SINCE MY PARENTS' DIVORCE WHEN I WAS SIXTEEN, MY father has remained financially supportive of me, but there has been little or no communication between us on a personal level. I am uncomfortable with him and never know what to say to him. My parents' divorce was a turning point in our relationship. When all of a sudden you have to spend one day a week alone with your father or call him every night, what do you say? When you're too old to be taken to the zoo, what do you *do* together?

Katherine, *twenty-four*

My father died when I was fourteen. He was an angry man, intelligent but not using his intelligence. He didn't like to take or give orders. In many ways, since after all I have no choice, it seems to be simpler that he's dead. He isn't around to interfere with my life. Still, after he died, I often dreamt that he came back, saying, "Oh, they made a mistake and I'm not dead."

Julia, *thirty*

The Absent Father, removed from his daughter's daily world by divorce or death, is no less powerful a figure than the father who sees his daughter every day. Unlike the Bystander, who teases with his physical presence but remains emotionally absent, the Absent Father may be physically removed but remains at the forefront of his daughter's life. In her fantasies he achieves a vibrant and compelling life of his own, fed by memory and hearsay, wish and fear. He may be idealized until he becomes as omnipotent and omniscient as a god. He may be caricatured or denigrated until he seems to personify evil incarnate, to be held responsible for every disappointment that follows in his wake. Or he may flip back and forth in fantasy between all-powerful and all-punishing, until his daughter is dizzied by her own dreams and sobered by her own apparent power to define and redefine her father's impact. If divorce has forced his absence, she will most likely still see him enough to compare and eventually integrate his idiosyncrasies with the personality in her head. And often with integration comes understanding and forgiveness for his alleged trespasses. But if death, not divorce, caused his absence, the process of adjusting fantasy to reality becomes all the more subtle and demanding, for there is no longer any reality to check the larger-than-life father figure who still looms in her mind.

A variety of circumstances influences the way father's absence is experienced by daughter and how the experience affects her in later life. Crucial are her age at the time of the separation, the web of reasons for the separation, and the quality of her relationship with her father beforehand. Whether father's absence is caused by divorce or death, the explanation to daughter can be pivotal in easing her response to the loss. And even with the most careful explanations, anger, self-blame, and guilt often flood her feelings, as she struggles with the fear that she somehow bears responsibility for the rupture. How her mother copes with the loss or separation, how she portrays the father in his absence, and how mother bonds with daughter afterward also have enormous influence on how the daughter will handle the loss. If mother becomes depressed and emotionally unavailable, daughter's loss is compounded: She has, in effect, lost both parents and faces the terrifying task of taking care of herself long before she is able to.

In a review of child-development research, "Separation from Parents During Early Childhood," Leon Yarrow explains how the loss of a father is painful at any stage of development, but possibly most difficult at the oedipal stage:

> . . . each developmental stage may be viewed as critical in terms of the child's capacities, in terms of the central developmental tasks or the focal psychological conflicts of specific developmental periods . . . each developmental period has its own sensitivities and vulnerabilities. . . . The data on father-absence suggest that father separation during the height of the Oedipal period may be particularly traumatic.[1]

When the family triangle is complete with father, mother, and daughter all present, the oedipal period typically allows the daughter the free play of fantasy about courting father's love, getting rid of mother and replacing her in father's affection. Usually these fantasies reach their peak between ages three and five, become buried during the latency years, and again resurface to be finally resolved during adolescence. With the resolution of oedipal fantasies, most girls relinquish their attachment to father and turn their attention to boys and other men. Mother is transformed from a feared and hated rival to a source of identification and support.

But when the family triangle is disrupted by divorce or death, the free play of oedipal fantasies is also disrupted. Explains child psychologist Peter Neubauer:

> In the absence of parental interplay—that is to say, in the absence of the primal scene with all its social equivalents—developmental forces crystallize too suddenly around events, rather than being slowly but continuously interwoven in experience and hence have an extraordinarily traumatic effect. . . . When a parent is absent, there is an absence of Oedipal reality. The absent parent becomes endowed with magical power either to gratify or to punish; aggression against him and the remaining parent as well, becomes repressed.[2]

The daughter who may, unconsciously, have wished that father leave mother, must now face the horrible consequences of her wishes. She may be paralyzed with self-blame and fear her own apparent omnipotence, which she believes caused the family breakup. Or she may blame one or the other of her parents, yet stifle her rage out of fear of recriminations at a time when she feels all the more vulnerable and dependent on them.

So for the daughter who loses her father either during the oedipal phase or during adolescence, both her erotic excitement and her endeavor excitement may take on a particularly dangerous quality. Without the ongoing, unfolding opportunity first to test out and then to desexualize and transform these early excitements, this daughter may fear her own powerfulness and the hidden dangers of sexuality and competent endeavor. For the daughter of the father who dies during her childhood, much depends on the opportunity to share her childish excitements with him beforehand. Finding father surrogates with whom to carry on these exploratory fantasies after her own father's death can also be enormously influential. For the daughter of the divorced father, the quality and intensity of the relationship following the divorce naturally influences the transformation of her erotic and endeavor excitements into her profound attitudes toward love and work later on.

The Absent Father who is separated from his daughter by divorce shows a range of fathering styles from the indifferent to the involved. On the most painful end of the spectrum is the Absent Father who estranges himself from his daughter as well as from his former wife. Whether from confusion, hostility, or ignorance, this father, having severed the tie with his wife, does not or cannot reestablish the connection with his daughter. This daughter must then grapple with her shattering feelings of rage at her father's abandonment. She must eventually come to terms with having to move forward into the world without any steady male guidance. For her, the path toward finding satisfying love and work is fraught with perplexity and anger. On the more positive end of the spectrum is the Absent Father who despite his break with his marriage is nevertheless able to establish a caring and involved relationship with his daughter. Whether through joint custody or an ongoing visiting schedule, this father continues to provide his daughter with a steady source of paternal love and guidance and remains a continuing model in love and work. This daughter's relationship with her father becomes surer groundwork for her quest in love and work.

The longing to have a father and to be fathered is so profound that if father is absent, daughter will seek passionately to replace him. Psychoanalyst Ernest Abelin calls this intrapsychic instinct "father thirst" and explains its role in development this way:

> There is evidence of a father thirst in the fact that children pick up father substitutes wherever they can. However, it is never enough, and the kind of continuity is not available in a triangular situation to allow the normal triangulation to occur. Children can substitute older brothers, grandfathers, and other males, but it is very important that their interest in men be supported by the single mother and that she endorse the child's interest in men. If the mother encourages and endorses relationships with men on the part of the child and herself, this can help to overcome the absence of the father. However, it is detrimental if the mother conveys the message that it is not important or necessary to relate to men.[3]

The single mother often paints the portrait of the Absent Father so convincingly that her portrait becomes as much an influence on her daughter's perceptions as the phenomenon of father's absence itself.

Frances Hodgson Burnett's classic, *A Little Princess,* is a gripping children's story about the daughter of an Absent Father, a poignant parable about the extremes of father thirst. I remember sobbing my way through reading it as a child—though my own father was happily present throughout—so deep are the psychological issues it touches, often buried and unconscious like the hidden themes of a fairy tale. Seven-year-old Sara Crewe is the "little princess," whose mother died when she was born. Her attachment to her father is fierce with seven-year-old passion. He in turn calls her "the little Missus." When he woefully leaves her in a proper girls' boarding school to embellish his considerable fortune in India, she consoles him: "I know you by heart. You are inside my heart."[4]

For several years she is the shining star of the school and lives the life of "a little princess," dressed in the loveliest dresses, attended by a personal maid, and provoking jealousy in some of the girls whose disdain she meets only with kind-ness. But in the midst of the fanfare and opulence of her eleventh birthday party, she receives the shattering blow—her father has died. He has died of a fever and the shock of a business failure, after his best friend had invested his money in a diamond mine that produced no diamonds.

Overnight the little princess has lost everything: her father, her fortune, her future. The harridan sisters who own the school agree, grudgingly, to keep her, but banish her to a cramped, rat-infested attic and the life of a drudge. Lying in her narrow bed, she mourns her father with a despair too overwhelming to be named:

> The first night she spent in her attic was a thing Sara never forgot. During its passing, she lived through a wild, unchildlike woe of which she never spoke to anyone about her. There was no one who would have understood. It was, indeed, well for her that as she lay awake in the darkness her mind was forcibly distracted, now and then, by the strangeness of her surroundings. It was, perhaps, well for her that she was reminded by her small body of material things. If this had not been so, the anguish of her young mind might have been too great for a child to bear.[5]

But the grim reality of her dejected state soon intrudes on her mourning. She is forced to slave for the tyrant sisters, cooking and cleaning and caring for the younger students. She does her duties so efficiently and uncomplainingly—and befriends several more unfortunate than she—that the reader, of course, realizes she is still a little princess, in inner if not outer riches.

Then, amidst the unremitting drudgery of daily life, the magic of the story unfolds. A mysterious gentleman from India moves in next door with his devoted servant. Wealthy, but ailing and weak in spirit, this gentleman is on a quest to find the lost daughter of his friend and business partner. When this friend died years before, he believed himself pen-niless, but was instead—surprise of surprises—rich from an unexpected discovery of diamonds. Though the gentleman considers his quest almost hopeless, he meanwhile takes a shine to the woebegone drudge next door and has his servant surprise her with sumptuous repasts, a kind of symbolic representation of the beginning of the slaking of her father thirst.

At the climax of the story, the connection—which the reader has guessed long before—is made. Sara is indeed the long-lost daughter of the gentleman's best friend. She has become the heiress to her father's fortune and is removed from the evil clutches of the boarding-school mistress to be safely and lovingly protected ever after by her father's dearest friend.

A Little Princess is an astute psychological fantasy that first allows the child to face the agonizing issue of father loss, but then provides a magical resolution in which the loss is assuaged, if not completely repaired. At the height of the father-daughter "romance," Sara loses her father, her beloved friend, support, and provider. Though she is devastated, her connection with him is so strong and her ability to internalize his protection so deft, she is able to carry on in his absence. Indeed, abased, she is curiously ennobled. Her own inner strength, which he has nurtured, serves her like a shield.

But the magic of the story also means that she is sent a surrogate protector in her father's absence. The sustenance, support, and riches he provides assure her that she will never feel the ache of father thirst again. The suggestion of the story is that Sara has somehow earned the magical protection of her father's friend, first by facing and working through the pain of her father's death, and then by dint of her own dignity, steadfastness, and, paradoxically, her own self-reliance. The moral of the tale seems to be that what a daughter *makes* of the trauma of losing her father, how she manages and carries on in his absence, is more significant than the fact of the loss itself.

How each daughter copes with the loss of her father has enormous influence on her development as a woman, on her strongest feelings about love, her deepest aspirations about work. Each daughter's response is colored by her unique family situation, by the comfort or neglect of mother and other siblings, by the advice or abandonment of friends and other relatives. "My family was divorced when I was twelve," recalled a woman in her forties. Her slip of the tongue revealed the truth of that divorce—and many others. For often not only the parents alone divorce, but the whole family suffers the rupture.

Of the many daughters of divorced or bereaved families whom I interviewed, responses varied with the fabric of family life: anger or denial, numbness or grief, a frantic search to replace the lost father or a gradual willingness to work through the painful details of the loss and learn to carry on beyond it. Shock and guilt often meet the initial announcement of a divorce—"Why is this happening to *me*?" with its corollary, "What did I do to cause this?" A thirty-eight-year-old Mexican-American woman still, in a corner of her heart, burns with anger and shame at her parents' divorce when she was nine. She had been sent to a boarding school in England "to sort of get me out of the way while the denouement was reached." Against her mother's wishes, her father wrote to tell her about the divorce:

It was quite a traumatic thing for a nine-year-old to take, especially since neither parent was there with me. I remember vividly how awful and abandoned I felt. I was absolutely convinced that I had done something unspeakable to make my father decide to leave me (I really felt the divorce involved him and me, not him and my mother). The terrible feelings of guilt and unworthiness that the divorce caused in me were to color the manner in which I related to my father (even to the idea of my father during the years in which he simply did not communicate with me) and from there to all men.

For almost three years—from the time she was nine until she was twelve—her father did not get in touch with her. Meanwhile she kept him alive with an elaborate—and heart-breaking—fantasy, another piece of evidence of the desperateness of father thirst:

I had a couple of photographs of my father as a young man, when he and my mother first courted. I got a girlfriend to fake a couple of love letters to me, and I used to show these and the pictures of that gloriously handsome Latin man to my other friends and tell them that this was my Mexican boyfriend and these were the letters he wrote me. Meanwhile, of course, my Mexican father was not writing me anything.

As she entered her teens, her father reestablished contact with her, and over the years they established the habit if not the heart of a relationship. But in the deepest sense the damage of the original split was irreparable:

He was affectionate with me, still proud of my achievements, nice to both my ex-husbands and a string of boyfriends. But there was always something missing: never any real interest in who I was inside; everything was always on his terms. I always felt as if I were wearing a mask when I was with him. I never felt free to let my hair down. I guess I was always afraid that if he ever saw me on a bad day, or saw some not-so-nice side of me, or if I shared a pain or a failure with him, well, he would probably just up and leave me again, just as he had done when I was nine.

Throughout her twenties they continued the semblance of a relationship, meeting for dinner once a week but keeping their emotional distance strictly and painfully defined. Finally a second separation occurred, this time precipitated by daughter, not father:

The separation occurred over a relatively meaningless incident involving a largish sum of money my father owed a friend of mine who had done a lot of carpentry work for him. My father simply refused to pay it, claiming that the job had been badly done. And I suddenly decided that I had had it, that I did not choose this man as a father and I would certainly not choose him as a friend, so why continue a meaningless relationship. So I broke with him. That was over ten years ago, and neither of us has ever made any attempt to get back in touch.

With a harsh logic that seemed to her to make sense of years of unresolved conflict, this daughter was repeating as an adult the separation from father that so wounded her as a child. She was punishing him for a debt he owed but would not pay, just as he had not made good on the debt he owed her as a father. But the pain and despair lurking beneath the surface of her story, like seaweed and algae beneath a bay, suggest that the second separation compounded the anguish of the first rather than easing or reversing it.

The groundwork for psychic healing and a newfound sense of joy came from an unexpected source:

Two and a half years ago, while I was living in Mexico, I adopted a tiny baby of a few days old, a boy, and fulfilled one of my deepest desires, namely to be a parent. In the middle of all the awfulness of what my father did and didn't do, I have, in fact, had such a good life with my mother that I have always felt I wanted to repeat the experience, but this time from the other side. I feel much happier and more comfortable raising my son by myself, with my mother's very important participation, than I would if there were a man around to share or not to share it with me. After all, the only model for childrearing that I have is that of a single mother raising me!

The experience of raising her son single-handedly seems, in part, to have validated her own experience of childhood, allowing her to appreciate and draw strength from her strong and loving mother and begin to let go of the rage at her negligent and abandoning father.

For another woman, twenty-five, denial rather than rage was the response to her parents' divorce. Like the rage that consumed the Mexican-American woman for so many years, this woman's denial of feelings also insidiously drained her energy, curtailed her choices, and impeded her progress in the world:

> Nothing seems significant up until my father moved out when I was fourteen. I was very disappointed but denied my feelings by telling myself that if others could get through it, so could I. Just when I had begun to get over some of my shyness and feelings of inferiority, my parents split up, and I was kind of like dead for a couple of years—uninvolved in activities and other people.

With her father preoccupied with a new marriage and her mother preoccupied with her own dashed hopes after the divorce, this daughter burrowed into the protective blanket of her own numbness. From years of stifling her feelings as if they were rebellious children, even her own desires became estranged from her:

> I've had many doubts and conflicts, especially since graduation from college. Three years of depression because I couldn't figure out what the hell I was supposed to do next.

The process of unearthing her own feelings has been an arduous one, and at times the anger, frustration, and grief blanketed by the numbness have threatened to overwhelm her. But with time, with therapy, and with an attempt to work out relationships with each of her parents as adults, her excavated feelings have brought energy and momentum back into her life. She has embarked on training as a nurse, her own sphere of compassion widened from what she herself has suffered and surmounted.

For other daughters a parents' divorce means a change in the relationship with father, but not a cataclysmic split. Many fathers and daughters I interviewed managed to maintain the continuity of their bond after the divorce, while adjusting to the differences in terms—scattered rather than steady contact, the presence of stepfamilies, the pressure of old patterns. A twenty-three-year-old student describes the bond that existed between her father and herself both before and after the divorce:

> My father and I were born on the same day, the day he turned thirty-four. He has always been an active part of my life. After a rough period when I was sixteen—the year my parents divorced—our relationship is better. He truly sees me as an adult, a very gratifying thing. We are close in a father-daughterly manner, rather than "friends." He has a tape deck set up in the shop at his house, and one day he played a song about a woman and how hard her struggles were, and he said it reminded him of me and how proud he is of me. I cried and he sniffled a little.

The early identification between this father and daughter, born on the same day of the year, helped sustain them through the "rough period" of the divorce. Now father is able to acknowledge and accept his daughter as an adult, recognizing and supporting her struggles as he realizes she acknowledges his own.

Many daughters who do not get this recognition or this guidance either during or after their parents divorce continue to yearn for it and attempt to quench their father thirst by transferring their needs to a father surrogate. A musician in her late twenties recalls the unnerving sense of abandonment she felt around the time of her parents' divorce:

Puberty was a bad time for all of us. I competed and fought with my older sister, and my parents' marriage slowly disintegrated. I felt especially abandoned during my junior and senior years of high school, when I was facing college and career decisions and sexuality. Because they never told me they were having troubles, I didn't consciously acknowledge that I needed more guidance in my own life than they could provide, didn't seek school counselors or relatives, just internalized. My father was jealous of my boyfriends, but probably thought he shouldn't be.

During the years following the divorce she found confiding in her father about heartfelt matters more and more problematic:

I didn't share much with him about my love life or intense philosophical/spiritual searching; he tended to be nonchalant about the former and so terrified of the latter that we rarely got very far.

As the gap between them widened, so did her troubling sense of questions unanswered, needs unmet. Without being able to name what exactly she searched for beyond the father she never had, she embarked on a personal quest that eventually led her to a spiritual teacher. Her commitment to this surrogate father aroused feelings of jealousy in her own father that resembled his jealousies of the boyfriends of her youth:

At twenty-two I became committed to a yoga society, and that got my father very upset, very afraid I would space out and forget my powers of rational analysis. He was also jealous of my guru, a man from India I had never met but whose spiritual guidance and ideas about people and society I still treasure. I thought that my father would think well of the concerns for social and economic justice that are part of what this second father figure was clarifying for me, but his prejudices against anything intuitive or group-oriented were too sharp. We had several bad fights in which I insisted he respect my friends and choices even if he disagreed; and he insisted I understand the intellectual and moral dangers of what I was doing. We would clumsily make up but not really learn how to stop hurting each other.

But beyond this battle of wills she was in fact being nourished by the yoga society and its spiritual master in a way that both healed her personally and eased her relationship with her father by relieving the burden of her expectations of him. By her late twenties she had married a man whom her "father took to easily" and had chosen to pursue a career in music, which was also her father's field. These two steps in love and work formed a bridge back to her father, a newfound closeness as adults that both of them needed to draw on when, several years later, her father became ill with cancer:

The last phase of our relationship happened when his cancer was accelerating. I was east on a tour and able to spend a couple of weeks with him, and he was coping with a lot of weakness and anxiety, though no pain. For the first time he had no energy to waste dominating or arguing, and he was becoming softer and more openhearted with everyone. I naturally had my share of helplessness and grief; it was a rough and intense time but on a deep spiritual level very satisfying as we seemed subtly sensitive to each other. I felt strong and grown-up and important to him rather than feeling judged and criticized. I got some clearer, specific advice from him about my music and theater work and he was openly very proud of me. My older sister's wedding happened at this time, and I will never forget giving my father a bath that morning! He'd been too weak to get into a tub for more than a week, and when I offered to assist, it worked out well, sweet and relaxed! Startling.

Her father's illness and dying became, paradoxically, a restorative time for their relationship, a gift that mitigated the devastation of the final loss. "Softer and more openhearted," her father was at last able to offer her the guidance, approval —and love—she had yearned for as a young girl. And, attending him at his bedside, she experienced the pleasure and consolation of feeling competent, complete, and adult enough to nurture him in return.

The timing of a father's death has everything to do with his daughter's ability to cope with and integrate the loss. Having a sense of unfinished business intensifies the pain of a father's loss, while having a sense of emotional closure helps ease the final separation. For the woman quoted above, her father's death, when she was twenty-eight, was made more bearable because it coincided with a period of rapprochement after years of alienation and struggle. But several of the less fortunate women I interviewed experienced their fathers' deaths as a shattering, agonizing, and often infuriating rupture. These daughters are forever left with the disorienting feeling that a pivotal conversation, begun with apparently good intentions, has suddenly been broken off in the middle—no explanations given, no chance for questions, no opportunity to splice the conversation into the rest of life.

The daughter who loses a father before she is grown naturally suffers the severest feelings of deprivation and abandonment. Having neither the understanding nor the emotional vocabulary to resolve the layers of issues surrounding the loss, she is left with an unbearable void, an overwhelming father thirst. Often her inexpressible needs are vented by a blast of anger or controlled by a kind of grim resignation. Julia, the thirty-year-old woman quoted at the opening of this chapter whose father died when she was fourteen, used anger and world-weary exasperation to defend herself against the searing disappointment of her loss. Her father's premature death coincided with the typical disgruntlement of adolescence, so the natural process of argument and resolution was forever short-circuited:

> My father was an okay friend, but he didn't want to take on the responsibility of being a father. But since he died, I didn't have to confront him about going to college and how he was going to pay for it or about sex or anything else.

Having been deprived of the opportunity to "confront" him about "college and sex," she tries to comfort herself by rationalizing that this loss will actually make things easier for her. Perhaps subliminally she also senses—but cannot acknowledge—that out of exactly such father-daughter confrontations would emerge the stronger and more satisfying relationship that her father's death has robbed her of.

At the other extreme from the angry, distant daughter is the daughter who copes with her father's death by idealizing him and keeping him alive in fantasy. For a twenty-seven-year-old woman whose father died when she was sixteen, her father's presence is still palpable, sustaining, at times even larger than life:

> Since my father is dead, our relationship is purely spiritual at this point. He was tall, very thin, energetic, had blue eyes and smiled a lot. A private man, he read a lot of American history books and played with us when we were kids. He was very honest: "You're only as good as your word." We were close. I still draw from his advice and how he would feel and react. His death was a major changing point for me. I became more aware of "what Daddy would feel" and "what Daddy would do."

In her essay "A Note on the Father's Contribution to the Daughter's Ways of Loving and Working," (as well as in her study *Children of Parting Parents*), psychologist Lora Heims Tessman describes her treatment of a journalist in her late twenties whose father died when she was ten. The process of the therapy revealed the daughter's need to acknowledge both extremes of feeling about father: the unrealistically positive and the crushingly negative or ambivalent. "She sought treatment," Tessman suggests, "in part to gain greater understanding of herself and the conflicting pulls of family and career and in part because she felt there was something 'unfinished' for her about the death of her father from cancer."[6] Early on, her father had shown a trust in her that nurtured her capabilities in love and work. Tessman cites in particular: "his support of her individuation and trust in her growing capacities; his acknowledgment and sensitive response to her libidinous wishes; their shared interests; and her love of the quality of his character per se."[7]

During the course of her three-year therapy, Tessman's patient, *Wendy S.*, now married and the mother of three, explored both extremes of responses to her father's death, both the idealization and the ambivalence, the fantasy and the fury. The picture she draws of him at the beginning is almost uniformly glowing: vibrant, energetic, funny, loving to her mother ("I remember only one real fight") and to her. Early in therapy, she admits, "My problem is that I idealize my relationship to my father. I have my favorite images and I cannot remember the rest."[8] But gradually the "rest" begins to emerge, the hidden drawbacks to his apparent virtues, which she faces with long-submerged anger and sadness. Explains Tessman, "Wendy decided that much as she loved her father, his need for mastery with which she identified and which was an asset to her, also hindered others from seeing her need to be dependent when she wanted support."[9]

As she recognizes the ambivalence as well as the adoration she still feels toward her father, she also faces the mixture of feelings toward that part of herself which is a kind of internalization of her father's memory. Her therapist comments about this conflict:

The kind of response you got from him has lasted inside you and become a part of how vibrant, direct, and caring you are all at the same time. Yet I think you resent it terribly, you are always disappointed when you don't get that kind of appreciation from [your husband] or others, or when your family gets threatened by those very qualities in you.[10]

Then, as her therapy comes to a close and termination arouses again the anxiety and grief over her father's death, she moves to another sobering, but liberating insight:

. . . when I can't show my wanting [support], everyone just assumes I don't need any support and I louse up my chances even more. By not asking for support I shut it off . . . *but to let go of the possibility that my father will somehow reappear . . . in someone else* [tears]. . . . I guess I have to realize it's not the same relationship with [my husband] before I can get taken care of too. In that way, sometimes the things I loved most about my father now get in my way.[11]

Acknowledging her need for support in her relationship with her husband prepares her for greater intimacy, but also makes her more vulnerable to the possibility of another loss.

Vulnerability to loss is an especially freighted issue for the daughter of an Absent Father. Having suffered the original trauma of losing her father, she unduly fears repeating this loss. She may protect herself, at times unnecessarily, from venturing forward in love or work and exposing herself to the risk of another loss. So facing her sensitivity to loss is an important first step toward feeling more freedom and satisfaction about making risky choices in the world.

How each daughter copes with the impact of her father's absence—whether from divorce or death—is mitigated for better or worse by her mother's presence and by their relationship. The picture mother presents of the Absent Father

—whether glowing or incriminating, distorted or accurate, fair or vindictive—will strongly influence the daughter's own image of her father and her feelings about him. The younger she is at the time of the loss, the more susceptible to mother's point of view. The older she is, the better she is able to counter her mother's image of her father with her own vivid memories and, if father and daughter continue a relationship, with her own unfolding impressions more and more tempered by age.

For the thirty-year-old daughter of parents who divorced when she was seven, mother's bitterness made a grotesque caricature out of father and kept father and daughter estranged for many years:

> My sister and I saw father only twice a year. Mother said she didn't want him to see us. She turned us against him. She never let any opportunity pass to criticize him. She said he was a womanizer. Later, sex became screwed up for me. She said he was a liar, that he stole things, that he was cheap. She exaggerated his qualities to the most negative extreme. My perceptions were always colored by Mother's terrible stories. I hated him until I was seventeen or eighteen. It was also hard for me to imagine a man who could love a woman and child.

But with maturity and distance from her mother came a new, more balanced and understanding perspective on her father and a willingness to initiate a relationship as adults, where she would be the judge of his foibles and charms:

> I decided to move to the city where he was living. Our relationship since then has been very close. It has almost been like getting to know a stranger. Now I've gotten to like him as a friend.

Not surprisingly, her reunion with her father also eased her inhibiting doubts about men and improved her relationships, which had been self-destructive and self-defeating. Getting to know father with all his ambiguities freed her from labeling all men either monsters or the hypothetical savior she could never find. When we spoke, she was contentedly married and expecting her first child.

But just as maturity softened her distorted picture of her father, opened her eyes to his virtues and enabled her to form a bond with him, she also adjusted her feelings about her mother and their relationship. Now she saw her mother in a more distant and dispassionate light and registered the bitterness, exaggeration, and self-interest that, as a child, she had believed was gospel. Now the alliances have shifted, and she shares her changing impressions of her mother with her father. But the difference is that as an adult she trusts her own perceptions more and feels readier to handle the ambiguities she finds:

> Father never tried to turn us against mother. I have gotten to where I can talk to him about mother. He can support my experiences from his own. He has helped me sort out my feelings about her. The net result is that I don't like her as much. She raised us to believe that life had given her a raw deal and that justified her bizarre behavior, including alcohol and drugs. But apparently that had been going on since before their marriage.

Though many daughters polarize their parents into "good" and "bad" camps, daughters of divorce often depend on this defense more desperately than most. After the upheaval and confusion of a divorce, many daughters struggle to control their own ambivalent and chaotic feelings about their parents by splitting their traits into positive and negative clusters. Then they will side with the "good" parent—now all the more dependent on this parent's protection—against the "bad" parent. This unconscious technique becomes self-defeating in the long run, for it curtails their possibilities for identification and their choices as adults. But in the short run taking sides seems to offer this daughter the shelter of at least one parent's steady love and prevents her from having to undertake the difficult task of coming to terms with each parent's ambiguities.

The thirty-eight-year-old Mexican-American woman whose father disappeared off the scene from the time she was nine until she was twelve sought refuge in her mother's supportive love. She instinctively labeled her father the bad guy and her mother the good. Dependent on her mother's love, she also became her mother's staunchest ally and defender. Together they struggled to form an intractable alliance against father, which over the years became a barrier against most other men as well:

> My mother is a strong, affectionate person, sometimes too opinionated, very flexible, but stubborn, too. Her outstanding traits are loyalty, lovingness, sensitivity, openness to new ideas, firmness in her principles. We share all kinds of interests: professional, cultural, political, personal. I have always considered my mother to be the most important person in my life.

For a thirty-one-year-old woman whose parents divorced when she was thirteen, the family alliances following the divorce were arranged along opposite lines. She remained close and sympathetic to father and designated mother the villain of the piece. Where the woman quoted above felt sustained by her mother's love and shut out by her father, this woman continued to feel nurtured by father but emotionally estranged from mother:

> Mother is strong-willed and frequently domineering. She's always had me "by the balls" emotionally. She's never approved of me yet thinks she has, rarely stops to listen to me, prejudges me, projects her fears onto me, has always tried

to run my life, is defensive when I want to talk feelings, puts me down a lot, and will not give me the space to rationally discuss anything with her that has any intrinsic value to me.

For this woman the trauma of her parents' divorce and the subsequent absence of father was compounded by the loss of mother's love. For the Mexican-American woman the crisis of her parents' divorce was intensified by the loss of father's love. For both daughters, polarizing their parents into enemy camps and siding with one while rejecting the other meant an emotional divorce from one parent that echoed the divorce between the parents themselves. For these daughters—and many others I interviewed—that emotional divorce from the parent also precipitated a kind of inner divorce, or estrangement between the part of the self that needs to identify with mother and the part that needs to identify with father. If the daughter blames and rejects her father after the divorce, she may also reject that part of herself that is modeled after the father, the part that wants to venture forth into the world, work, accomplish, achieve. If instead she faults and rejects her mother, she may also reject that part of herself that is nurturing, supportive, sensitive in relationships.

Before she can sally forth into the world, feeling whole and autonomous, ready for love, bolstered for work, the daughter of a divorce must often go through a complex recovery and healing process that allows her to resolve both the outer and the inner split. Often, with age and distance, she begins to see each parent's participation in the divorce, each parent's shortcomings and each one's strengths, rather than the culpability of one and the innocence of the other. Gradually, blaming neither, she may forgive them both. And forgiving them, she may also be able to forgive and unite the warring parts of herself.

Sometimes this sense of perspective arrives with maturity— or with the arduous search and struggle of psychotherapy.

Other times another relationship, either inside or outside the family, might provide the healing balance. For many daughters of Absent Fathers, the relationship with a brother becomes an encouraging and restorative influence, an alternative model of masculinity as well as a connection sustained beyond father's absence, a source of continuity and, often, comfort. This woman, whose parents divorced when she was in her early teens, describes the equilibrium her brother's example offered her:

> I've learned equanimity from my brother and peace of mind (or striving for it). Acceptance of life. He's been more creative and alternative in his approach to life, and so have I, than Dad. But he's also the product of a new-age generation and therefore is a seeker, whereas Dad has been sort of a muddler. My brother frequently gives a lot of himself and subsequently gets burned. I've learned to flow somewhere between his extreme and my mother's paranoid extreme. Both he and Dad have given of themselves to others. I've learned a lot about healing myself from my brother. Primarily, I've learned how to take care of myself inside from my brother and more how to deal with the outside world from my dad.

At thirty-two and the daughter of an Absent Father, Mimi Leonard is a contemporary woman whose journey toward security in adulthood reflects the upheavals and ironies of the past three decades. Her father, George Leonard, rebelled against the values of the fifties and felt most at home with the inner explorations of the seventies. Editor of *Look* magazine for seventeen years, he moved from the three-piece suits and martini lunches of the eastern Establishment to the aikido robes and encounter sessions of the West Coast, finding himself in the forefront of the human-potential movement. The titles of the books he has written over the past twenty years pinpoint the junctions of his quest: *The Man-Woman Thing, Education and Ecstasy, The Ultimate Athlete, The Transformation, The Silent Pulse, The End of Sex.*

Mimi Leonard's husband, Jerry Rubin, is a symbol of the sixties. His books—*Do It!, Growing (Up) at Thirty-Seven,* and *The War Between the Sexes* (which Mimi co-wrote)—reveal another apocalyptic and hortatory imagination not unlike her father's. Mimi Leonard has both synthesized the messages of her father and husband and detached herself from them. Conscious of their shadows and of the imprint of the fifties, sixties, and seventies, she has nevertheless fashioned herself as a woman of the eighties. After years of being in school and out of school, of drifting and rebelling, of experimenting and resisting experimentation, Mimi Leonard has found her niche as a stockbroker with Conti Commodities, one of the giants of Wall Street. If security eluded her as a child, now securities have become her bread and butter.

We meet at a restaurant in the towering World Trade Center, and Mimi Leonard is dressed to blend in with the other brokers and businesspeople who swarm around us. In her conservative brown knit dress and jacket, she still stands out as an exceptionally pretty woman: soft blond hair, blue eyes, and delicately chiseled features that seem as fitting for a southern belle or a flower child as for a high-powered businesswoman.

"I'm really not all that fascinated by looks," her father had confided in an earlier conversation, in his rambling old house in California's Marin County. "Looks can be a terrible detriment to a woman, a threat, a problem, a challenge. And all four of my daughters have had to meet that challenge. I'm not really bragging. It's just that physical beauty has been a terrible problem for all of them. They're all four rather attractive to look at." About sixty, George Leonard is still an attractive man himself: tall and lean, silver-haired but still boyish. Father and daughter share the same watery blue eyes, the same instinctive sense of their own charm, the same gift of charisma. They are two people who appear used to getting what they want. But for Mimi the early years were troubled by disappointments.

Sipping a glass of white wine, she sketches in the outlines of her relationship with her father, a relationship that was inalterably wrenched by her parents' divorce when she was only seven. "My relationship with Daddy has gone through four basic periods. First, childhood. Then, from the time the divorce occurred until I was maybe seventeen or eighteen, I really worshipped him in every way. He was like a hero. And then, from eighteen till about twenty-six, I was having just the opposite feeling—having a lot of difficulty with him, and at times wanting to hurt him as much as possible. And I guess in the last few years it's kind of mellowed out and there's more of a balance between those two."

Like most little girls, she glorified and romanticized her father—and he fanned her fantasies, first happily, then, more guiltily. "He was heroic, mythic," she recalls. From early childhood she remembers him doing tricks for her, watching cartoons every Saturday morning and enjoying them as much as she did, orchestrating a fabulous sixth-birthday party with the whole basement covered with newspapers, so that no light came in and hanging fish from the ceiling. "Everyone was horrified and excited. It was one of the best parties I've ever been to." Then, after the divorce and after her father's remarriage, he tried to maintain this same feverish pitch of excitement and entertainment. For most of the year Mimi and her sister lived with their mother according to her staid and conservative tempo. But every summer the sisters would go to visit their father and his new wife, and he would take them swimming each day and to the theater at night. But beneath the razzle-dazzle, the mood had changed. "After the divorce, there was a melancholy aspect to our relationship. There was a sadness. And tension and guilt on Daddy's part, and I'm sure a tremendous amount of resentment on my part. And I think it was very, very difficult on us." Over the years the difficulties intensified. Without Daddy as a daily presence to temper the adoration and ease the resentment with a dose of reality, Mimi's emotions seethed past the boiling point, like an unwatched stew. At seventeen, champing at the bit after years of a proper girls'-school education, Mimi Leonard was ripe for rebellion. And finally it was her father who set the stage for it.

"At seventeen I graduated from high school and went to Esalen for the summer. What a transition! I went from being the speaker at my high-school graduation in a long white dress to about three weeks later living at Esalen, where Daddy rented me a room, and having a very wild summer. I studied Gestalt therapy with Fritz Perls that summer, and of course I got into my resentments. And that kind of attitude kind of progressively grew for three or four years until at twenty-one I went back to school. And from twenty-one to twenty-five I was going through a very low period in my life. And I took out a lot of it—as much as possible—I really seemed to blame my father for everything."

She fiddles with her wineglass, and although the anger has long cooled, the hurt is still palpable, like a bum knee that has never entirely healed and flares up under adversity, pressure, too long a hike. "I think I desperately wanted to be close to him. Desperately. And I felt it to be impossible. There was something about the magical quality that I saw in him as a child and as a teenager that grew into a distant, unobtainable quality. I think Daddy is somebody who is quite difficult and just doesn't do really warm, cozy, maternal type of things. He just isn't that type of person. I wonder if I was trying to get his attention by shocking him, by doing more and more bizarre, dangerous things."

But even her outrageous behavior failed to rivet his attention and reverse the frustrating fact of his absence. Looking back on this era now, she explains, "I wasn't able to get a reaction out of him. I guess I wanted the kind of father who was concerned with what your grades were, with how you're doing, someone who centers a little bit of his life on you. But Daddy so much had his own life—a rich, full life—and there was so little I felt I could contribute. And there wasn't that much real interest from him, except that he wanted me to be happy. But in terms of the details of my life, he wasn't interested in them, I didn't feel. He didn't want to know what color I was going to paint my bedroom. And I think that's what I really wanted, and he was unable to provide me."

So during this period of her early twenties, her need for her father's attention—and her rage when she did not get it—was unleashed with a fury that shook both father and daughter. "I kept going after it, and I kept getting no. And it was just very painful for me." And meanwhile she played out the same self-punishing psychodrama in her relationships with men. "During the same period I had a couple of very painful unrequited love situations with cold, self-involved men who were wonderful, witty, and charming at the same time. They were really representations of rejections from Daddy. Also I gained weight. I didn't look good. I was doing everything I could do to be rejected, but on the other hand was trying as hard as I could to be totally accepted."

But out of that agonizing cycle of pushing and pulling some new ground was gained. By her late twenties Mimi was jockeying less for acceptance in the eyes of others, felt more contentment with her life the way she was shaping it. Defining an interest in business after several false starts, opening herself to a relationship with a man who truly cared about her, she also noticed the dynamics with her father changing. "I'm more able to appreciate what he does give me and stop so much demanding what I particularly want that he can't give me anyway." Now, many years after the fact, she also acknowledges the anguish of letting go of her life's most poignant romance. "I had a real hard time falling out of love with Daddy to be able to fall in love with anybody else. There couldn't be a man who would be more perfect. And in a way I still feel that. If Daddy were not my father, he would be ideal for me."

Instead she found in Jerry Rubin, a man who mirrored certain seductive characteristics of her father, but was also able to offer her the intense involvement her father could not or would not share. "Jerry very much does provide me with that total attention and concern I wanted from Daddy, but he couldn't give. He's just totally interested in my every little thought or desire. He calls me four or five times a day. Just everything I always wanted." Adds the father about his son-in-law, "Jerry Rubin is a very controversial character. But he shines a searchlight of love and adoration at Mimi. It's dazzling."

Mimi sees in Jerry both the image and the opposite of her father. As many daughters of Absent Fathers discover, finding a lover who is a reconciliation of opposites can also provide a reconciliation with father. If the lover seems too similar to father, he may also seem too threatening. If he seems too different, he does not emotionally compensate for the early lack of father's attention. But as a combination of like and unlike father, he shines with the luster of the ideal mate. Mimi illuminates the contrasts and connections: "Jerry is five six and Daddy's six four. But the very fact that they're both extremes makes it a similarity. Jerry is absolutely obsessed with me and every detail of my life, whereas Daddy was the opposite, I felt. Jerry can be loud and emotional and lose his temper and fuck up and scream, and Daddy's just the opposite. Everything's under perfect control. He has that kind of Nordic quality that is more like me. So that's an opposite.

"Now the similarities are they're both visionaries—they're both charismatic leaders. They're both on the fringe. They're both challenging the established order of things. They're both extremely gutsy. They both believe that they're truly impor-

tant people, or else they wouldn't, I suppose, be such noncon-
formists. They're large—I mean, they have large spaces
around them. They both accept me as companion instead of as
a woman. They—neither one of them pulls women trips on me
at all. And both of them want me to be as powerful as possible
and encourage me when I am."

Indeed, it was Jerry who encouraged Mimi to go into commodities trading. Not only did he want her to be as powerful
as possible, but in some sense he forced her to be that powerful, unwilling, despite his devotion, to be her sole source of
support. Her story of finding her way to working on Wall
Street is a curious turnabout of the classic feminist job search.
"Jerry and I had been working together. We put on a large-
scale human-potential Event and then we wrote a book together. Then I had to figure out what to do with the rest of
my life. And I was really kind of starting at ground zero,
because there was nothing I had done in my past that particularly drew me. And Jerry really very, very much wanted me to
be a strong, independent, powerful woman, and I think he
very much wanted not to bear the total financial responsibility."

She tells the rest of the tale without irony or embarrassment, as if almost enjoying the paternal interference she had
earlier longed for, however inappropriate now. "So he
wanted me to get a job—not a twelve-thousand-dollar-a-year
job in publishing or a sixteen-thousand-dollar-a-year job in
news or on a paper. He wanted me to get a job where I
would seriously be carrying at least half the financial burden. He gave me the direction. I wouldn't have thought of
it. But I guess it appealed to me when I started thinking
about it. I thought, Gee, I really would like to be independent and financially self-sufficient. And so we thought of
sales. And then I really picked out this job. Jerry never could
have, he didn't know what it was, and I didn't either until I
found it. I networked my way to it."

And as it turned out, the commodities futures market—

where investors gamble on the future prices of internationally traded commodities like wheat, corn, or precious metals—turned out to be something Mimi Leonard had a knack for. Her quick mind, her grace under pressure, her ease maneuvering with people, her own willingness to gamble with the future, having somewhere come to terms with the insecurity of the past—all these skills were developed in spite or because of her father's early absence and cashed in on now.

And meanwhile the two rebels in her life—father and husband—from whose choices she was diverging radically, still rallied around her with pleasure. Who knows but she was responding to their covert messages for success, however padded with layers of rhetoric. "The fact that I started off at a very, very high salary and had good potential was very impressive to Jerry and I think it excited him a lot." And as if inspired by the triumph he had helped generate, the former revolutionary soon followed suit and signed on with another Wall Street brokerage house that specialized in solar investments.

As for her father, he, too, could not be prouder of his daughter's professional course. Although Mimi feels now that "there was no question that Daddy probably didn't think when we were growing up that his daughters would end up working, because his mother didn't work, his sister didn't work, my mother didn't work," his attitude has, of course, been tempered by the times. Now he crows about his daughter, "When she went to work for Conti Commodities, she had not spent one day in business school and had no training whatever in business. She got the job and went through the training program. There were twenty-five in each of the classes, and I assume every one of the others was an M.B.A. with many years of business training. She had zero, and she graduated first or second in her class. And she's kind of marvelously ingenuous. Blond hair and big blue eyes, she said, 'Well, I read *The Wall Street Journal* for three months.'"

He is as pleased with her as if her achievements were drawn to his own specifications. But in another mood he can also acknowledge the boomerang affect of his influence. "For many kids of the sixties the thing to do to rebel was to go to the Fillmore, be a hippie," he suggests. "But I was already there, at the Fillmore. How can you become part of the youth culture when your father is already a part of it himself?" With and without her father's help Mimi Leonard has synthesized the conservatism of the fifties, the upheavals of the sixties, and the self-absorption of the seventies to secure for herself the comforts of the eighties.

But these comforts do not remain entirely unalloyed. A year or so after our first conversation, Mimi and Jerry legally separated for seven months. A newspaper article rumored divorce. But instead they got back together and seemed from the outside at least, to be more intertwined than ever. "We understand each other and are able to adjust to each other better now," says Mimi now, staying safely with generalities about the changes their separation has wrought. But she has left Conti Commodities ("I've kept commodity futures as a hobby," she says) and is working alongside her husband in a company he started several years earlier called America's Network Marketing. Among a "number of entrepreneurial projects," they run "networking parties" at New York's Studio 54 every week for professionals of various stripes to meet, greet, and make business contacts with each other. Interestingly, Mimi has taken her husband's name now, and when she answers the phone at the office they share, she is no longer Mimi Leonard, but Mimi Rubin. After the separation the desire for merger seems to be more powerful than ever. It is as if their marital separation aroused fearful memories of the earlier separation from father, and this time she is more determined than ever to make this relationship last.

In her search for love as an adult, the daughter of the Absent Father finds herself coping with confusion, discouragement, and a driving need—often self-sabotaging—to create the happy, romantic ending she never knew as a child. She feels confusion, because she has not had the psychological comfort of continuity in her first and foremost attachment with a man. The loss of her father has left her with unresolved questions, which she may unconsciously continue to hammer out with her new partners. More than many other daughters she feels torn between seeking a lover in her father's image and seeking his opposite. Often having found one, she will rebound to the other, as if ricocheting between repeating and embellishing the short-lived bond with father and replacing it with someone more secure. The search for father's double sometimes leads this daughter to a relationship with a much older man; the search for his opposite at times leads her to relationships with women.

The sense of discouragement this daughter feels often comes from her powerlessness at preventing the original separation from father. Falling in love and forming an intimate attachment with a man arouse all the old anxieties over another possible loss. So, more than many daughters, the daughter of the Absent Father agonizes over commitment. Trying everything to defend herself against the possibility that her man will leave her—and repeat the original trauma —she often becomes the first to leave. Thus, she inadvertently perpetuates a negative cycle that is hurtful rather than healing. In the furious grasping for the happy ending, she often pushes herself farther and farther away from it.

In her essay "Loss, Rage, and Repetition," Martha Wolfenstein explores the self-sabotaging romantic patterns of daughters whose fathers died when the girls were still young. Acknowledging the difficulty of the young child to mourn for the lost parent, Wolfenstein outlines instead the child's typical reaction to the parent's death: "the persistent quest for the lost parent, rage rather than grief, repetition of disappointments and the vindictive determination to prove no one can help."[12] Wolfenstein uses as an illustration the case of a nineteen-year-old patient named Mary whose father died when she was fifteen. She traces Mary's series of disappointing love affairs, each time with a slightly unwilling lover whose hesitation is repeatedly overlooked. In analyzing her patient's consistent emotional denial of the loss that will repeat the initial loss of her father, Wolfenstein explains:

> In the pursuit of the unhappy love-affair there is the same splitting of the ego as had been instituted in response to her father's death. The setting up of the predicament of pining for an absent lover, while cherishing the hope of eventual reunion, represented a repetition of the situation vis-à-vis her father, whose death she could not accept as something irreversible. To an immature individual the death of a parent deals an intolerable blow to the sense of omnipotence. In willfully precipitating a later situation which portends a similar loss, the individual is not aiming at a total repetition, but expects a last-minute reprieve. It appears that the same drama is being played again, but the earlier outcome has not been accepted, and there is the insistent hope that this time it will turn out differently. . . . The underlying motive . . . is one of undoing a past disaster, of recovering the injured sense of omnipotence, of coercing fate, rewriting the tragedy with a happy ending.[13]

As long as this daughter denies her rage and grief at her father's death and tries to assuage her feelings rather than coming to terms with them, she exposes herself to repeated and wrenching incidents of loss. And repetition, of course, brings only wilder rage, rather than comfort.

The confusion and self-defeating circularity of her romantic quest is described from another perspective by a woman whose parents divorced when she was sixteen, and who now, at twenty-three, has already been married and divorced:

> I seem to choose men who have a character flaw that prevents me from marrying them. I have a need for romantic

involvements, although that does not include marriage, so I pick men based on other criteria than marriageability. An example would be the man I'm dating now: He doesn't like kids and is very selfish (thus ruling him out for marriage), yet he is a great companion.

Watching the bitter disintegration of her parents' marriage forced this daughter to draw an imaginary but inviolable line between romance and companionship on the one side and marriage and kids on the other. As her parents were not able to integrate the two, neither is she. And for now the prospect of romance and companionship is the safer, more pleasurable option, since marriage and kids, at least in her parents' experience, lead only to rupture and pain.

Consciously or not, in her love relationships the daughter of the Absent Father seeks to repair or undo the damage of her original loss. She will look for security where her father created insecurity, continuity where he represented interruption, sustained involvement where his was detached. For a number of women I interviewed, this search led to relationships with older men. In exchange for offering these men the potent elixir of youth, their liaisons provided the chance to replay the role of daughter with—they hoped—a readier and more willing partner. The thirty-eight-year-old Mexican-American woman introduced earlier, whose relationship with her father was damaged by years of desertion and fraught with bitterness, found in her father's colleague the worldly and caring father she never knew. She draws the connections as she tells the story:

My second lover, and definitely still one of the most important ones, was a man twenty years my senior. The whole episode is interesting in the context of my relationship with my father. I met this man—let's call him Gabriel—in Europe, when I was eighteen and had traveled there to spend the summer with my father. Gabriel and my father worked for the same organization and my father was attending to his stay. In the normal course of protocolary events, my father and stepmother had a lavish cocktail party for Gabriel. At that point I saw him simply as a colleague of my father's, albeit quite handsome, though gray-haired and distinguished and very much of another generation.

But several weeks later she ran into him in the airport of another city and they struck up a conversation that soon enthralled them both:

We spent about five days in that city, registered at separate hotels but very soon were spending each night together in his room. I was eighteen—he was thirty-eight (the age I am now!) and seemed tremendously grown-up, mature, sophisticated, experienced, self-assured, wonderful to me. He was so much of what my father had never been.

Not only did he provide an emotional intimacy she had never experienced with her father, but he also created an intellectual intimacy that was foreign as well:

He cared about my mind a great deal: he talked to me for hours about European literature (he is French) and about music and how to listen to it, and he asked me about myself, my interests, my friends. The loving and the sex were incredible to my eighteen-year-old terrified and curious self, but what was most important was that other kind of interest. And when I finally had to return home, after those initial five days and then another week in another city, his letters kept me going for months. And he would send me books. And he would suggest records for me to buy—to him I owe the discovery of the B-Minor Mass of Bach. Gabriel was definitely a father figure.

During their relatively brief romance he kindled both the erotic excitement and the endeavor excitement her father had so neglected during her childhood. Just on the impressionable brink between adolescence and womanhood, she found the combination intoxicating, and at least partially healing. But the damage her father caused by his desertion and cruelty was not entirely undone by this one interlude. During the years that followed, she became involved in one disappointing liaison after another, each time replaying the original scenario with father, trying to undo the original disappointment:

> There has been a certain pattern of choosing cold, distant, impossible men—and it seems to me that each time I have struggled to win them or to hold them or whatever, I have been reliving that battle I kept up as a child and adolescent and young woman to try and gain my father's love back.

Many daughters of Absent Fathers try to cope with and assuage their anger at the loss of father's love by seeking to replace it with the love affairs of adulthood. Others are either so consumed or numbed by their anger at father that they find themselves turning away from relationships with men and gravitating instead to women. Especially if mother provided a safe haven after the divorce or death, these daughters seem to consider alliances with women more comforting and secure than relationships with men. Women represent the safe and known, men the unknown, uncontrollable, and potentially harmful, and these daughters hover perilously between the two shores. A woman in her early twenties describes the conflict:

> I desire a settled, monogamous relationship and at the same time feel discouraged by most men I know. I enjoy my women friends so much more than men.

Or again, a thirty-year-old woman confesses to the pull between the safety offered by women and the excitement offered by men:

I used to fear at times that I would be a homosexual, because of some dreams I had and some conscious recognition of feeling attracted to women. I've always felt more comfortable (less threatened) around women, but one of my weaknesses is that I do like to flirt and get attention from men and like to feel that I'm attractive to them.

Another woman whose alcoholic father left her at fifteen to her mother's sole support chose, in her late twenties, to limit her romantic attachments only to the company of women. Involved for the past two years with a woman who is physically like her father—"tall, heavy, blond"—she still finds herself plagued by the same conflict that nags the women described above who remain open to relationships with men. Despite the best intentions of ideology, this lesbian woman still yearns for the steady paternal protector she never knew—and yet chastises herself for that yearning:

I have always wanted and not wanted a monogamous, supporting relationship. I mean that I fight with myself over wanting to be supported so I can stay home and be essentially a "housewife" (since I am not financially secure). I usually don't want the seemingly necessary and emotionally complex intimacies involved in a "marriage," but I am so attracted to it that I hve gotten involved many times up to the point of "marriage" and then disengaged. Now I am really working on building a job/career that will give me the time at home I want so I don't have to be in a relationship like the ones I described.

Like many daughters of Absent Fathers, this woman struggled at first to assuage her father thirst by seeking the solace in others that her father was not able to provide. But when the dream of romance, of marriage, of perpetual care failed to offer the comfort she craved, she gradually began to turn inward, ferreting out her own inner strength, her own resources. For the daughter of the Absent Father, the central challenge of adulthood is to find and nurture her own inner security, her own capability for caring for herself. Though as a child she may have known only shifting sands, her task as an adult is to create a secure base for herself. Then from that base she can venture forth in love and work, augmenting her inner strength rather than flailing around desperately trying to shore up a self which otherwise she may fear is achingly absent.

In the process of making adult decisions about working, the daughter of the Absent Father once again confronts the fact of her father's absence. Once again she must face the effort or challenge of moving forward in the world—that outside world, menacing or tantalizing—that her father once represented. But now, as an adult, she must approach that world without the continuity of his support, guidance, or involvement. Once again she must consider those issues of venture and impermanence, success and failure that his absence may have provoked for the first time—and perhaps long before she was ready to assimilate the contradictions.

Meeting the challenge of work is a frightening, even overwhelming task for some daughters of Absent Fathers. For many years these daughters may flounder, vacillate between a variety of unsatisfying choices, or simply throw up their hands and retreat altogether from the pressures of professional responsibility and the working world. But for other daughters, father's absence may work as a curious catalyst. For these women the crisis of father's absence, whether by death or divorce, may prove an acceleration to development, a spur to motivation. Instead of crumbling in the face of loss, these women become remarkably energized by it. Coping with father's absence, they plumb their own powers of ingenuity, creativity, and responsibility. Then these assets arm them for success in the working world later on.

Martha Wolfenstein describes two cases of daughters of Absent Fathers whose confrontations with work and achievement illustrate these contrasting responses to loss. Her example of a flounderer is the nineteen-year-old Mary, introduced earlier, whose father, an artist, died when she was fifteen. Mary had been a "conscientious and excellent" student in school, but after her father's death her "performance became erratic," and she drifted away from her studies and into promiscuous affairs. Wolfenstein explains this not uncommon response to a parent's death:

> The deterioration of school performance is a recurrent (though by no means invariant) finding in cases of children who have lost a parent. . . . In the absence of external ego support and with the loss of narcissistic supplies provided by parental praise and pride, the incentive for achievement is radically reduced. The surviving parent often, as in Mary's case, is so lost in incapacitating grief as to afford little support.[14]

Furthermore, precociously artistic, Mary had looked to her father to praise and inspire her talent. Her loss of his support was compounded when he bequeathed to her brother the art supplies that she felt were her due. Increasingly discouraged by the initial loss and subsequent perceived deprivation, Mary became even more agitated when she graduated from college and had to face earning a living. Comments Wolfenstein, "It was as if further proof were being forced on her that she had no father to provide for her."[15]

By contrast, Wolfenstein cites the case of a young woman doctor, the daughter of a doctor as well, whose death when she was ten proved an incentive to achievement rather than a hindrance. From the time of her father's death she showed a "determined and precocious independence." She chose to go away to school and worked to pay for her own tuition so she would not have to be financially dependent on her mother and stepfather. As Wolfenstein suggests, by identifying in a constructive way with her lost parent, she learned to parent herself:

> She herself became the only substitute for her father. It was she who would get the now greatly improved school reports which he should have seen and rewarded her for. Instead of declining in her achievements . . . this girl made marked and continuing improvement . . . But the father would seem to have been incorporated into the ego ideal and to have given an increased impetus to striving and achievement.[16]

Mary and the young doctor operated under magical but opposite assumptions about the fantasized return of their lost parent:

> The young woman doctor believed for some time following her father's death that if she was good enough, he would come back. Mary lived on the implicit assumption that if she suffered and floundered sufficiently, her father would have to return. For the doctor her father was a model for effort and achievement. In Mary's case the father remained a need-gratifying object.[17]

My interviews with daughters of Absent Fathers offer examples of both patterns of response: the flounderer, like Mary, whose father's absence leaves her without moorings in the world of work, and the coper or achiever, like the young woman doctor, whose father's absence seems to mobilize her to great feats of competence. An example of the flounderer pattern is a twenty-four-year-old woman whose parents divorced when she was sixteen. She has remained a perpetual student, supported by her father, and though she does volunteer work, she is too conflicted about her sustained dependence either to enjoy or value what she does:

> My father is a great philanthropist and told me as a teenager that he would support me "forever" if I did full-time volunteer work. I have always done volunteer work and been a student, since I was sixteen. Even though I feel good about

what I do, I feel a failure, as I do not bring home a paycheck. I have almost a fear of getting a full-time paid position.

Coupled with his absence, her father's "support"—perhaps conceived as guilt money—has proved more millstone than incentive for this young woman. Having deprived her of the steady involvement she craved as a teenager, her father cannot now try to compensate by putting her on a perpetual dole. In fact, this dole has perpetuated her dependence at a period of life when she needs to be drawing on her own reserves and gaining the self-esteem and satisfaction of paying her own way, in both the literal and pscyhological sense.

A thirty-year-old woman who now runs a small costume jewelry business is another example of a wanderer in the world of work. After her parents divorced, when she was seven, her father moved across the country. He would make a couple of brief but intense and guilt-ridden visits each year to see her. Her mother, restless and dissatisfied herself, was unable to provide the nurturing support that might have eased the ache of father's absence. This woman reached adolescence and her early twenties in a vacuum of expectation and guidance. "I never got any leads from my parents about what was awaiting me after college. I wish Father had directed me more. The things he suggested were things like waitressing. He never thought of me as a career-oriented person. He imagined I'd work for a few years and then settle down." For most of her twenties she bounced haphazardly from one unsatisfying job to the next: a stint on a kibbutz in Israel, then assistant to a private eye, then six months as a Playboy Bunny, which she calls "just a waitress job in an uncomfortable costume." In her spare time she pursued an old interest in designing costume jewelry, found she had a talent for it, eventually set up her own small company, which is by now modestly successful and modestly rewarding. Married to a doctor and expecting her first child, she is more content than she has ever been. Yet an unresolved anger still nags at her: "I got channeled into doing things that don't count. Like my company. I think it's outstanding that I manage it. But it's just a frill, it's expendable. Whereas my husband's career as a doctor affects life and death. But I was raised to think of doctors and lawyers as superhuman, people way out of my league."

Ironically, her father, who is an artist, offers another interpretation of his behavior, self-serving perhaps, but not unreasonable. "I never wanted to decide what my children should do. My parents thought I should be a doctor or a lawyer, so I rebelled and became an artist. I haven't put pressure on my daughter toward any career." What he called benevolent indifference, his daughter considered neglect—with his absence exacerbating her frustration.

As always, what this daughter made of her father's absence was more influential on her adult choices than the phenomenon of the absence itself. Despite her father's apparent good intentions, she perceived his absence as hurtful, neglectful, and ultimately debilitating. But other daughters seem to take the similar fact of father's absence and turn it to their advantage. In a series of articles for *The New York Times* on eight outstanding American women leaders, Gail Sheehy concluded that all of them "confronted a crisis in childhood: the death or abandonment of a parent or chronic insecurity due to the failings of a father."[18] From Gloria Steinem, whose "free-spirited" father abandoned the family when she was twelve, to Jane Fonda, whose father left the family shortly before her twelfth birthday to keep company with a girlfriend barely out of her teens, from Rosalynn Carter, whose father stopped working when she was thirteen and gave her mother the reins of the family, to Carolyn Reed, the black household-worker activist whose father deserted her in infancy—each of these women turned the experience of being deprived of a steady, providing father into an impetus for development and initiative. Out of hardship they unearthed the savvy, confidence, and responsibility that is the stuff of leadership. Sheehy reveals their common bond:

> To discover in childhood that you cannot depend on one of your parents is an experience of terrifying helplessness. A child has no way of knowing whether things will ever improve. Yet in each instance, while compensating for the weaker parent, these adolescent daughters identified with the stronger one. What makes these women singular is not so much the similarities in the triggering crisis, or the fact it usually came at the turning into adolescence, but the way they responded to it. Rather than falling back on earlier modes of dependency, or accepting a fate as victims, even in crisis they pulled *forward.* They took over as substitute adults, and in the process, their own development was accelerated.[19]

Grace Brown is a forty-three-year-old black woman, artist, activist, and sometime housekeeper for other women's houses. She is a slim woman with a strong face on which life has written of both hurt and healing. Grace's mother was thirteen when Grace was born. Throughout Grace's childhood her mother was often remote and unstable, hounded by "nervous breakdowns." Grace never knew her father existed until she met him through a fluke at thirty-three. Her mother lived with a man who became the steadiest presence in her life, a "happy-go-lucky guy" who would drink only every two weeks when he got paid and come home and cook up a slew of food. Grace Brown is not a national leader, but she is respected and cherished in her own community. She is unknown as an artist, but her art gives her pleasure, its meaning deepening with the years. She has raised four children, with and without their fathers, and provided them with more security than she ever knew. When people ask her if she fears that she, too, will go crazy like her grandmother and mother before her, she answers simply and with confidence born of struggle, "I don't try to hold it all in. If I feel like screaming, I do. I'm different in other ways. I keep a journal. I have goals.

I didn't want to be the average person raised in Harlem. I wanted to be outstanding." Out of the rocky soil of father's absence, mother's indifference, and a community caught in its own turmoil, incapable of much sustenance, Grace Brown took what nurturance she found and improvised the rest. Now she has grown strong and bold, proudly taking care of others, learning to take care of herself.

Sitting in the apartment she has artfully decorated for a song from flea markets and garage sales, she talks about growing up in Harlem, as if explaining the mores of a foreign country. "You have to understand the levels," she says. "My family didn't drink or abuse their kids. We were respected in the neighborhood." While other kids were experimenting with drugs or sex, Grace "was a tomboy fighting for my rights." Her talent as an artist flourished early and was appreciated by her family but never encouraged as the sort of work that could become capital for adulthood. Her mother's boyfriend "worked for an advertising agency—carrying products," and it was this practical and useful work that was valued. Art was considered a frill, an indulgence. If she felt at all bitter about this, she has long since put the bitterness aside. She understands her family's limits in their context and has struggled to outgrow them on her own. Meanwhile, about her past, she takes the philosophical long view: "On the whole, I had a pretty stable life. I was never raped or robbed." She laughs, as if knowing damn well this is not enough to say about a life and yet somehow knowing she is lucky to be able to say it.

At first she looked to marriage as her ticket out of the ghetto, to freedom, independence, and adulthood. At eighteen she fell in love and married a man fifteen years her senior. She describes his attraction straightforwardly; "I was hungry a lot growing up, and he fed me." After four years and four babies, of whom her second son died, the marriage was over. "My husband was a gambler. And he would hit me. I took him to court and divorced him. Black people didn't get divorced. That's how aggressive I am."

She is proud of herself and tells this story with a swagger. But she also admits her vulnerability. After the divorce she took all the photographs of him out of her albums. "I wanted to get rid of all the memories of him" is her explanation now. After three years she married again. "That was an enjoyable thing for the kids and me. Then he fell in love with another woman, a white woman at that. Was I bitter? I almost went—" She breaks off and changes her phrasing. "I didn't want it to end." But with some hard-won hindsight, she also admits, "He was immature. He was into music. I was into education and studying. I was changing at that point. I was very serious. I outgrew him in a couple of years."

The past few years have been a period of retrenchment for Grace Brown. Living on her own, without a man, she has been raising her children, pursuing her art, dedicating herself to the political work of her community. Closer to her women friends, more honest with her children, she can feel her own strength gathering, her sense of purpose sharpening, the boundaries between self and others, self and the world growing clearer, more secure. She has learned how to nurture herself with humor. She has also learned how to take risks and how to retreat when necessary. "My goal now is to be an art therapist," she says. "That's the safe way to go. People want to hear that, especially from a black woman. But deep in my heart I still want to be an artist. I want to go to the country and paint and bring change to my people that way."

And during these years, as her sense of herself has been focusing and deepening, so, too, has her sense of what she seeks in a man. "I want someone who can appreciate me for who I am. I don't want to have to be too fabulous. I don't want to dye my hair. If I get odor under my arms, I can wash it. I want a man who will appreciate my art, someone who can communicate. Mostly I take the attitude, it's not going to happen. I feel I'm old now and not as attractive as I used to be. But I want someone who has a sense of humor and fun and who I'd enjoy sexually."

Having put her energy these past few years into digging deep into her own resources and finding herself changed, she is not sure she will find someone to match her changes. Resisting the undertow of her past and bucking her own culture in the present, she cannot be certain she will find someone to share her future. As our conversation ends, I feel her pride in herself, her growing sense of her own security blooming forth with the surprise of the first spring bulbs, buried beneath the cold ground all winter, ready for their show. But beneath that pride there is also a certain hesitancy that has not entirely been lost, the hesitancy of the little girl who was uncertain she had a father until she was thirty-three, whose mother opted out with illness, whose culture left her to her own devices. So I am startled but not surprised when, walking me to my car, she gently catches hold of my arm. "There's one thing I want you to be sure to put in your book," she says. "I wish women didn't have to be so dependent on a man's love." She looks at me intensely, grimacing slightly. "I wish I could say I have my art and that's enough. But I can't. It's not."

PART TWO

Daughters, Lovers, and Others

7

MR. WRONG AND MR. RIGHT

FOR MANY YEARS I THOUGHT I'VE FOUND MR. RIGHT—OVER and over again. But something always turns horribly wrong. First there was the mellow spiritual seeker. But when I got to know him better, he had a nasty violent streak. Then there was the revolutionary who thought he wanted to save the world. But he really only wanted me to massage his ego. Now there is my latest lover, who is adoring and attentive—but only on alternate Wednesday nights, because he's married. Does a man exist who can make me happy?

Lillian, *thirty-three*

For most women the path away from father's house leads eventually to the quest for a partner, marked for better or worse with the legacy of father's image, his wishes and words of wisdom. Rarely is this path straightforward and clearly marked. More often experimentation makes it circuitous, indecision interrupts it, and self-doubt clouds it like a dense thicket. As we journey along this path, most of us are both guided and encumbered by fantasies and dreams left over from the unfinished business of childhood. The unconscious needs that may never have been fulfilled, the expectations raised wittingly or unwittingly by father still hover in memory like the faint but persistent beating of birds' wings in a night forest. And of these early and hypnotic fantasies, none is more potent or more crippling than the myth of Mr. Right—and his inevitable counterpart, Mr. Wrong.

Typically Mr. Right is the all-knowing, all-powerful, and benevolent Prince Charming who will magically make everything about our lives all right. He will enable us to be everything we want to be but cannot be on our own. This Mr. Right will be perfectly loving, understanding, and supportive, a mate who answers our every need—even before it is voiced. If Mr. Right is the empowerer, Mr. Wrong is his antithesis—the underminer and colossal disappointer. Mr. Wrong can be as powerfully seductive as Mr. Right, but his magic sabotages rather than assists. Mr. Right appeals to a woman's best sense of herself, to her image of greatest potential; Mr. Wrong's attraction is to her worst fears, her most frightening self-doubts and hatreds. Mr. Wrong is the seducer, the punisher, the withholder. He is the one who will always promise more than he can deliver. He can be counted on to treat a woman badly—and is perversely chosen, again and again, for this very reason.

The fantasies of Mr. Right and Mr. Wrong can be seen in one sense as embodiments of the tenacious wish to stay attached to Daddy. Mr. Right seems to personify—and exaggerate—father's most idealized nature, the side of him that, the child believes, will forever protect her, enrich her, enable her to do everything she cannot do on her own. Mr. Wrong, on the other hand, often uncannily resembles the part of father that seems harsh or punishing or inaccessible. So Mr. Right often stands in for the image of the good father and Mr. Wrong for the image of the bad father. Both remain fundamentally reflections of the daughter's powerlessness. They are limiting dreams of a little girl rather than a woman's mature desire for an equal and caring partner to share a life of mutual support and love.

The search for a lover and for a life mate is necessarily exploratory and experimental. This search may be fueled by the deepest connections to the past, to the unresolved wishes still attached to father. It may also carry the most intoxicating possibilities for the future, seductive hints of who we will become. In her searing essay "First Love," writer and poet Andrea Dworkin explores what she calls the "drive to become"—that profound wish for self-definition and self-revelation—which both drew her toward her first lover and then forced her to leave him. At twenty-nine, with the maturity of ten intervening years, she writes an imaginary letter to the Greek lover she met on Crete at nineteen:

I want to describe in some way the *drive to become* that impelled me to go to you and to go from you, that has driven me from person to person, place to place, bed to bed, street to street, and which somehow coheres, finds cogency when I say, I want to write, or I want to be a writer, or I am a writer. I want to tell you that this *drive to become* is why I left you and why I never returned as I had promised.[1]

As she explores her passion for this man who turned out to be both hero and betrayer, she also reveals the flickering and far-reaching shadows of the myth of Mr. Right and Mr. Wrong. First, she draws a portrait of a lover who is all-loving and enabling. Later, when feeling has soured and adoration turned to fury, she depicts a lover who seems evil and malice incarnate. The way these two images are inextricably intertwined is also essential to the mythology. For the threat of the evil lover forever lurks in the captivating embrace of the good lover. And the promise of the good lover also peeks like a lure from the stranglehold of the punishing lover. And part of the seduction is her fantasy that she will be able to transform Mr. Wrong into Mr. Right. Her secret hope is that the sheer force of her will or charm or simply perseverance will soothe the angry brow of her lover, undo his inaccessibility, secure his heart forever. This time she imagines she will triumph where she failed in childhood; she will manage to make Daddy love her forever.

As she recounts in her essay, Andrea Dworkin journeyed to Crete at nineteen to find love—and to find herself. After months of wine and talk and lover after lover, she finally came upon the man whose magnetism separated him from the others. Her description of their first meeting is unabashedly apocalyptic:

> I had been on Crete maybe three months when I first saw you.
> Glorious, golden moment. I was drinking vermouth at an outdoor
> café. The day was dark and drizzly. You stepped out of a doorway,
> looked around, stepped back in out of sight. You were so beauti-
> ful, so incredibly beautiful, radiating light, yr eyes so huge and
> deep and dark. I don't remember how we began to talk or when
> we first made love, but it did really happen that way, I saw you
> and the earth stood still, everything in me reached out to you.[2]

The dark stranger, appearing in a burst of light, he was a kind
of messianic figure who would save her from herself—indeed,
give her to herself:

> I was happy. I loved you. I was consumed by my love for you. It
> was as if I breathed you instead of the air. Sometimes I felt a peace
> so great that I thought it would lift me off the earth. I felt in you
> and through you and because of you. Later, when you were so
> much a part of me that I didn't know where you ended and I
> began, I would still sometimes marvel at yr physical beauty.
> Sometimes I would think that my life would be complete if I
> would always be able to look at you.[3]

For almost a year the love affair continued to burn with this
intensity. When their lovemaking decreased from all day and
all night to only once a day and once each night, she worried
to a friend that he no longer loved her. But the merger with
him that she believed she craved also entailed a shocking loss
of self. Sharing not language nor customs nor values, they had
no common reference when passion went awry. And when
they began to fight, their fights became as vicious as their
lovemaking had been divine. The lover whose benevolence
seemed to breathe life into her threatened to crush her with
his malevolence. The angel of her liberation turned on her
and became her tyrant. Mr. Right was hideously unmasked as
Mr. Wrong:

> I don't know exactly when or why yr anger took explicit sexual
> forms. You began fucking me in the ass, brutally, brutally. I began
> to have rectal bleeding. I told you, I implored you. You ignored

my screams of pain, my whispers begging you to stop. You said, A woman who loves a man stands the pain. I was a woman who loved a man; I submitted, screamed, cried out, submitted. To refuse was, I thought, to lose you, and any pain was smaller than that pain, or even the contemplation of that pain. I wondered even then, how can he take such pleasure when I am in such pain. My pain increased, and so did yr pleasure.[4]

First out of awe, then devotion, finally out of mindless fear, she gave her power to him, and he exploited that power. By the end, he was denigrating her in the vilest way. Their love-making had become rape.

But finally, when the dream of her lover as savior died completely, the glimmer of a new dream began to take its place. From the ashes of her own powerlessness, disappointment, and rage, a sense of her own destiny began to emerge. Gradually she generated the energy to leave her lover and take up her own quest. This decision was not made without wrenching pain, but once made, it was irrevocable. And only when the dream of Mr. Right—and the nightmare of Mr. Wrong—were put to rest could the vision of the self as an adult and as an artist begin:

The decision to leave was not rational. It was made, in fact, long before the worst happened. It was a feeling, an impulse, that inhabited my body like a fever. Once I felt it I knew that I would leave no matter what. I describe it to you now as the *desire to become* that lives in the part of me that did not breathe in you, that is a writer, and that even my identity as a woman could not entirely silence. It is that part of me that enraged you even as it enthralled you, the part that could not be subsumed by seduction or anal assault or any sort of domination. It is that part that could not even be conquered, or quieted, by tenderness. It is the part of me that was, even then, most alive, and that no man, not even you who were for me the air that I breathed, could ever take from me. . . . I had a drive to become, to live, to imagine, to create, and it could not be contained in what took place between us.[5]

More intoxicating than the charms of Mr. Right, more alluring than the promises of Mr. Wrong, was this "drive to become," this life-embracing urge toward self-assertion and self-expression that Andrea Dworkin discovered. For her it became the drive to become an artist, a writer. For others it may be, more basically, the wish for autonomy, the need for an independent and separate self. And a major step toward this separate self may be relinquishing the adoration of a Mr. Right or submission to a Mr. Wrong. Only after this autonomy is achieved can a new kind of relationship—that is, the meeting of equals—be possible.

Often the insidious intertwining of the dreams of Mr. Right and Mr. Wrong makes their unraveling and eventual abandonment all the more complicated. In *Their Eyes Were Watching God* Zora Neale Hurston pinpoints the moment when her heroine—young, black, unschooled and unsophisticated—realizes that the husband she chose, dreaming him Mr. Right, has turned out to be another man entirely. It is an agonizing moment when all her beliefs are thrown into disarray. But it is also to become an epiphany leading to her liberation:

She wasn't petal-open anymore with him. She was twenty-four and seven years married when she knew. She found that out one day when he slapped her face in the kitchen. . . . When the bread didn't rise, and the fish wasn't quite done at the bone, and the rice was scorched, he slapped Janie until she had a ringing sound in her ears and told her about her brains before he stalked on back to the store.

Janie stood where he left her for unmeasured time and thought. She stood there until something fell off the shelf inside her. Then she went inside there to see what it was. It was her image of Jody tumbled down and shattered. But looking at it she saw that it never was the flesh and blood figure of her dreams. Just something she had grabbed up to drape her dreams over. In a way she turned her back upon the image where it lay and looked further. She had no more blossomy openings dusting pollen over her man, neither any glistening young fruit where the petals used to be. She found that she had a host of thoughts she had never expressed to him, and numerous emotions she had never let Jody know about. Things packed up and put away in parts of her heart where he could never find them. She was saving up feelings for some man she had never seen. She had an inside and an outside now and suddenly she knew how not to mix them.[6]

When the image of her husband as Mr. Right falls "off the shelf inside of her," her image of herself is also radically reshuffled. Life's possibilities become all at once more dangerous and more complicated—but also more promising of fulfillment. Holding on to the false image of her husband's power keeps her a powerless child; letting go of that image opens her up to the challenges of adulthood.

The fantasies of Mr. Wrong and Mr. Right have their roots in the fantasies of childhood and the child's distorted images of father. One day he is the white knight who will magically lead her to the kingdom of eternal happiness. The next day he is the dark betrayer who will punish her wrongdoings and make her eternally miserable. Clinging to these fantasies, being driven by their promises of hope, then disappointment again and again keeps a woman perpetually attached to her childhood. But sometimes the frustration of encounter after heartbreaking encounter with a Mr. Right who turns out to be Mr. Wrong will produce enough self-awareness for change. And this psychic redefinition may become a most powerful catalyst toward adulthood.

Many psychologists feel that one explanation for the seductive pull of the Mr. Wrong fantasy, despite all evidence toward its inevitable failure, lies in what Freud called "the repetition compulsion." Repeating relationship after relationship with an unobtainable, punishing, or disappointing man replays the relationship with the first unobtainable man—that is, father. This time, the woman believes, she will master what eluded her in childhood. This time, she hopes against hope, she will obtain the unobtainable, appease the punisher, and undo the disappointment, still smarting beneath layers and years of camouflage. But just as she failed in childhood, this time she is destined to fail again. Her methods are still the antiquated ploys of childhood, her candidates uncannily familiar, and her needs have become all the more boundless with the frustrations of time. Writer Anne Roiphe describes the origins and impact of this self-sabotaging mechanism:

> All children take their father's rejection as an accurate judgment on themselves. Children can't see a father's indifference as a result of alcoholism or of daddy's unfortunate dislike of women or as a logical outcome of his relationship with mommy or as comment on his immaturity. Many rejected girl children grow into women who must woo man after man to undo the first wound and fill the emptiness that has now become infinite.[7]

Besides the repetition compulsion there can also be a masochistic motivation in a woman's repeated encounters with Mr. Wrong. Some psychologists trace this motivation to the child's first, distorted inkling of what happens during sex between mother and father. Psychologist John Munder Ross explains, "The little girl's early perception of the primal scene is sadomasochistic, whether or not she actually witnesses it. She imagines father's huge penis tearing her apart and worries about how he would get that big thing inside of her. Her attraction to a Svengali or Mr. Wrong is a masochistic one that repeats her earliest perception of what went on between mother and father." Ross stresses that these early misapprehensions are reversible—but sometimes only with considerable struggle. "The repetitive attraction to a Mr. Wrong can be unraveled in therapy, but it can take a long time and can sometimes be murderous. Often the guilt over consummating a relationship with a man and having a baby is too threatening, so the woman stays attached to a Mr. Wrong who will never give her a baby."

Entanglements with Mr. Wrong have their origins in childhood misconceptions and often serve to keep a woman mired in this early era rather than freeing her to experience adulthood, mutual love—and eventually to raise children of her own. But infatuations with Mr. Wrong can also, paradoxically, nurture rather than inhibit the development of an adult and independent self. Experimenting with a series of Mr. Wrongs can be a way to experience unacknowledged or hidden aspects of ourselves we would be unable to express otherwise. Jungian psychotherapist Katherine Whiteside Taylor connects this experimentation with Jung's notion of "the shadow" and explains, "Perhaps our own dark side hasn't been brought to light, so we project it onto others. That is how we find our way, over and over, to the dark, devil lover. And then we develop a very strong attachment to those we project onto."

In her poem "The Man Under the Bed" Erica Jong conjures up this demon lover who is part shadow, part mirror, part other, part self. His image begins with the terrors of childhood, and his shape is illuminated by the encounters of adulthood:

The man under the bed
The man who has been there for years waiting . . .
The man whose breathing I hear when I pick up the phone
The man in the mirror whose breath blackens silver
The boneman in closets who rattles the mothballs
The man at the end of the end of the line . . .

I met him tonight I always meet him
He stands in the amber air of a bar . . .
For years he has waited to drag me down
& now he tells me
he has only waited to take me home
We waltz through the street like death & the maiden
We float through the wall of the wall of my room

If he's my dream he will fold back into my body
His breath writes letters of mist on the glass of my cheeks

I wrap myself around him like the darkness
I breathe into his mouth
& make him real[8]

"The Man Under the Bed" begins as a phantom of our imaginations, created from our deepest fears about ourselves. Then he becomes manifest as we project his demon energies, his menacing magic onto a parade of lovers with whom we entangle as we move out into the world. But as we waltz and tango with these Mr. Wrongs, we are also giving ourselves the chance to explore and exhibit, then integrate or reject parts of ourselves that otherwise would remain taboo. Not only does this experimentation allow us to define more carefully what we would like in a lover but more important, it also allows us to define more deeply who we ourselves are.

Of the many types of Mr. Wrong who may entrap a woman but ultimately enhance her understanding of herself, one of the most magnetically seductive is the Charismatic Lover. The Charismatic Lover comes in many guises and disguises. He may be a wild and crazy artist or sensitive and searching intellectual whose charisma is his genius—or at least his convincing obsession with his own talent. Or he may be a free-wheeling and free-dealing cowboy or adventurer, whose shoes may be under our bed one morning and on the road the next. His charisma is the lure of freedom and the wide world, though it may remain a lasso out of reach. Then, too, the Charismatic Lover may also be the public personage, inflated with his own prestige, whose charisma is the heady promise of power.

The woman who falls for the Charismatic Lover has grave doubts about her weight in the world on her own. Inadequate and incomplete alone, she hopes his charisma, like a magic elixir, will nourish and enrich her till she is whole. Perhaps, she imagines, his wild genius will ignite her own—or at least disguise her own intellectual doubts. Or maybe his wander-lust will kindle her own yen to explore the world, which has for too long been stifled by fears and inhibitions. Or she dreams that his power and prestige will be contagious and vaunt her station in the world without any hard effort of her own. Secretly she would like to be this man and have his coups for her own. But failing that, she will attach herself to him and do everything in her power to hold on for dear life.

The charm of the Charismatic Lover who seems to be Mr. Right inevitably turns out to be the quality that makes him Mr. Wrong. His allure is his genius, his freedom, or his power. But obsessed with his own genius, rabid about his own freedom, or heady with his own power, he turns out to be far too preoccupied with himself to have the time or inclination to sustain a reciprocal relationship. His ego may appear at first to be ample enough to shelter two. But it turns out to be too shaky even to provide for one.

Falling in love with a Charismatic Lover invariably begins with intoxicating dreams of glory. How marvelous I will look with him—even in his shadow—we imagine, how powerful and impressive. But when these dreams do not pan out, shattering disappointment is inevitable. Still, from this dev-astation can also emerge untapped momentum toward self-discovery and self-realization. For the Charismatic Lover, in spite of himself, gives us the opportunity to acknowledge what we thought we wanted for ourselves, be it accomplish-ment, adventure, or prestige. Coming to grips with the disappointing fact that no man will hand these goodies to us on a silver platter, we must then consider using our re-sources to secure them for ourselves. And sometimes a closer look at our lover's cachet reveals the illusion of what we had once yearned for. Leaving him, we will proceed in an entirely different course.

Maria Gomez is the twenty-eight-year-old daughter of a re-served and withdrawn immigrant whose ambition for her was to join the civil service, as he himself had done. But she had a streak of wildness and a vision of creativity that, in her twenties, she was hot to explore. No sooner at college and away from her father's repressive clutches than she attached herself to a Charismatic Lover who, she fervently hoped, would give her permission to pursue her dream. "The first man I fell in love with in college looked like my father—tall and thin with thick black hair—but he was nothing like him. He was the big director on campus, and I was the aspiring actress. He was a crazy, sensitive artist who wasn't in love with me, though I was crazy about him. He was screwing around a lot, but I wouldn't sleep with him because I felt he should love me. Still, I had the strong impression that he respected me more than the other women."

Just as her "big director" flaunted the promise of theatrical glory but withheld it along with his love, she retaliated by holding on to the only coinage she felt she had—her virginity. But after another collapsed romance with an actor "who was not into a sexual thing," she felt her "sexual drive was coming out of [her] ears," and soon gave up her virginity to the first taker. With that mission accomplished, she returned to the director—still her great love—and literally offered herself to him. For two weeks they had a passionate affair, and she was giddy with her love for him—and for the artistic vision he could offer. But then, without warning, he stopped the relationship cold. "He became my father figure and my oppressor. It was easier to rebel against an oppressor than to take my life into my own hands."

For six years, on and off, she remained in an ego-crushing, push-and-pull relationship with this director, always hoping that she would win his love, and his sense of direction with it. For years depression muffled her. Finally she joined a therapy group and began to release her own energies for self-direction, which for so long she had subsumed in her lover's. After long, hard thought she realized that her dream of theatrical glory was bringing her as little satisfaction as was her lover.

She began to explore the possibilities of a career in social service. Then, too, she allowed a new lover into her life: "short, blond, totally unlike my father." And he had a newly magnetic quality that both her father and her director lacked; he listened to her. "He didn't have to be the center of attention. He thought I was wonderful, intellectually and sexually. I flowered under that. I had believed until then that no man could love me, but after him I never believed that again, even in my darker moments."

For *Carol Taylor,* a hard-driving, go-getting government professor, the specter of the Charismatic Lover was inhibiting in a different way, but purging that specter provided a similar awakening. At thirty-five Carol had already worked her way through a frustrating sequence of Charismatic Mr. Wrongs— "brilliant but neurotic." Finally she settled in with a man who was kind and dependable—"but too boring to marry." One night they were invited to a dinner party given by one of the leading lights of the government department. The other guests were dazzling luminaries, heavyweights in science and politics. Before dinner the guests listened to a televised presidential address and tossed out comments while he spoke. To Carol's surprise, the luminaries' comments were less than luminous. "It turned out that unless they had to be 'on,' they were not that brilliant. My friend's observations were much more interesting. He wasn't at all boring. He turned out to be genuinely interested in the world outside, rather than in his own head." At that dinner party some crucial and constricting romantic images were reshuffled and reshelved. The clay figure of the Charismatic Lover tumbled from its pedestal and shattered for good. And in its place she allowed herself to respond to the idea of marriage to a thoughtful, loving man who truly cared for her, who could both listen and converse.

Even more insidious and more inexplicable in his attractions than the Charismatic Lover is the Mr. Wrong I will call the SuperMacho. The SuperMacho offers a distorted version of masculinity that seems to appeal to the woman whose confidence in her femininity is shaky. For genuine strength and virility the SuperMacho substitutes arrogance and abuse. His is the unerring instinct to go for the exposed nerve, the center of vulnerability. The woman who responds to him confuses submissiveness with femininity. And her dependence on a SuperMacho keeps her perpetually the little girl waiting for Daddy's approval and his permission to grow up. The Super-Macho, of course, will never grant this permission. The woman who falls for him finally has no choice but to leave him —if she wants to stand on her own feet. "Never offer your heart/to someone who eats hearts," is the cool advice of the poet Alice Walker about the snare of the SuperMacho lover. "Refrain from kissing/lest he in revenge/dampen the spark/ in your soul."[9]

The SuperMacho is the lover who, living under his own storm cloud, emerges only to bellow and shake his fists. His romantic overtures are to berate, belittle, and bedevil. And he thrives only as long as he is tolerated. When he meets with resistance—in the form of strength of character—he beats a hasty retreat. The SuperMacho is all swagger and braggadocio. Genuine strength unmasks the cowardice that his cockiness tries to conceal.

The SuperMacho preys on the woman who doubts her worth. The woman who is drawn to him, drawn against her better instincts, like a collie to a piece of poisoned meat, is often the one who feels perpetually guilty over some nameless wrong. Like the crippled and troubled heroine of *Looking for Mr. Goodbar,* she feels, in the most unfathomable part of her psyche, that she deserves and needs to be punished. The SuperMacho is all too willing to comply. At first she may find his menacing advances curiously attractive. But sooner or later they become repellent. And this is the moment she is ready to stop visiting punishment on herself. She has come to realize she deserves something better.

The relationship with the SuperMacho lover may begin with a blaze of rehabilitative zeal. I will change him, we boast to ourselves; I will tame him and turn his destructive energies around. But when transformation occurs, the woman is far likelier to change than is her lover. The dark embrace of the SuperMacho lover allows her the chance to explore her own shadowside, to experience her own most devilish impulses. Often this powerful part of her has been buried beneath the childish veneer of having to remain "the good girl" at all costs. Liberating and coming to terms with this submerged self allows her a more three-dimensional approach to adulthood and to the possibility of finding a partner who will know and love her for everything she is.

Thirty-three years old and a college administrator, *Naomi Stein* has always seen herself as the most sexual person in a family that seemed to value—and understand—the mind over the body, accomplishments over the longings of the heart. Her father, a classic Patriarch, a well-respected scholar and presidential adviser, "was not a very warm man who did not give lots of strokes and hugs. But when he did," she adds, "they were nice." Her mother was also intellectual and remote, "very cold, very restrained, and kind of proper, uncomfortable with her body and giving affection to her kids." From an early age Naomi sought outside the family the affection she craved that was not available inside the family. From the fifth grade on, her diary sizzled with her amorous fantasies: "I love him. I have to have him. He is my best boy."

That early adolescent craving for attention, that fervent wish for affection raised so ardently in childhood but never satisfied made Naomi Stein ripe prey for a SuperMacho lover. Her longings—sexual and romantic both—had become complicated over the years by a sticky sense of guilt about fulfilling them. Most influential was the fateful father-daughter talk the night before she left for college. "The first thing I want you to know," advised her father, while her mother eavesdropped on the stairs, "is that I know you can do well at school. The second thing I want you to know is that we don't want you to hang around with beatniks. And the third thing I want you to know is, don't get knocked up. But if you do get knocked up, you call your daddy."

"Testing every limit I could test," she says, by the end of her sophomore year she was on academic probation for poor grades, had befriended several of the dreaded beatniks and—more to the point here—found herself pregnant by her "romantic, totally irresponsible boyfriend who had sent [her] red roses after their second date." Ashamed and confused, she felt driven to call Daddy. "He was speechless. He had to think. He said he would get back to me." These were the sixties, when abortion was still a back-room job. When he got back to her, he had arranged an abortion in Mexico. He met her in Tucson and drove her to the strange, forbidding clinic. When she woke up from the anaesthetic, he was sitting near her, reading his scholarly journals. "He was incredible," she remembers, her awe of him still confused with her own guilt. "From that point on and for several years, I was jumping over backward to do right in this man's eyes. I was so ashamed of myself. I wanted to pay him back so badly." "Just forget about it" was his response. "Go back to school and forget about it." "That," his daughter knows now, "is his way of dealing with emotional stuff."

But her father was unable to take his own advice. Two months later she was visiting home and had a brief conversation with her mother about birth control. An hour or so later her father got wind of their discussion. "He came storming into my room, literally slamming the door open with his hand. It was the most unbelievable thing I've ever seen. He said, 'I've just heard what your mother and you have been talking about and I can tell you this, no daughter of mine is going to go sleeping around. And if you get pregnant again, don't you come to me. That's all I can tell you.' " Though knocked for a loop by his outburst, she still idolized him—and denigrated herself—enough to call his tantrum justified. "That was the first time he allowed any kind of feelings about the abortion to come out—especially his anger, which I had earned, rightfully. He was Mr. Magnanimous. He had taken me on that trip. He had paid for it. He hadn't charged a thing for it."

The only price "Mr. Magnanimous" exacted turned out to be a psychological one, and the cost was high. In a family of intellectuals and academics, Naomi had always worried that her own intense sexuality and longings for love were somehow inappropriate, an affront to civilized company, like a flasher disrupting a distinguished scholarly lecture. Her unwanted pregnancy, the harrowing abortion, and her father's livid recriminations only confirmed her worst fears about herself and the perils of her own sexuality. For months after her confrontation with her father, she retreated from sex altogether. "After the abortion," she remembers, "I was scared of just letting anyone inside of me." When she recovered and sought the company of men again, she stumbled—not surprisingly—right into the unsafe arms of a SuperMacho lover.

"I started going with a guy named Gino who could not have been more opposite from my father and my upbringing. This guy was from a Catholic, Sicilian family. I still have a strong suspicion that they may have been Mafioso. He was a football-player type, a burly, mean-looking guy. He had a moustache that he would wax and it would come down to his chin. He was a huge guy, and he always wore a leather jacket."

Early in the relationship Naomi's parents met this shady character and were predictably horrified. But some instinct, deeper even than the unbridled passion she felt for Gino, allowed her to assure them that this was *not* the man she was going to marry. "I just felt this need to have this kind of relationship," she offers now. "He was so different, so attractive to me. But I knew that this was not the man I was going to end up with for the rest of my life."

What she found in Gino was a man whose perversities meshed perfectly with her own scariest sexual fears and fantasies. And nowhere was this more apparent than in bed. "He was abusive sexually in subversive ways. He made me feel really, really bad about myself as a woman. He would say in front of people to scare me that one day he was going to surprise me when I came home from work to find him and his friends at the house, naked, having a Mazola oil party. He would threaten me with group sex, saying, 'That would show your true womanness.' Or he'd say, 'Wouldn't it be great to get into bed with me and another woman?' and I'd have the feeling that I would lose him if I didn't—although I never did. I was really scared that one day I would come home and there would be another woman there."

She winces at her own narrative, at the kind of person she could have loved, at the kind of person she must have been to be with him. But given her sexual history, her choice of this SuperMacho lover served several purposes. Guilty and confused about her early sexual stirrings, and guiltier and even more ashamed when sexual romance led to pregnancy and then her father's harsh disapproval, she felt she needed to be punished. Gino provided this punishment in his sexual taunting and abuse. And he punished her all in the name of making her more "womanly"—that distant state she both feared and desired. Meanwhile he became the incarnation of her own wildest sexuality. All her most bizarre and self-destructive fantasies were expressed through him, projected onto him in their most extreme form, so that she could experience them and eventually move beyond them. Finally, choosing someone so awesomely inappropriate that even in her most passionate moments she knew she would not marry him allowed her to stay attached to Daddy, to remain that little girl who still needed permission to become a sexual woman.

Naomi spent two miserable years with Gino, and finally, out of that whirlwind of self-destructiveness, a new attitude, more self-confident and self-loving, began to emerge. "He had been my fantasy of what a motorcycle person would be like in bed. He was harsh on me. It took me a long time to realize that I didn't need to be treated harshly. I needed to be treated gently.

"Finally I had worked through the fantasy so well, I was so clear about why I was going with him, that suddenly one day I said, I don't want this anymore. I guess I'm like my father in that way. When he decides he wants something, he goes out and gets it. I decided I didn't want this anymore, and I came back from work one night and I said, 'Time for you to go. We have to stop this. I don't want it anymore.' And so he moved out."

Months later she ran into Gino unexpectedly at a party. By then she was seeing another man, a gentle and thoughtful person who cherished her—mind, soul, and body—for the woman she had become. He was the man she would marry. Stumbling on Gino at that party meant having to confront a discarded part of herself, and that confrontation hurt, but also reminded her of how much she had grown. "Gino was sitting in a chair in a corner of the living room, big and burly as ever. I took one look at him and honestly got sick to my stomach thinking, How could I have done this to myself? On the other hand, I know that if I hadn't had that relationship, I don't think I could have had the healthy one that my husband and I have now."

A third and prevalent Mr. Wrong is the perpetually enticing but perpetually Unavailable Lover. Like the Charismatic Lover, the Unavailable man seduces with a passionate fanfare of promise and potential. But once the conquest is made, there is rarely any follow-through, any staying power. The Unavailable man keeps himself at a constant but provocative distance, close enough to set the bait but far enough away never to be caught. He may be a married man, bearing assurances of his flagging marriage like a bouquet of roses that blush crimson for an evening but brown around the edges the morning after. Or he may be a homosexual who makes delightful company as an escort to any locale but the bedroom. Or there may be no evident excuse for his emotional unavailability; he may simply be driven away by his own internal conflicts. This is the hot-and-cold lover who tightly controls his own emotional thermostat. When the romance gets too hot, he turns cold and withdraws.

The woman who is attracted to the Unavailable Lover has fears and fantasies about love that his behavior complements. She may still be locked in a struggle to win the battle over the first and foremost Unavailable man, who is, of course, her father. Repeating this battle as an adult may give the illusion of mastery, but that illusion is usually transitory. One forty-year-old woman I interviewed had picked lover after Unavailable Lover in an effort to repair the heartbreak of her father's absence after her parents' divorce. "I didn't go looking for men like my father," she explained, "but I ended up with them. I picked attractive men who were not emotionally available and then worked hard to get them to like me. If I win that one, I will have won the earlier battle." The first time we spoke, she had recently extracted a promise of commitment from a formerly noncommittal lover, and she was gleeful. "I'm winning!" she beamed, clapping her hands. But when I checked back several months later, her erstwhile lover had flown the coop, and her glee had become despondency.

Another impetus toward the Unavailable Lover may be a women's own complex fears of intimacy, which she equates with engulfment. If she has seen her mother give up too much of her own identity and potential to keep her marriage afloat, the daughter may feel that marriage for her, too, will become entrapment. So for her, a married lover represents the thrill of romance without the worrisome bonds of commitment. Then, too, if her own womanliness and sexuality still feel threatening, she may prefer a nonsexual relationship that allows her to remain psychologically in the safer harbor of girlhood, still the pleasing companion at her father's knee. So for her, a homosexual lover offers the appeal of companionship without the demands of sexual love.

She may also doubt her own weight and worth in the world, her own substantiveness. Still privately defining herself as the little girl who must share her great love with mother, she does not yet feel powerful enough to have a man all to herself. In her bitter and bittersweet poem "For My Lover, Returning to His Wife," Anne Sexton rages against her Unavailable Lover but ends acknowledging her own sad complicity in the affair. With all her desperate attraction to her married lover, she still cannot rid herself of the demeaning contrast between his wife's imposing presence and her own insignificance:

> She is so naked and singular.
> She is the sum of yourself and your dream.
> Climb her like a monument, step after step.
> She is solid.
>
> As for me, I am a watercolor.
> I wash off.[10]

Behind every woman's doomed relationship with the Unavailable Lover lurk the footprints of earlier years, and particularly of her relationship with her father. *Diana Stewart* had been raised by her Pal father to be as chaste as the goddess of the moon for whom she was named. He was a driven research scientist who spent most of his life in the company of men. He scorned most women as oversexed and intellectually insubstantial except for the rare characters he defined as "special." In order to be included in the pantheon of the "special" ones, Diana was encouraged by her father to refine her intellect and sublimate her sexuality. "To this day," she observes at thirty-two, I have always kept up appearances so that he wouldn't know I was sexually active."

Diana Stewart's first serious love turned out to be a classically Unavailable Lover whose seduction was to dazzle with the intellect and bury the passions, just as she was raised to believe was appropriate. She met Peter after college and after a frustrating spate of two-week affairs. He was a medical researcher, easily as hard-driving as her father, a "charming and socially able" young man who identified with Christopher Newman in Henry James's *The American*. "He was the first person I had a long-term relationship with. The others would last only for a week or two, until they realized how 'uptight and cold' I was. But Peter liked the sexually repressed person I was. We could talk endlessly about music and art. The first two years, it was only a date once every two or three weeks. He would ask me to sleep with him, but was secretly relieved when I said no. Finally, at twenty-three, we both began to have some sexual impulses and we did sleep together."

They lived together secretly for a year and a half. Peter enrolled in a double doctorate program in science and business, working till dawn every night and most weekends. To keep herself busy, Diana, too, began graduate work in sociology and soon became engrossed in it. As the months wore on, instead of deepening, their intimacy faltered. Peter especially started pulling back, and finally suggested they separate. Not too reluctantly, Diana moved across the country to follow her favorite professor and continue her studies. For three years she heard nothing from Peter, not a Christmas card or a call on her birthday.

Suddenly one spring vacation he appeared out of the blue, amorous and attentive. They spent an idyllic month together, talking around the clock with the feverish intensity of their college days. "He wanted very much to get married," Diana remembers, "and he talked me into it." They got married secretly with neither parents nor friends in attendance and kept the marriage hush-hush. Then they retreated to their opposite sides of the country, agreeing that the plan was practical for the time being, but only temporary.

Married, Diana resumed her life exactly as she had before. She threw herself into her studies, got restless, drifted into a desultory affair with an old lover. Letters and calls from Peter became more and more sporadic. She was not entirely surprised, or even wrenchingly disappointed, when a month or two after they married he wrote to suggest a divorce, for he had found someone else. But she could not remain unruffled, when she read at the end of the letter that his someone else was another man.

Looking back on that phantom marriage now, a decade later, she realizes, "Peter actually had a similar history to my father. He was a man who didn't really like women, except the 'special' woman. I think he wanted me for a cover, something to put on his résumé." But in a less obvious way Peter also served as a cover for Diana. Offering her a protracted and comparatively chaste courtship and then a long-distance and nonsexual marriage, he allowed her to retain the separation between her intellect and her sexuality that her father had raised her to believe in. And as long as she forced her mind and her body to live at cross purposes rather than integrated and whole, she continued to impede herself from growing up and growing away from her father's stifling controls.

The belief in a Mr. Right who will magically deliver us from our own humdrum fate into a painless and perfect existence is by its very definition limiting and inhibiting. If we turn over our hopes and wishes to this larger-than-life creation, we necessarily circumscribe our own possibilities, narrow our own options, and, most crippling, undermine our own power to make things happen for ourselves. But on the road to meeting Mr. Right, as we invariably encounter a parade of swashbuckling, denigrating, or simply unavailable Mr. Wrongs, we may eventually be pushed—by an onslaught of romatic hard knocks—to take our destinies back into our own hands. So the fantasy of finding a Mr. Right, inhibiting at its origins, may paradoxically become empowering, as it leads us first through the inevitable series of Mr. Wrongs—and finally back to ourselves.

High in an apartment in the fabled Dakota, presiding over a view of Manhattan that sweeps from Central Park to the city's skyline, Jamie Bernstein sits at her father's baby grand piano, playing her own music, singing her own tunes. This apartment was once the studio of her father, the conductor and impresario Leonard Bernstein. Now he lives upstairs and the studio has become a pied-à-terre for his daughters when they are in town. The decor is a mix of the generations. There are plushy elegant couches as well as duffels and college clutter. There is a handmade collage of the Beatles, a totem of Jamie's childhood. (She idolized John Lennon and was at this very piano the day she heard from the street the shot that killed him. "It was the worst thing that could have happened," she says, "the way my parents must have felt when JFK was assassinated.") Next to the Beatles is an imposing Saul Steinberg print that proclaims in cartoonlike letters, "I have. I am. I do," a credo that could be her father's as well as her father's wish for her.

Jamie is dressed for our interview, casually but self-consciously chic. She wears an oversize black sweater with a string of pearls, a long plaid skirt, and cowboy boots. Her thick, wavy hair is butterscotch-colored and restrained in a ponytail, with a shock uncontrollable in front, reminiscent of her father's at the podium. She looks like a very well bred young woman who now wants to come into her own as an artist. Conventionality is gradually being phased out by originality.

Clustered on the piano as if watching her fingers on the keys are photographs of the family, who still in many ways keep a keen eye on her, although she is thirty now and works as a musician in California. There is a picture of her father wearing a pink shirt, looking grand and mystical, salt-and-pepper hair waving with a life of its own. "My father was always larger than life," she confides as she shows me the photographs one wintery afternoon. "He was always a star. He was always really handsome and my mother was gorgeous. To this day it's hard to look at my family and figure out what is real about it, because everything has been in sort of mythic proportions. And so my problems about my family have mythic qualities, too. Everything seems a little larger than life." There is also a picture of her mother, Chilean-born Felicia Montealegre, who died painfully several years ago of lung cancer, but for the photograph sat glamorous and willowy in evening clothes, a fashion arbiter, all elegance. "My mother was a master of the visual," Jamie observes, "and what she said, went. As a result I always felt like a bumbler in her presence. I never felt I knew how to dress. I couldn't do anything that was visual. I didn't feel I could draw. I assumed that I had no sense of style. To this day I have dreams in which I have to get dressed to go to a concert of my father's, and I'm going through my closet trying to find something to wear, and nothing seems right, and finally I go out and my mother says, 'You're not going out in those shoes. You can't wear that shirt with those pants.' But," Jamie adds poignantly, "she'd like me so much better now. It's such a shame she's not around to see the person I turned into."

Then, too, there are pictures of her younger brother and sister, Alexander and Nina. They are posed both as carefree children (Nina in a sweatshirt boasting "I am a little tax exemption") and as young adults, struggling, like Jamie, to leave their mark as performers in a world where their father looms so large. Alexander is twenty-seven, feeling the pressures of being a famous father's only son. Grown restless as a production assistant for documentaries never produced, he is now a hopeful actor in New York. Nina is twenty, still growing into her sophisticated image, a student and aspiring actress at Harvard, which is Jamie's alma mater as well. About her relationship with her siblings, Jamie is warm and enthusiastic: "My brother and I grew up being best friends, because my sister came along later on. My relationship with her was more golden. We didn't spar. But I know my brother like I know my own hand." About the children's artistic relationship with their father, she is more equivocal: "My father being the big performer, I guess we felt we had to keep our distance from that—but ultimately we couldn't resist."

Jamie's memories of growing up are unabashedly rhapsodic, full of a dewy-eyed idolatry that would make breaking away all the more wrenching. "My earliest childhood memories are basically golden. I remember no stress. My parents never fought. They were beautiful. They were full of fun. Our friends were full of fun. There was a lot of laughter and carrying on and silliness. Summers were fabulous. There was a period when we would go to Martha's Vineyard every summer. I remember those summers as endless sailing and beaches and sun. And my father was great with us—talking to us and teaching us things. He was the eternal teacher and we were the eternal students."

Nowhere was his teaching more powerfully affecting than in the realm of music. "He was always giving little mini–Young People's Concerts about tonics and dominants and the sonata form. The Young People's Concerts were just culled from what was going on every day." Jamie watched her father perform from such an early age that "it seemed like a perfectly natural thing." Seeing anyone else conduct was unsettling, and most unnerving of all was the one occasion when she saw an orchestra play with no conductor at all. "It was the hundredth-anniversary New York Philharmonic concert. My father conducted most of it. But the final piece the orchestra played by itself without a conductor. That really freaked me out. You mean they can do it without him? Then why is he up there? You mean he doesn't have to be there? It was like the puppet moves without a puppeteer." For the little girl who believed her father was larger than life, this performance provided the first inkling that perhaps he was only human after all.

Many years later, with aching jolts of recognition, she became aware of the cracks in her mythic and untarnished family portrait. "Everything seemed very perfect, but it wasn't so perfect. I didn't find that out for a long time. In the last years of my mother's life, the marriage really suffered. They separated for a year and then just about the time they got back together, she got sick. So the last year of their marriage together was basically my father taking care of my mother. It was very painful for everybody. What once had seemed so perfect—now the fire had gone out like that. And in retrospect I realize that a lot of what seemed totally secure and blissful was actually sometimes superficial. And it has been very difficult for me to go back and sort of reedit everything."

Becoming a person in her own right, both psychologically and artistically, has involved a reexamination of the family mythology, acknowledging both its tug on her and her need to separate from it. "The family as a unit was very close, and to this day it's a problem for me," she realizes now, "because the centrifugal force in my family is tremendous. It takes all my strength to maintain my independence and sense of integrity that I am a discrete entity with my own solar system, my own gravity and all that stuff.

"My father is really the center of this whirlpool we're talking about," she continues. "His whole life is a vastly complex network of personal relationships and business relationships. He has this incredibly complicated life and schedule that is mapped out five years in advance. And there are thousands of people all over the world who care desperately about him and about whom he cares desperately. He's a very emotional guy and he gets involved with everybody's life, and as a result of this he stretches his attention to the limits and doesn't always have enough time for his kids."

Every choice Jamie has made, in both love and work, has forced her to acknowledge the "centrifugal force" of her family—especially the whirlpool that is her father—while at the same time to garner her strength to become a "discrete entity." Professionally she is making her way as a musician, always conscious of her father's name, nevertheless trying to make her own. She wishes she did not hunger for his approval but cannot deny that she does. "All I could think of when I was taping my latest songs," she says, "was 'Boy, wait till Daddy hears this one. Sure hope he likes this one.' " I try to pretend that I don't care, but I do, very much."

Romantically she is also caught in a contradiction: wanting yet not wanting a lover in her father's image, another hero, another conductor of her destiny. "Boy-crazy" since high school, she has had a succession of lovers who sparkled like Mr. Right—their looks, their talents, their seductiveness— then soured like Mr. Wrong. But after each relationship her self-definition has also sharpened, as if a new portion of herself has emerged out of shadow. And with each new relationship her relationship to her family has also altered, as she becomes more independent, more grounded, and centered beyond their vortex.

For Jamie, as for many daughters of close-knit families, falling for Mr. Wrong has helped catalyze a separation that could not have been effected single-handedly. "I think I deliberately fall in love with people who don't get along with my family," Jamie explains, "because then it's a way of driving a wedge between my family and myself. It's a manipulative thing to do, but I think I've done that in the past. I do it because I recognize that I've got to pull away somehow. I'd never find out who I am unless I create some distance. In the past I think I would use my boyfriends as a means of creating distance."

She got together with her first serious boyfriend, *Greg*, senior year in high school, and their stormy relationship continued till the end of her freshman year at Radcliffe. Now with undisguised scorn for her former self, she calls their affair "the most unbelievable, unenlightened relationship." Greg was a classic SuperMacho lover, possessive and domineering. She recalls one telling incident after a triumphant high-school production of *Guys and Dolls,* in which she had one of the leading roles. At the rollicking cast party at her house, Greg watched her give the male lead an affectionate kiss good-bye. Incensed at some imagined slur to his ego, he took her into the library, called her a whore, and started to slap her around. At this point several friends and her aunt, who was chaperoning, burst in "like a scene out of some bad play." They dragged him off, "raging and roaring like a bull." "After this incident," she remarks, "he was *persona non grata* forever."

She met Greg at a pivotal time of late adolescence, when her sense of her own identity was as slippery and shapeless as loose mercury. He fanned both her doubts about herself and her doubts about her family and pushed her to the first of several brinks of separation from their tight hold on her. "He and my father didn't get along at all," she observes now, "and it was an awful time for me, because suddenly I became angry at my father, and I started going through the normal adolescent feelings and frustrations. But I just didn't know which end was up, and I was so unhappy with this guy. I was sort of masochistic. He was mean to me and made me feel small. But that was good, because that would make him look big, and I wanted him to look big. So I had to make myself very small to make him look big. And so it went for quite a while."

The relationship with Greg allowed her to regress to an earlier time when she was the small, dependent child and Daddy the big and powerful hero. But replaying that scene as a young adult, she began to realize how inappropriate and outmoded it had become. Having allowed herself to become that small, she could then give herself permission to begin to grow up, to stand on her own feet, to carve out her own niche.

The period that followed her breakup with Greg was a time of both adventure and anxiety. "I spent the next three years sort of celebrating my freedom and getting high and partying and having a great time—sort of. I was wildly anxious. I didn't know who the hell I was and I was much too frightened really to do anything extracurricular." Writing, especially poetry, became a central focus of her attention. But when her one venture—to get on the campus humor magazine—was met with rejection, she withdrew from the competition and kept her achievements vicarious. "What I did instead was go out with guys who did what I wanted to do. I went out with the managing editor of the *Crimson,* the star forward of the soccer team, and a guy who was in a rock and roll band." Her dreams of glory were keen, but she did not yet have the courage to fly them on her own.

The year or two after she graduated, she continued to experiment in the arts, sometimes with direction and purpose, sometimes without. She worked for a children's television action group in Boston, then enrolled for a few semesters as a "special student" in writing at Columbia, then came back to Boston and worked for a public television consulting firm. The "guy who ran this outfit," as she puts it, was a kind of *What Makes Sammy Run?* character—driven, seductive, and undependable—an Unavailable Mr. Wrong. "I didn't know at the time that he was a type," she confesses, "but he was one of these really energetic fast-talking, sharp, witty, California Jewish guys. With Malamute blue eyes—very startling, very attractive. And how was I supposed to know that this was a syndrome? That he would talk a good game, and then not come up with the goods."

Like the classic Unavailable Lover, he led her on until he caught her—and then turned his back on her. "We never had an affair, but he sort of seduced me into working for him for peanuts. I would have done anything for this guy, because I thought he was so wonderful. I started setting up an office with him in New York and making all these contacts and pulling all my family strings. But eventually, about a year and a half later, I quit, because I just wasn't getting any support from him. I couldn't get him on the phone. I suddenly felt, 'Where are you? You promised me so much and it's not happening. I can't do it all myself.' The work had no reality. So I quit.''

But his very unavailability threw her back on her own resources. Perhaps for the first time, she began to plumb her own talents and take her own desires seriously. After she quit the phantom job in New York, she drew back from television, drew back from writing poetry and moved toward what she allowed herself to realize was her first and greatest love: music. She took up her guitar and began writing songs. Though painfully shy and uncertain at first, she knew in her heart she was at last on the right track.

During this most recent period, she has had a succession of musician lovers, charismatic and beguiling figures who have helped her, in one way or another, open musical doors. One was a drummer who moved into the apartment downstairs from hers and "turned out to be the first person to try and get me to play with other people." Another was a guitarist friend of his named Jamie, whom she ended up living with for two years and playing with in a local bar as a duo called, of course, Jamie and Jamie. Still another was a rock and roll musician, a young friend of her father's, who persuaded her to come out to California to make a demo tape in his studio. "I was so excited, I felt like Cinderella going to the ball. It was just what I needed," she gushes, remembering the turning point of that trip out west. "He got the musicians together. We went into the studio—a twenty-four-track studio, the real thing. We did five songs and worked our tails off. It was certainly far better than anything I'd ever done in my life. It was really professional. I was never so proud of anything I did." Though the rock and roll musician eventually rocked out on his own, reneging on a promise that the two would work together, Jamie took from their relationship a new confidence in her own promise. "I was very quietly writing new material, making a life for myself in California, and starting to find out who I was. In a funny way, maybe it was a good thing that I didn't get a record deal right away, because I had time to think about a lot of things." And in the meantime, director Franco Zeffirelli—"an old family friend"—asked her to provide a song for a scene in his movie *Endless Love.* And though the song itself "wound up on the cutting room floor," her cameo appearance in the scene remained.

During the ten years since she had graduated from high school and first left home, she had come a long way toward defining herself as a presence, strong and separate from her family—and most especially from her father. Her love affairs with one after another flamboyant Mr. Wrong played a major part in this separation. Each one allowed her to experience out, in the extreme, another dimension of her relationship with her father—his dominance, his unavailability, and, most inescapable, his charisma. And after each affair ended, she learned how to discover in herself those strengths that her father had in fact helped nourish and that now belonged to her: her resilience, her resourcefulness, and her own talent and charisma.

When she was asked to write and sing a song for her father the night Jimmy Carter honored him with several other artists at the Kennedy Center, the timing felt absolutely right. She wore a gorgeous painted-silk dress that had belonged to her mother (only later did she realize she had it on backward!). Poised before an audience that included millions of TV viewers, as well as Jimmy Carter and John Travolta, she was "dying of fear. You must understand, this was somebody who three years earlier couldn't play for her best friend." But her own heart was entirely in her song—which was called "The Big Heart"—and that gave her confidence:

> Some people say it's crazy
> To believe in people
> I used to be afraid
> They might be right
> Until I saw the way
> You shine your brightest light
> Ooh, you never know
> Who's gonna start to glow. . . .
>
> Thank you, thank you
> For the big heart
> Making room for everyone
> Is the hardest part. . . .[11]

Her new distance from her father was allowing her to forgive him—and reach out to him again.

"He was in the balcony directly across from the stage," she remembers, "far away, but very visible. I could see him weeping away as I was singing. It was great, because as I was writing the song, I was crying, thinking, 'Boy, is this gonna break him up.' And when they showed it on television, they split the screen, and you saw me singing and my father crying. Apparently it was very effective." She is enough her father's daughter to appreciate the emotion being milked for artistic effect.

Jamie's most recent swain is yet another musician whose talent she reveres and whose influence on her work she feels has been electric. "He has a record collection that is unparalleled. He knows everything about everything about music. He played me things I'd never heard before. Music from Burundi, from Mongolia and Tibet, music from the most exotic places. And stuff that made my ears go—" She breaks off to make an almost supernatural "Boinng." "It was an electrifying thing. All of a sudden I started writing music that was coming out of left field. I saw that something had clicked, something had happened. That jarred me at my foundations. So the music I've been writing since I met him has been substantially different—much more exciting to me and to everybody who hears it." She plays me a tape of a song she has recently written about their relationship. The song is called "Trance Music," and it spins into the room in a burst of wild exuberance. In the end the song is perhaps less a tribute to the spell he has cast on her than a testimony to the spell she is now working on her own creative force. Loving him has helped her liberate her own most intangible tunes, but the voice that is blasting them, belting them, beaming them is unmistakably her own.

8

THE MENTOR

I BELIEVE I WOULD RATHER HAVE STIEGLITZ LIKE SOME-
thing—anything I had done—than anyone else I know of
—I have always felt that—If I ever make anything that
satisfies me even ever so little—I am going to show it to
him to find out if it is any good. Don't you often wish you
could make something he would like? . . . I don't see why
we ever think of what others think of what we do—no
matter who they are—isn't it enough just to express yourself?

Georgia O'Keeffe at *twenty-eight,* in a letter to her
friend Anita Pollitzer[1]

A woman's relationship with a male mentor—like Georgia O'Keeffe's with Alfred Stieglitz, Simone de Beauvoir's with Jean Paul Sartre, Jane Fonda's with Tom Hayden—resembles at times the daughter's with her father and at times the lover's with her mate. Adviser, teacher, guide, wise friend—the mentor offers a relationship that may repeat and synthesize earlier bonds with father or lover, yet becomes more complex than an amalgam of both. Usually about half a generation older than his protégée, the mentor is often more effective with some professional distance as well (Having a boss as mentor may mean serving two different masters at once). A mentor's attention and commitment to his protégée can often dramatically step up the momentum of her career.

Like a father, the mentor is older, wiser, more knowledgeable and powerful. He is a figure of authority who can both criticize and praise, empower and deflate. His gift to his protégée is the paradoxical permission to grab hold of her own power, and like the most selfless parent, he must simultaneously lead and let go. Like a lover, the mentor is exciting and appreciative. Enamored, he is dazzled by the talents of his protégée and thus draws out her best performance. He turns her on—with the heady promise of her own potential. But sharing traits with both, he is finally neither parent nor peer. He is, instead, a transitional figure who helps the younger woman make the transformation from daughter to independent adult, from naïve to accomplished, from novice to professional. Just as an involvement with Mr. Wrong or Mr. Right, however problematic, ultimately helps us define ourselves as a lover, a relationship with a mentor helps us clarify ourselves as a worker, helps us realize our needs, our strengths, and our contributions.

In the ongoing struggle between working to win approval ("Don't you often wish you could make something [Stieglitz] would like?" O'Keeffe implores her friend) and working to please oneself ("Isn't it enough just to express yourself?" she also asks), the mentor may be a pivotal mediator. Ideally the force of his impact wanes with the development of an inner assurance. At first he provides an external source of encouragement and reinforcement during the most tentative phase of a career and then gradually withdraws—or is withdrawn from—as his protégée becomes more confident of her own capabilities. As in a therapeutic relationship, the mentor allows the protégée to use him as a foil until she has internalized his voice and his authority. Fatherlike, he provides her with the chance to be reparented. Loverlike, he permits her to fall in love with his possibilities, but, more important, with her own.

Yale sociologist Daniel Levinson has probed the role of the mentor in facilitating for the young person what he calls "the realization of the dream." Although his work focuses on young men, his concept of the mentor also emphasizes the qualities the mentor shares with parent and lover:

> Mentoring is best understood as a form of love. Invariably intense, lasting several years, when the mentor is a man and the

protégée a woman, there may often be an erotic element; even when sex is not involved, outside observers tend to think it must be. . . .

> A mentor does for the young adult, in the context of a specific reality—a profession, a corporate hierarchy—what the parent does for the young child in a more general way: helps her navigate obstacles and dangers, gain confidence in her own abilities, learn the language and values she will have to speak and act through, and stands as an example of full-fledged adult success.[2]

Levinson also explains why the most effective mentor will not be parent or peer, but instead a mixture of both:

> If he is entirely a peer, he cannot represent the advanced level toward which the younger [person] is striving. If he is very parental, it is difficult for both of them to overcome the generational difference and move toward the peer relationship that is the ultimate (though never fully realized) goal of the relationship. The actual parents can serve certain mentoring functions, but they are too closely tied to their offspring's pre-adult development (in both his mind and theirs) to be primary mentor figures.[3]

The notion of looking to a mentor for guidance negotiating life's vagaries is at least as old as the Greeks: Odysseus left his son Telemachus in the hands of his wise friend, Mentor, when he set out on his own odyssey. But where women in the past may have found mentors in their clergymen, therapists, or professors, only recently—with the explosion of women into the work force—have they sought out that profound kind of guidance in their professional lives. Now suddenly the media hype the necessity of having a mentor ("Everyone Who Makes It Has a Mentor," claims the *Harvard Business Review,* and *The New York Times* headlines, "On Ladder to Top, Mentor Is Key Step"). "Mentor mania"—as writer Kathleen Fury has labeled it—seems the newest craze for professional women since dressing for success.

My own interviews suggest that although many of today's

productive and creative working women do (or did) have mentors, at least as many do not. And while the women without mentors may regret their perceived deprivation and envy their colleagues who do get guidance, the women with mentors may still have ambivalent feelings about them. *Not* having a mentor raises the anxiety about whether a woman has the guts or smarts or stamina to make her way on her own. But *having* a mentor does not necessarily prevent this anxiety—may even exaggerate its importance while holding it at bay.

The high-powered women I interviewed who lacked mentors cited a variety of reasons from sex to sexism to corporate self-absorption. One young attorney, who had found support from professors in law school and summer jobs but found no one in her firm willing to play mentor, voiced a common complaint. "To get into a prestigious law firm like ours," she said, "people have to give up a lot. So they become very focused on their own careers. They also feel that they made it on their own. They don't see that their success or future is linked to others. They only see the link to the people ahead of them. The people beneath them are perceived as a threat. Furthermore, the male-female interaction is still so heated because there are relatively few women in the profession. The young male attorneys have many opportunities to socialize with the senior partners—squash, tennis, lunch dates—and can find a mentor that way. But many of the men in the firm are afraid to be seen on the street with me." Adds one of her women colleagues in the firm, "If you ask for too much guidance, you are perceived as being weak. The feeling you get from the senior partners is that figuring out a problem on your own is character-building." So in many fields competitiveness, self-interest, sexism, and the old-fashioned feeling that "I made it on my own—so can you," all serve to thwart a mentoring system that may in fact be as beneficial to the mentor as to the protégée.

For the women who does forge a relationship with a mentor, the benefits can be far-reaching, as much of this chapter will explore. But working with a mentor can also have its drawbacks. "The mentor relationship can be a trap," observed one academic who first found her mentor as a graduate student. "You are seduced into a role that is all too familiar and then find yourself unable to extricate from it." In a study of mentors and protégées, Marianne LaFrance at Boston College concluded that too much male support can sometimes diminish a woman's confidence in her own abilities. A relationship with a mentor that becomes too cozy and ingrown can be detrimental to a woman's professional development if she finds herself copying her mentor's work instead of breaking new ground of her own. So a sense of balance between dependence and independence, between a strong concept of self and an easy professional cooperation, becomes as important in the student's relationship with a mentor as in the daughter's with her father or the lover's with a mate. An economist who was afraid to look for a mentor because her relationship with an authoritarian father was so difficult summed up the challenge this way: "There seems to be an art to asking the right questions and being guided by a mentor without losing your sense of integrity."

Such a balance is likelier to be achieved by first understanding the two extremes of the mentor-protégée relationship—the psychological echoes of the paternal and the romantic bonds. Anthropologist Margaret Mead's relationship with her anthropology professor, Franz Boas, is an example of the most old-fashioned paternalistic model. And yet the assertiveness and strong sense of professional purpose that Margaret Mead developed within its constraints are decidedly contemporary. As an undergraduate at Barnard, Mead recalls in her autobiography, *Blackberry Winter*, she considered Boas "a surprising and somewhat frightening teacher,"[4] who would pose rhetorical questions that no one dared to answer. But ever the well-trained and dutiful daughter, Margaret Mead eventually won him over with her diligence. Her habit of jotting down an answer and nodding when it turned out to be right earned her an excuse from the exam for "helpful participation in class discussion" as well as the attention of Boas and his assistant, Ruth Benedict. Nearing graduation, Mead asked Benedict for advice about whether to pursue psychology or sociology. Neither, countered Benedict. "Professor Boas and I have nothing to offer but an opportunity to do work that matters." Their appeal to her deepest sense of social commitment seemed to settle the matter for Margaret Mead. "Anthropology could be done *now*. Other things could wait."[5]

Boas's *modus operandi* was consistently, if gently, authoritarian. His students called him "Papa Franz," and he treated them "rather like grandchildren." "He had to plan," Mead writes, "much as if he were a general with only a handful of troops available to save a whole country—where to place each student most strategically, so that each piece of work would count. . . ."[6] But despite their vast difference in age and experience, Margaret Mead honed her will by matching it against her mentor's, as they jockeyed for which direction her field studies should take:

> . . . he was very definite about what he wanted done.
> I was equally definite. I wanted to go to Polynesia, the area on which I had read so extensively. He thought it was too dangerous. . . . He wanted me to work among American Indians.
> I wanted to study culture change, a subject that was not yet on his agenda, although it was soon to be. He wanted me to study adolescence.[7]

Eventually they worked out a compromise. Margaret Mead went to Polynesia, as she wanted; but she studied adolescence, as her professor wanted her to. To negotiate this settlement, she "did what I had learned to do when I had to work things out with my father." She appealed to the "liberal,

democratic, modern man" in Boas, not to the "Prussian auto-
crat." "Unable to bear the implied accusation that he was
bullying me," she concludes, "Boas gave in."[8] Using the wiles
and strategies perfected as her father's oldest daughter, Margaret Mead made adult collateral out of them. She carved out
for herself a professional niche that was to put her at the
forefront of anthropology; in time her reputation would
eclipse her mentor's, and she herself would become a mentor
to hundreds of young anthropologists.

My own interviews revealed again and again, both articulated and unconscious, the reverberations of the daughter's bond with father on her relationship with a mentor.
Often she uses the experience with a mentor as an opportunity to be reparented, to ask for—and ideally receive—the
attention, guidance, or encouragement that she missed the
first time around. Or in other cases, even if she did receive
early support from her father for her developing competence
and her endeavor excitement, she is more able to make use
of that support in her adult relationship with her mentor.
Often the protégée's relationship with her mentor will repeat
the developmental stages between daughter and father: the
initiation, indoctrination, and even adulation of childhood;
then the resistance and eventual separation of adolescence
and young adulthood; and finally the transformation of maturity to equality and reciprocity. How mentor and protégée
diverge is often as instructive as how they work together.

For a twenty-eight-year-old accountant, a mentor during a
summer job came to represent a parent in both his positive
and negative guises. "Mentoring can be like a fun version of
parenting," she observed, thinking about her early contacts
with her boss and mentor, how he enjoyed handing her assignments that were more and more challenging, urging her
on to handle and master each one and be ready for the next.
"The mentor has the fun of watching the younger person
learn without having the burdens and responsibilities of

being her actual parent. A big part of mentoring is opening doors—and being there when the door slams back. Everybody needs a cheering squad." Though her mentor cheered her on for project after project, when she came to a turning point in her career—whether to consider a large, prestigious firm or go for the smaller, safer one—he suddenly traded his encouraging stance for a cautious and pessimistic one and urged her toward the safer and less demanding option. Like the insecure parent, he became inhibiting and overprotective. "That was an inadequate form of mentoring," she concluded, and soon parted company with him. Yet disappointment in him pushed her more quickly to find her own strength. Diverging from him, she found the confidence in her choices and went ahead and established herself in the larger, prestigious firm.

A fifty-year-old vice-president of a major bank recalls a similar moment of diverging from her first mentor's paternalistic guidance. "My first mentor was my boss when I worked in computer sales. He took a special liking to me and was willing to train me and educate me in the ways of the world. It was like a father-daughter relationship, and we were comfortable with it, because we were both used to it." Their moment of truth occurred when his parental overprotectiveness became a roadblock. "He didn't want me to drive into the valley on a sales trip because of the dangerous fog. He wouldn't have minded if a man went. Because I felt comfortable with him, I said I appreciated his concern but hoped he'd have the same for a male counterpart. Then, of course, I went anyway." Differing from her mentor reaffirmed her conviction about her own sense of direction. But unlike the accountant, she retained rather than rejected the relationship with her mentor, having renegotiated its terms, because she still felt his support could spur on her career.

A social worker and professor in her sixties benefited from her mentor's faith in her early in her career just as she had benefited from her father's faith in her in childhood. But finally, parting from her mentor, like parting from her father, kindled her faith in herself and in her choices. "I had a very good relationship with my father," she remembers. "I always felt very loved, appreciated, and cherished. I took it for granted that men would like me. Also, my father really took pride in my intellectual achievements. Whatever I did felt right to him. But at the same time I had some slight brain damage and was considered noneducable. I couldn't work with figures, learn to ride, bike, or skate. So there was a significant difference between that reality and my father's idealization of me."

Just as her father's idealization of her encouraged her to reach for intellectual heights that others defined as beyond her, her mentor's faith also catapulted her forward. When she met him, she was twenty-two and a student at an adolescent treatment program. He, at thirty, was a first-year social worker. He spotted her talent for working with children and helped her deepen her perceptions and commitment. "The most crucial lesson he taught me was that the most important thing a therapist—and parent—could do was to give the adolescent the faith he could solve his own problems. It was critical for the adolescent to introject that voice and believe in himself."

For years her mentor encouraged her progress, hiring her to work at the centers he headed, guiding her intellectual development—even introducing her to music ("He played me Beethoven's Ninth for the first time and that was a peak experience"). She flowered under his benign attentions, and he became more and more admiring of the person who unfolded. "My reputation was enhanced," she says, "by his idealized picture of me." He had dreams of her rising to the top in his field, but she had dreams of her own. She wanted to be a pioneer in her own field, so she chose another direction from his. "My mentor could never entirely understand this," she says now. "We differed, but there was no acrimony." Their parting was amicable, because each allowed the relationship to be transformed. He was generous enough to see her go her own way without defining her shift as a rejection of him. And she, in turn, could leave him while also "introjecting" his voice—his confidence and belief in her. This faith—his in her and then hers in herself—helped bolster her to meet the challenges ahead of her. Just as her mentor urged her to instill in the adolescents she counseled the faith that they could solve their own problems, he instilled that same faith in her.

In this mentor-protégée relationship, the echoes of the daughter's experience with her father are particularly striking—the learning and seeking advice, the reverence of older by younger, the introjection of the paternal voice, the eventual need to separate and ultimately transform the bond. But between the lines of the daughterly and fatherly devotion, there is also the suggestion of another kind of love. Their relationship is at times as intense and passionate as a love affair. But the love exchanged—the admiration, the idealization, the absorption in each other's lives—does not have a sexual expression, but instead a creative, professional, even spiritual one. It is a kind of psychic kindling—the "peak experience" of hearing Beethoven's Ninth for the first time—a kind of nonsexual seduction where both are seduced by the very magnitude of the protégée's possibilities as a social worker, a professional, a woman. "He fell in love with me as an idealized object" is her rather clinical appraisal of the formative relationship that is now decades in the past. But even these many years past her mentor's death, there is something in her voice that belies the clinical dismissal—a gentle affection, a shy pleasure that suggests that each of them was indeed a little bit in love with the other, and that it was this love that prompted the most important mentoring.

Many mentor-protégée relationships are fueled by the kind

of love or admiration that is usually the province of lovers. More often than not this love becomes neither romantic nor sexual. But beneath the surface of an apparently professional liaison, it can add interest or intensity or simply extra motivation to the exchange of information, advice and ideas. Occasionally the involvement between mentor and protégée does become sexual. The affair—or at times marriage—that develops becomes a curious hybrid of love and work, where the rhythms of attachment and separation in the relationship become complexly interwoven with the satisfactions and limitations in the professional affiliation.

Georgia O'Keeffe's relationship with photographer Alfred Stieglitz—her mentor, lover, and later husband—illustrates the complicated connections between artist and adviser, lover and beloved, even daughter and father. Twenty-five years his junior, O'Keeffe met Stieglitz in her late twenties when she was an unknown but immensely gifted young artist and he was a celebrated and influential photographer with a knack for making artists' reputations. Without asking her permission, Stieglitz exhibited some of O'Keeffe's drawings for the first time at his gallery, "291"; soon after, he gave her her first solo show. Meeting him for the first time, O'Keeffe was intrigued, entranced, frightened, and a little put off—a mixture of emotions that continued to describe her feelings for Stieglitz long after their lives were permanently joined. "There was such a power when he spoke," she remembered after his death. "People seemed to believe what he said, even when they knew it wasn't their truth. . . . If [his listeners] crossed him in any way, his power to destroy was as destructive as his power to build—the extremes went together. I have experienced both and survived, but I think I only crossed him when I had to— to survive."[9]

As for Stieglitz, he responded to O'Keeffe quite passionately both as a woman and an artist. Stifled in a long and loveless marriage, he warmed to the young woman's beauty, her mystery, her sexuality quietly contained beneath the somber black costumes that were even then her trademark. As an aging artist, he saw in O'Keeffe's burning talent a spark he might further ignite as indeed she might again ignite his own. "What appealed to him" about O'Keeffe, observes her biographer, Laurie Lisle, "was that she had her whole creative life ahead of her, whereas his, he thought, had ended."[10]

In the early years of their relationship, first friends and then lovers, Stieglitz played the role of godfather to O'Keeffe's eager and willing initiate. Once she admired a Marsden Hartley painting exhibited at Stieglitz's gallery. He simply gave it to her, adding casually, "If you get tired of it, bring it back." Some years later, when O'Keeffe was living and painting in a brownstone studio that belonged to his niece, Stieglitz asked, "If you could do anything you wanted for a year, what would it be?" Recalls O'Keeffe, "I promptly said I would like to have a year to paint. . . . He thought for a while and then remarked that he thought he could arrange that—so I kept on painting in the studio."[11]

While Stieglitz was adding momentum to O'Keeffe's burgeoning career, O'Keeffe, in another way, was revitalizing his own. From the first time he photographed her—capable and lyrical hands entwined in front of one of her own sinuous drawings—he found in the younger artist a captivating and engrossing subject. In less than three years he made two hundred prints of her; by the time he stopped at age seventy-three, there were five hundred. He conceived of the photographs as a composite portrait of his lover, friend, and protégée, and they seem to capture her many selves. In one she sits in an open robe, hair loosened down her back, her face pained and yearning. In another he shows us the proud and public self, black cape wrapped around her shoulders, black bowler hat rakish against a huge sky, daring all comers. Sometimes his piercing eye settles only on her torso: lean and angular in certain moods, soft and round in others.

And often his camera sees only her hands—sensuous and strong, talking, dancing, working, even resting suggestively on the shiny hubcap of an automobile tire.

Stieglitz's photographic portrait of O'Keeffe makes tangible the mentor's gift to his protégée—that is, to reveal to her her own power, her own depths, her own possibilities. O'Keeffe responded to the prints with awe and fascination. Gradually she became able to accept, her biographer believes, Stieglitz's "inspired image of herself."[12] That image, and her mentor's faith in it, in turn became a catalyst to further accomplishment. "I can see myself," she once remarked, reflecting on the personas Stieglitz's photographs revealed, "and it has helped me to say what I want to say—in paint."[13]

As their relationship deepened and intensified—first as lovers, later as husband and wife—that, too, nourished O'Keeffe's talent and expanded her reaches as an artist. When she first began living with Stieglitz, she boasted to a friend that every woman should have him as a lover. And although the links between sexuality and creativity inevitably remain mysterious, her biographer speculates that "as her awareness of her sexuality was heightened, she started painting marvelously original abstractions in exuberant, uninhibited rainbows of pastel colors that appeared to melodiously celebrate her happiness."[14] Then, too, the paintings O'Keeffe produced during their union were treated almost like children: "Stieglitz had said repeatedly that Georgia's paintings often came out of a moment between them—out of their lifeblood, like children. After Georgia created a painting, she would turn it over to him, its guardian, so that he might find a foster parent who would take it, appreciate it and care for it tenderly."[15] So all of Stieglitz's different roles—mentor, lover, husband, even father to her "children"—fused in his complex relationship to O'Keeffe's art.

But over the years as this first flush of excitement, both artistic and sexual, began to wane, as O'Keeffe's powers augmented and Stieglitz's began to diminish, a change in the balance between them became inevitable. When Stieglitz's health deteriorated, he became more and more insular, wanting to stay put at his family's house at Lake George, which O'Keeffe found increasingly oppressive. O'Keeffe meanwhile, in her forties and at the peak of her powers, found herself needing more and more creative space and distance from her mentor. Drawn to New Mexico, a place whose vistas she loved and symbolically identified with, she chose eventually to live there for as much as six months of the year. Stieglitz respected her creative imperatives but, naturally enough, resented her lengthy absences. What would have been an inevitable parting of the ways between protégée and mentor became in the context of their marriage a more painful and irresolvable issue.

During one of O'Keeffe's absences Stieglitz took up with a still younger woman, Dorothy Norman, who, though married herself, became a kind of helpmate to him in matters of art and business. She enjoyed the more traditional wifely role that O'Keeffe had never wanted. He began photographing Dorothy Norman as he had photographed O'Keeffe in their first years together. Despite her growing distance from Stieglitz, O'Keeffe was naturally wounded when she found out about the liaison. That news as well as other self-doubts precipitated a depression for which she had to be hospitalized. During her recovery Stieglitz continued to offer support and encouragement for her art, but their marriage became redefined as a "cooler kind of companionship."[16] O'Keeffe's image of herself after this psychic upheaval was that she needed to be "fully individuated and alone, upon a mesa."[17]

As their relationship drew to a close, the wonderful vibrancy that had animated it at the beginning faded to the pale light of memory. By the end of Stieglitz's life, when illness had incapacitated him, O'Keeffe moved him into an apartment that presumably she paid for. Now their roles were fully reversed; she was providing for him as once he had so power-fully provided for her. When Stieglitz died, his obituaries all identified him as the husband of Georgia O'Keeffe. At her mentor's death O'Keeffe's paintings were hanging in a retro-spective at the Museum of Modern Art. She had become as well known and influential as her renowned husband.

Now in her nineties and sequestered on her ranch in New Mexico, O'Keeffe has nonetheless provided a postscript to this story. Several years ago an artist in his late twenties ap-peared at her doorstep offering himself as an assistant cum apprentice. Although O'Keeffe had never taken on a student before, something in her resonated to Juan Hamilton's crea-tive spirit, and she began to involve herself deeply in his work. She urged him to concentrate on pottery and became a god-mother to his career, just as Stieglitz had become a godfather to hers. And in return—just as she had given her mentor a restorative creative gift by providing him with a subject of endless fascination—Juan Hamilton also gave her a gift: He taught her how to make pots. And though her eyesight was badly deteriorating, he helped her use her sense of touch to accomplish this art. So, at the end of her life, Juan Hamilton gave her through the touch of the clay what Stieglitz had given through the sight of his photographic portrait—a renewed sense of her own strength and efficacy and an increased plea-sure in existence. Both early and late in life, the mentor-protégée relationship inspired her vision as an artist and renewed her spirits as a woman.

My own interviews suggest a number of connections be-tween mentor and lover, creative inspiration and sexual expression. The intimacy, the heightened energy and involve-ment, the admiration—often mutual—all these characteristics of the mentor-protégée relationship also describe the bond between lovers. The sexual energy implicit between mentor and protégée—even when left unexpressed—adds liveliness to the relationship. But when the sexual attraction develops into a full-fledged affair, the results can be more problematic—particularly if the affair turns sour.

Deirdre Rosen is an enterprising young therapist who specializes in treating women with eating disorders. The daughter of an entrepreneur who was a self-made millionaire at thirty, Deirdre at thirty-four has a practice that is growing faster than she can handle. Beginning with a father who exposed her to a lot of "wheeling and dealing" early in childhood, she is forthright about the men in her life who have aided and abetted her progress. "There have been men all along the way who have been helpful" is how she puts it. "They have come into my life when I needed them." She is matter-of-fact about these liaisons. "Some became lovers. Some stayed friends without becoming sexualized."

Her first mentor was a consultant to small businesses. He interviewed her for a job, and although she did not land the job, she did snag his interest. "We became lovers. He gave me moral support to leave a job I hated. He hired me to do some free-lance jobs. I learned a lot from him about putting together a class and about finances. He also taught me book-keeping, which is a very useful tool." But ironically, the better the student mastered her lessons, the more anxious her mentor became. "I was an eager student with him, but never vice versa. I came to realize I was a good income generator, but he was not. During the time we were together, his business went under and mine quadrupled. I became very involved in making my practice successful. It began to be like a baby. He felt I was feeding it rather than him."

This pattern was repeated with her second mentor, a newspaperman and publicist whose own career and marriage, at the time they met, had become rather lackluster. "He took me under his wing and helped me produce a brochure. He showed me how to do it, and I saw I could do it myself. With both mentors, their primary contribution has been to demystify the working world." But the more competent and powerful she became, the less attractive she became to her mentor and lover. "The less needy I was, the less he could Pygmalion me. As I became less needful, he became less interested and eventually found someone else."

The fiasco of these two relationships suggests that although the bond between lovers and the one between mentor and protégée may share certain external similarities, the inner imperatives of each liaison are actually very different. An affair between lovers flourishes on reciprocity, mutual support and concern, with each taking a turn nurturing or encouraging or bolstering the other's delicate ego. But to be a mentor requires a certain detachment, even selflessness, a willingness to encourage the protégée without expecting a return in kind, a pleasure in watching her grow, even if she grows away from or beyond her mentor.

Certainly the mentor stands to benefit a great deal from the relationship. Deirdre describes her first mentor's transformation in response to their involvement: "Within six months he had lost thirty pounds, gotten contacts and a new wardrobe. He found me an attractive woman, and his sense of his masculinity was enhanced." Apart from the sexual dividends, the mentor often gets other ego boosts as well: someone who admires, contributes to, and often promulgates his ideas and whose accomplishments can add considerably to his own standing. But if the mentor comes to depend on these benefits, he adds unnecessary constraints to his protégée's progress. Sometimes when the two relationships—professional and romantic—overlap, a conflict of interests becomes almost inevitable.

In the portraits of Judy Dater taken by Jack Welpott—her mentor and lover, husband and then ex-husband—the camera hints of the energy that drew them together as well as the friction that drove them apart. Like Stieglitz examining

O'Keeffe, Welpott searches out his lover's many selves. Now she is erect in an overcoat with arms crossed in front of a gnarled tree. Under the brim of a floppy, Garboesque hat, her eyes are half closed, looking in and looking out—mysterious and supercilious, contained, but also self-consciously posing for effect. In others she is naked and vulnerable. In one her elbow bends forward by her face in shadow; in another the back of her torso glistens under the light. In both every hair and freckle is exposed. In a final one the camera sees her from the back, bending over a washbasin, washing between her legs. She is naked except for little cotton booties. Her tie-dyed shirt and jeans hang over the back of a chair, promising adventures past and to come. Jack Welpott sees the sensuality and strength of his lover. He hears her saying, Come hither. But he also hears her saying, Leave me be.

Almost ten years have passed since those portraits appeared, part of a collaborative book of photographs called *Women and Other Visions,* in which Welpott and Dater each turned an eye to the subject of women. The book became a celebration of their own intensity and sexuality, of a partnership that had begun when he was the experienced mentor and she the eager and willing apprentice, then gradually flowered into the shared excitement of taking pictures together. But in these past ten years, mentor and protegée, husband and wife, have gone their separate ways. Judy Dater's reputation as a photographer is enough established now so that she can support herself by selling her work and teaching workshops around the country. Her subject began in imitation of her lover's; then it turned—with him—to the portraits of other women. But now, completely separated from her mentor and husband, her eye is turning inward for self-portraits, and her subject has become herself.

At forty-two Judy Dater is the first to tell you, "I have never looked better in my life." With fine features and dark hair cut to her shoulders, she is thinner and more elegant than earlier pictures I had seen of her. Puttering around her kitchen, fixing herself a cappuccino, she is her own art piece: black T-shirt with bright pink hearts dancing across it, blue jeans, purple belt and purple shoes, pink punk earrings. In the house in California's Marin County hills she once bought with Jack Welpott and now shares with another lover, she clearly enjoys her own aesthetic, her own sensuality. The sun filters in through the thicket of trees and ferns and lights up the colorful pieces of Mexican folk art perched on the redwood shelves, the Oriental rug and plushy caramel-colored couch, the Mexican tiles of the kitchen floor. From an overhead kitchen rack hangs her collection of kitschy mugs gathered from her photographic travels around the country. She pours her cappuccino into the most recent one—from Billings, Montana, where she has just judged a photography show—and begins the tale of her birth as an artist.

"I always wanted to be an artist. The idea of a free life appealed to me. I wouldn't say my parents encouraged me, but they didn't discourage me. They thought my fantasy was cute, but they didn't take it seriously." Her close relationship with her father—a movie theater-owner in Hollywood—fanned her fantasy by exposing her to the magic of movies. "Every Saturday morning I would go with him to 'film row,' where all the movie-theater-owners gathered to get popcorn and posters. I'd meet his cronies. He would also take me to private screenings. I have very fond memories of sitting in those dark screening rooms.

"My father and I always got along very well. There was never any conflict. I talked to him and confided in him more than in my mother. He was very quiet, sweet, and even-tempered. He never tried to tell me what to do. But he was always trying to get me not to go off the deep end. He used the image of a thermometer in a freezer—he wanted me to stay in a certain zone, whereas I had a tendency to want to go to extremes." Her mother was rational, too, but more

emotional than her father, also more of an authority figure with more responsibility for Judy. "Of my parents'
qualities," she says now, "I see in myself a combination of
passive and aggressive. Sometimes I'm passive, stoic, uncomplaining. Other times I have zero tolerance and can be
pushy and aggressive. As a kid I saw my father as passive
and my mother as more aggressive. She was more vocal,
getting me to do what she wanted me to do."

Although her parents would have preferred she become a
doctor or lawyer ("or at least married one"), they sanctioned
her artistic ambitions—but urged her to get a teaching cre-
dential as a backup. For three years she went to UCLA and
lived at home, all the while restless to break free. Eventually
she took the first available route out—she got married. "I got
married at twenty," she says, nervously fiddling with her cappuccino mug, "someone I met at UCLA. It was a disaster from
the beginning. We had nothing in common. We weren't
ready, but I pushed him into it. I'm convinced I did it as a way
to get out of the house."

Soon after they married, her husband enlisted in the army,
was transferred to San Francisco and then to Korea. Left
behind in San Francisco, Judy enrolled in a photography class
at San Francisco State. "Jack Welpott was the teacher," she
says and laughs, "and that was the end of the marriage."
Never once does she call her first husband by name; he remains in memory, several lifetimes away. When she met Jack
Welpott—and fell in love with him and with photography—
she seemed to begin another lifetime. "That first photography class was wonderful and shocking. The photography part
was really exciting, a revelation. Soon everything got mixed
up together—my interest in photography and my interest in
Jack. It was"—she chooses her words carefully—"very potent." Jack Welpott was eighteen years her senior, a married
and established thirty-nine to her married but footloose
twenty-one. Remembering her impressions of him then, she

laughs and blushes, somehow the teenager who has just seduced her father's best friend. "My sense as a student was that
he was kind, intelligent, thoughtful, intellectual, stimulating
—at that time. He seemed to have a lot of latent sexual potential. But it was contained. There was a lot of sexual tension
and energy coming from both of us." In three months they
had become lovers.

But if their love affair was impetuous, her commitment to
photography evolved more slowly. "It took a long time before
I realized how serious I was about photography—a couple of
years." With her husband back from Korea and her marriage
falling apart, she took a job teaching art at a junior high
school, the safety net her parents guided her toward. But one
day she confided in a colleague that she couldn't stand her
marriage or her job and wanted to get her master's in photography. "Just do it," he said, and those chance words became
the permission she needed. "I left a note for my husband to
get out, and he did. Jack hadn't wanted the responsibility of
making me leave my husband. I had to do it on my own."

Back at San Francisco State—this time to get her M.A. in
photography—she felt her own seriousness about her art for
the first time. It was also the first time she had lived on her
own, and that, too, was a heady feeling. She made a darkroom
in her kitchen and stayed up till three in the morning printing
pictures. Meanwhile her love affair and apprenticeship with
Jack Welpott also continued to thrive. At first she took cues
for her subjects from his, photographing landscapes and
close-ups of rocks at Point Lobos just as he did. "I started out
doing landscapes because I thought that was what we were
supposed to do. But then I began putting people into the
landscape." Soon people, not landscapes, had become her
true subject. Even as their themes diverged, Jack Welpott
continued to try to shape her thinking. He was particularly
interested in Zen and psychology and in their meaning in
photography, and he urged on her books by Jung, Alan Watts,

and other Zen philosophers. "I read them and was kind of interested," she confesses, "but I was more interested in working intuitively than in picking up on someone else's ideas." Even under the sheltering wing of her mentor, she was already beginning to rely on her own voice. A crucial turning point turned out to be the day she presented her photography project to her master's committee. Though Jack usually sat on this committee and could be counted on for support, the day of her presentation, an emergency—his brother's funeral—forced him out of town. She panicked, but got her degree anyway, even without his support. Inadvertently the first step toward artistic separation had been forced upon her.

Still, years after they have gone their individual ways, she is forthright about the benefits of the relationship to each. "In the beginning, our involvement was always helpful. I always had someone to talk to about my work. I'd be in the darkroom printing and I'd call Jack in to ask what he thought, even though I wouldn't always take his suggestions. Then, too, I met a lot of interesting people I wouldn't have met otherwise —Ansel Adams, Wynn Bullock, Brett Weston.

"As for what Jack got out of the relationship"—she smiles a slow, knowing smile—"it's hard to know—besides the sex. That was certainly something." After a pause she changes gears and continues, "I was his best student and he really wanted me to acknowledge him as his teacher. He took pride that I was doing well. It was also good for his ego that he was with someone so much younger." Then, too, besides the delights of a mistress and the loyalties of a student, she also offered the attentions of a wife—first in addition to his own wife and then instead of her. "I'd take care of him," she remembers. "Before we were married, I'd make him all sorts of fancy things to eat. Also, I was always dragging him off to do adventurous things. Early on, we traveled in Europe together for about six months. After we were married, I still went out of my way to do all the housewifely chores that he complained his first wife hadn't done, until I couldn't stand it either."

When they had gotten back from their European foray, Jack had gotten a divorce and they had started living together. Soon they were immersed in a collaborative project photographing women that eventually grew into their book *Women and Other Visions*. Judy describes how the project began: "We were walking on Grant Avenue in North Beach in San Francisco one day. We saw a woman and were both struck by how she looked. We asked if we could photograph her and she said we could, so she became our first subject." In their two portraits of her in the book, she stares at the camera, eyes wide and made up under a cap of curls. Jack's is a close-up of her face, starkly lit, unrelenting; Judy's shows her full body, skirt hiked above her thigh, eyes coquettish, longing.

Gradually over the course of several years they amassed a series of portraits that were as much a study of women as a portrait of their own marriage, their own dialogue. In his introduction to their book, Henry Holmes Smith observed, "We learn what Judy Dater and Jack Welpott think and feel and sometimes know about sex, their own and the opposite. The games, the pleasures, the hurts—that danger and madness the ancient Greeks feared: Eros." From Judy's cover portrait of a confident blonde sitting stripped to the waist and smoking to Jack's reclining black woman, moody and naked except for a gold necklace, the pictures are bold, sexual, troubling.

"What I was doing," explains Judy, differentiating her vision from her lover's "partially consciously and partially not, was to strip away the stereotype of the women we were seeing. I wanted portraits that showed intensity, strength, beauty, flaws. I was not trying to exploit their sexuality. But Jack wanted to make the women more glamorous, sexier from the male point of view. He was less interested in a one-to-one confrontation, less interested in fierceness. But now I look at his pictures, and they really bother me. They seem too sexist, too exploitative. He would defend himself. He felt he had a right to express his male sexuality."

Since my own eye does not discern such a striking difference between the two sets of portraits, I take her comments to be as much about their relationship as about the pictures themselves, a growing resistance to Jack's vision of the world, which more and more she wanted to differentiate from her own. For the time they were working on this project together was also the time their relationship, by now a marriage, was realigning. As her talent and competence matured, Judy felt an increasing need to take risks on her own, follow her own leads, exercise her own vision. But the understandable urge of the protégée to rebel against and separate from her mentor became more fraught with complications when the mentor was also her husband. "At first we were together as teacher and student," Judy realizes now. "Then we became colleagues. We did workshops together. But then I started getting a reputation on my own. People were not always interested in our doing things together. That created serious problems. At first I felt guilty, worried, almost insulted that they'd ask me and not Jack. I turned down some things without question. But eventually I realized I had to stop apologizing to him. He was afraid he'd lose me by having me go off without him, afraid I'd meet someone else, and also afraid of my freedom."

Gradually her husband's fears and her own resentments began to take their toll on the marriage. "For most of our years together I was not doing much questioning. I was doing my work and doing what I thought I should do as his wife. It was okay for most of the time. But then I started to realize I was feeling very anxious. I knew something was wrong when I'd get up and feel anxious and not know why."

Just as years before she had used a romance to escape her parents' clutches, this time she used the same solution to escape her marriage. "Then a funny thing happened. I discovered I had a crush on another person. It was an incredible shock that I was falling out of love with Jack and that I would have to do something. It took about a year, but eventually we got a divorce." Breaking away from her husband was painfully intertwined with establishing her separate identity as a photographer. "All the time we were working and married," she explains, "I never felt Jack's equal. I thought I might be, but I couldn't assert it until the very end. I had to leave him, to do this thing that was bigger than both of us. Before, I had always had the sense that he would come first as a man, a husband, a photographer. I was inhibited about exposing myself. But toward the end I began to feel that my own ideas were valid and that I didn't always have to rely on him."

The affair that broke up her marriage—"wonderful, glorious," she calls it—nevertheless lasted only a year. But catapulted out of her marriage and out of her protracted apprenticeship, she began to blossom in her artistic and personal freedom. Her next lover turned out to be a "much younger man," and today, more than five years later, they are still together. She shows me his snapshot—a kinetic, intense-looking fellow—with obvious pride. "He's a conceptual artist, a video person," she says. "I met him when my career was established, and he was working, too. I've learned a lot from him about the avant-garde. But he's learned a few things from me as well: an appreciation of quality, a dedication toward what you believe in. Now I've been the one who has maybe tempered his going off the deep end. He's very volatile."

Clearly the balance of power has shifted in this relationship with her younger lover. Speculating about how this shift occurred, she first draws the connection back to her relationship with her father. "Superficially I used to think that because I was very close to my father when I was younger, that may have influenced my attraction to Jack and to the man I had the affair with after Jack, since they were both older and married. There was a thing about male power that was appealing in both these people, because they were both older, established, respected. I find it interesting that I went for someone younger once I felt I had my own power. I had less need to find those qualities in men that I felt I hadn't possessed early on."

The sense of integration and balance that she now feels in her emotional life is also reflected in her creative work. Self-awareness—and self-satisfaction—in one sphere have prompted self-exploration in the other. "For the past two years I have been doing self-portraits," she reports and adds, "Isn't that perfect? Almost too perfect!" Laughing at herself, she continues more seriously, "The self-portraits have been connected with turning forty and taking stock. I was worrying about getting old, losing my attractiveness and sexuality. But when I got to be forty, I stopped worrying about it. I was tickled to have that birthday over with. It was a big release!"

The self-portraits have just been mailed back to her from an exhibit in Oregon, and together we open the box and spread them out on the floor to examine them. About half are nudes in black and white. Most were taken on the Badlands in South Dakota and show her lying on huge boulders, curled in the fetal position on gigantic rocks. The landscape is lunar, desolate, suggests in metaphor a time of inner devastation and struggle. In one she stands on a barren plain, naked back to her camera, as if poised on the edge of the world. "That's just how I felt," she says.

The self-portraits in color have an entirely different tone: more antic, witty, self-parodic, they are caricatures of the woman's role. In these she poses in costumes and often in a blond wig. In one she is curled up in a nightgown, munching bonbons; in another, dressed like a chambermaid, she juggles a duster, a broom, an iron, and soap; in yet a third she wears a leopardskin body suit, open to reveal her breasts. Posing next to a gory lamb's head, she becomes her own mixed message about the lure and taboo of sexuality.

Compared with her earlier work—the portraits taken with Jack Welpott for *Women and Other Visions*—these photographs seem both more confident and intense as well as more humorous and lighthearted. It is confidence and intensity born of a long struggle to become her own person, humor and light-heartedness that admit she is at last also able to laugh at this struggle and move on.

The woman's relationship with her mentor may recapitulate the dynamics of the daughter's relationship with her father and the lover's with her mate and may repeat the pleasures and pitfalls of both. Like the daughter with her father, the protégée may warm to her mentor's protectiveness—but resist when the sheltering arm becomes overprotective. Sometimes the mentor, like the father, will impose limits against which the protégée will chafe—and that way have an opportunity to grow. Like the lover with her mate, the protégée may thrive in the encouraging glow of her mentor's appreciation and admiration. But she may also rebel when keeping in his good graces seems to require a clipping of her wings, a submissiveness or dependence more like subservience than devotion.

But understanding these two influences—the paternal and the sexual—can also lead to working out a more balanced mentor-protégée arrangement that may occasionally recall the earlier relationships, yet provide benefits that are uniquely influential. For though the mentor may be older, wiser, and therefore more paternal, still, *unlike* the father, he meets the younger woman as an adult. From the outset of their relationship he expects her to meet his challenges with competence and maturity. Without the psychological baggage of shared childhood history, she rises to the occasion of his belief in her with an increased professionalism of her own. And though the mentor may offer admiration and support the way a lover does, his protégée does not expect to be his primary emotional involvement. Knowing that she can be encouraged but not controlled, guided but not tied down, gives her the necessary psychological leeway to move forward confidently in her career.

First, a mentor often provides an initial intellectual spark that becomes a catalyst to his protégée's development. Usually this first contact will be in person—a professor's lecture, a supervisor's critique, a teacher's words of wisdom. But the connection may also be symbolic—an intellectual awakening, even camaraderie, provided by a writer's novels, a composer's music, an artist's paintings. A forty-year-old librarian whose father was a rather rigid and authoritarian professor found an entirely different kind of intellectual model in her symbolic mentor. "From the time I was nineteen until I was twenty-one," she recalls, "my mentor was Aldous Huxley. He was symbolic, but I read all his books, collected memorabilia about him, wrote to him. He was my idol." In an intangible, but deeply influential way, Huxley nourished her intellectual search and encouraged her own quest.

More concretely the mentor also offers his protégée advice, expertise, words of wisdom. These words may make an impression at the moment or else register below the surface and show their influence years after the two have gone their separate ways. When Jane Rosenmann first went to work as editorial assistant to Henry Robbins, one of the country's most renowned editors, she did not exactly define him as her mentor. But during the three years she worked for him, his philosophy about publishing, his attitudes about editing and writers made an indelible impression on her. When Henry Robbins died, Jane Rosenmann, still in her late twenties, inherited several of his writers, including John Irving, whose *World According to Garp* had been a major best seller. Then, and even more now that she has moved to another publishing house and is in charge of her own books and authors, Rosenmann hears the echoes of Henry Robbins's credo about publishing.

"The only thing you have to go on is your own judgment," she remembers him teaching her. "You only have a worthwhile opinion on the kind of book you yourself are interested in. If you don't read pop novels, don't try to pick a first pop novel." Then, too, she remembers his counsel about taking the long view, going for excellence, not faddishness. "The idea is not to try a writer once and if he doesn't work out, let him loose," Robbins would say, "but rather to build a list over the long term. And always remember, it's the writer's book, not the editor's!" Now that Robbins is gone, Rosenmann often thinks, "There are so many things I'd like to ask Henry about now that I've been publishing myself." But she also realizes that long past his death she has made his wisdom her own, drawing on what she needs as she pursues an independent course.

The mentor also offers the perspective of his own greater experience and maturity and fosters in his protégée more far-reaching vision, deeper understanding, and more ambitious goals. A psychologist who specializes in treating disturbed youngsters recalls how her mentor, a prominent clinician in that field, expanded her own frame of reference some forty years ago. "When he talked about youngsters," she remembers, "he had a much wider reference than was typical at that time. He saw the influence of sociology and of the family on troubled children long before others did. He was willing to go outside traditional lines. He opened me up to be more honest with youngsters. He was never afraid of using himself with a person and of touching the humanity in others." The scope of her mentor's vision inspired her to widen her own scope, both as a counselor and as an adult.

The mentor's position of greater influence and respect can also become a helpful stamp of approval for his protégée. Adding credibility to her ideas and broadcasting her abilities and achievements are crucial ways he can contribute to the upward mobility of her career. A forty-year-old government professor, who, although a brilliant thinker, looks far younger than her years, described how her mentor, a senior and admired professor, threw his weight behind her during her stressful struggle for tenure. "No one ever listened to me during faculty meetings," she realizes now, "unless my mentor would say, 'Susan made a very good point.' Then everybody would turn toward me admiringly." Gradually, with his backing, she built up her own credibility and her own power base. Now that she is a tenured professor, other faculty take her remarks seriously without her mentor underlining their worth.

Similarly, a young attorney in a large law firm felt that being touted by her mentor, a senior partner in the firm, meant the difference between blending in with the dozen other first-year lawyers and standing out as competent enough for the more important assignments and eventually for promotion. "Having someone broadcast your good work," she concludes, "is more important than *doing* good work." Although her good work and canny legal mind drew her mentor to her in the first place, she also acknowledges that her mentor's recognition of her accomplishments added to her reputation in the firm.

At different stages in a woman's career, different mentors may provide distinct and valuable functions. Nancy Collins, an enterprising businesswoman and author of *Professional Women and Their Mentors,* cites her own three mentors to illustrate how their influences differed according to her needs at three important junctures of her career. "At the very beginning of my career, when I was in my twenties, my mentor was a role model. He was a senior vice-president at the large Fortune 500 corporation where I worked right after I graduated from college. He taught me by his example that I wanted a career, not a job, and that I, like he, enjoyed working with high-level people. His philosophy shaped my life, and he taught me to 'think big.'

"Halfway in a career a mentor can give you protection. He

can also get you on committees and get you visibility. I met my second mentor when I was in my early thirties. He was the director of a program at the Stanford Business School in which I became the assistant director. He gave me a lot of responsibility, but he also taught me that women don't always get credit for what they do, so to ask for responsibility and then to ask to get credit. He was loyal and really went to bat for me. When someone has that much confidence in you, you wouldn't dare let him down.

"Then, nearer the end of a career, a mentor can push you toward senior management. My third mentor, whom I met in my early forties, was outside my business structure. He is a certified public accountant and a recognized authority in the field of corporate taxation. While we never worked together, his main contribution was to help me get my career in focus. He helped me set my sights a lot higher and to get more visibility. He was also one of the people with whom I could do reality-testing: Were my ideas good ones? How were others perceiving me? This process was at times painful, but it was also necessary for growth."

Of all the benefits the protégée receives from her mentor —his intellectual spark, his expertise and evaluation, his perspective and vision, his credibility and weight added to her own—his most profound gift is to lead her back to herself, back to her own authority. This may be a delicate dance in which the mentor senses when to lead—when to give advice, bolster self-esteem, point out new directions—but, more important, recognizes when to relinquish the lead. The best mentor, like the best therapist or indeed the best parent, must know how to guide while gradually letting go. And his influence may, paradoxically, be felt more intensely as he himself becomes more invisible. He must first create the illusion and then the certainty that his protégée is capable of doing everything she wants and needs to on her own.

For *Eva Tanner*, a theology student in her fifties studying now to be a minister after another lifetime of being a doctor's wife, mother, and community volunteer, psychologist Carl Rogers functioned as such a mentor. He helped her retrieve her faith in her own capabilities, which, before she met him, had gotten badly frayed around the edges. After twenty years of a marriage endured but not enjoyed, years of raising three children and muffling her own needs to meet theirs, years of endless volunteer projects that filled a gap without creating a whole, Eva Tanner ached for change. Chafing against her marriage, but without the courage or means to leave it and yearning to study and make her mark as a professional, she signed up for a seminar with Rogers at his Center for the Study of the Person in La Jolla. Eager if not desperate for his guidance, she volunteered to play the client in a counseling session to which the rest of the group bore silent witness.

As she began to speak, first haltingly, then with growing insistence about her fears and desires, her ambivalence about her marriage, and her yearning to make something of herself, she waited apprehensively for Rogers to respond, to tell her what to do, which path to choose. But instead he simply sat there quietly, patiently reflecting back to her everything she said, occasionally asking her to clarify her meaning, repeat and rework a complex point. She began to warm to the process, lend herself to it more and more, until gradually, between the lines, she began to see how he was leading her back to herself. "At first when I started talking, I felt as if I were in a hole, digging myself in deeper and deeper. But then at some point Carl suggested that we change the position of the chairs, to make our roles more equal. It sounds like a small point, but it was like a bolt of lightning. My marriage to a classic medical-model person had always made me feel I couldn't ask the right questions. But under the guidance of Carl Rogers I felt a tremendous release—I recognized that I could solve my own problems. From then on, a sturdy inner self has continued to grow." Eva Tanner's epiphany illuminates the most valuable lesson the protégée can learn from her mentor—the confidence in her own ability to ask the right questions, to solve her own problems, to shape her own future.

Having the confidence to leave her mentor without acrimony is a protégée's highest compliment to the effectiveness of their relationship. "A woman should go into a relationship with a mentor with the idea that it is temporary," suggests Nancy Collins after researching several hundred mentor-protégée relationships for her study. "Many women realize, looking back on it, that they kept things going longer than they should have. I think a woman should stay with a mentor as long as he is giving her career upward mobility. At some point, if that peaks out, if she has learned as much as she can from a particular person, she needs to end the relationship and find someone else or move on." Exploring the psychological dynamics of such a leave-taking, Gail Sheehy observed in *Passages*, "Sooner or later every apprentice must refute the absolute power of the mentor if he (or she) is to emerge as owner of his own authority."[18]

Parting from the mentor almost invariably involves a complex process of turning inward, of reclaiming the inner authority that the mentor—that external authority—has helped the apprentice generate or unearth. Like the voice of the parent that the child internalizes for guidance as she grows to adulthood, the voice of the mentor is also incorporated by the protégée to assist her as she makes her way in the working world on her own. The relationship with the mentor, explains Daniel Levinson, "enables the recipient to identify with a person who exemplifies many of the qualities he [or she] seeks. It enables him to form an internal figure who offers love, admiration and encouragement in his struggles."[19]

In her introspective essay "Birth of the Amateur," Pamela Daniels traces the development of her authority as a writer, teacher, and psychologist by exploring the shifts in her inner world precipitated by her relationship with her mentor, Erik Erikson. Her childhood pose was the classic Dutiful Daughter: A firstborn, she was "bright and unquestioning, a very good girl. To please my father (and over the years, the gifted and encouraging teachers . . . who were like him) was purpose enough."[20] Her father's authority in her inner world was pervasive. She describes it as the "lifelong primacy in my inner world of the figure of the 'good father' bestowing benevolent praise and wishing me well—indeed, the best."[21] When Pamela was two and a half, the birth of her brother diverted some of her father's attentions from her to the baby. So Pamela re-created the parental voice—its "standards and expectations"—in the form of an imaginary companion, a "sober little boy of about four." Just learning to talk, she dubbed him not "judge" but "Gudge." She internalized Gudge as her constant inner critic: "He was my secret mentor. He set the pace, called the shots, knew right from wrong, took me across the street, kept me a prudent distance from that baby brother. Whatever Gudge told me to do, I did."[22]

Her intellectual apprenticeship as a student and graduate student was calculated to appease these inner voices of parental authority. Her father dreamed she would become a foreign service officer, so she majored in political science. She became, she realized now, "an involuntary participant in my own career development . . . as I moved up, grade by grade, achievement by achievement, no one consulted me, least of all me."[23] But after many years of this knee-jerk dutifulness, married, pregnant with her first child, and just about to begin her Ph.D. thesis, she balked. Years of work and study undertaken to please others had finally taken their toll. The need to discover what she herself *loved* had become mandatory. She defined it as the need to become "an amateur—*one who loves:* herself, others, her work."[24]

Meeting Erik Erikson at this time of internal upheaval proved decisive for both her professional and personal growth. For more than seven years she taught sections of Erikson's Human Life Cycle course at Harvard, assisted in the historical research that became *Gandhi's Truth*, and edited some of his other writings. During this time he functioned as her mentor both in her work life and in her increasingly complex inner journey. "Part teacher, part father figure, part collaborator, part friend," she called him, "both more and less than a professional mentor," and summarized his contribution to her career this way:

> First, my unorthodox apprenticeship in clinical thinking and psychobiographic method converted my intellectual interests from political history to life history. Second, working as his editorial collaborator, I developed skill, experience, and a reputation as a good editor who knew the literature of developmental psychology. . . . Third, the years of section work in the Human Life Cycle created close ties with an entire generation of students, some of whom, now thirty years old, have become my "sample" in a longitudinal field study of adult lives.[25]

But Erikson's most profound contribution, she acknowledges, was not his assistance in the professional sphere, but rather in the intrapsychic one. "I didn't need a career mentor," she explains, "so much as authoritative permission to step back from a premature professional commitment and take some affirmative action on the inner ground of my own psyche."[26] Like the most empowering therapeutic relationship, her relationship with her mentor allowed her first to regress under the beneficent guidance of his authority and then to burrow into her own inner world and retrieve her own authority:

> My intense positive transference to Erikson "worked" without conventional psychoanalytic intervention on his part; the dutiful daughter identity was perfected and played out. It may seem improbable that I would outgrow the dependency—the "clinch" —of daughterhood in a relationship that so intensified it; how-

ever, when transference works, it works that way. Moreover, Erikson took me seriously in adult roles; he engaged me as a co-worker, admired me as a mother, eventually became my friend. Matter-of-factly trusting that I could become someone new, he did not intrude on that process, but provided me with a "margin of freedom" to look inward—if *I* chose to do so.[27]

For Pamela Daniels the process of finding her own authority, of becoming "someone new" meant a subtle and intricate inner realignment. Her relationship with Erikson allowed her to confront the voice of male authority at both its most intense and its most benevolent. Gradually she redefined her professional focus, allowing herself the leeway to "become the amateur" and do what she loved rather than what she ought. Her attention became absorbed by the study of life history. She dropped the thesis in political science that seemed to have outgrown its usefulness—along with the self driven to please her father's wishes and Gudge's commands.

Gradually she found herself diverging from her mentor, and this also meant diverging from the voice of male authority and turning deeper inward to listen to and begin to reclaim another voice, a feminine voice. "For almost thirty years, my convictions about what counted, and who, had depended on men," she realized. "I knew I was my father's daughter."[28] But now, at last, she began to see how she was her mother's daughter as well. And though her mother had died suddenly three years before her daughter became a mother herself, Daniels explored the relationship in memory—its ambivalences and contradictions, its distance and desires. Slowly she allowed herself to acknowledge her identification with her mother and with her own sex. "I finally cut through a lifetime of male orientation and dependence," she concluded, "and for the first time identified wholeheartedly with my sex."[29]

And during this inner transformation, not surprisingly, her Gudge—her childhood companion, her inner critic, her "secret mentor"—was transformed as well. In the language of her dreams, she began to see Gudge as more playful, more humanized, indeed, more feminine. The coercive voice of male authority that for too long had ordered her "inner household" was at first replaced by a kindly voice, but still one of male authority, and at last replaced by an encouraging, enabling female voice. Her "secret mentor" had become her own fullest self.

CONCLUSION:
THE MEN IN OUR INNER
LIVES

IN THE MOST VIVID DREAM I'VE EVER HAD ABOUT MY FATHER, he was in a room with absolutely every other man I had ever known in my life—including my sons. Each of them had come to see me, but found that they so very much enjoyed one another's company that they became a group that excluded me—and left. I was not able to follow; my mother was with me, but totally oblivious to any of the action—her back was turned.

Marianne, *fifty-one*

As often happened in reality, in this dream—the most vivid I've had about my father—he was driving me to the store. He stayed in the car when we got there, and I went in to buy bread. After dealing with poor service, getting ready to walk out without paying, because the clerk, a young guy, wouldn't come out of the back room to be paid, I returned to the car to find my friend Ellen waiting behind the wheel. We women went to a play park to collect our little children and drove with them to my house for lunch—as also often happened in reality. I think this dream means that my father drove me, carried me where I wanted to go, and became my friend.

Barbara, *thirty-one*

Listening to our dreams helps us explore the way that the men in our lives can lead us back to ourselves. For in our dreams, in our fantasies, in the idle wanderings of our imaginations, we find the images and imprints of the men we have lived with and loved, the men we have feared and avoided, the men we have worshipped and revered, the men who turn out to be everything—or nothing—like us. In the language of our dreams we hear and translate the messages of our fathers, transform the authority that they wield for us, the wisdom that they offer, and begin to make that wisdom our own. In our memories and musings we play with our images of our brothers, our imaginary twins and comrades, and the characters we imagine we might have been had we been born the opposite sex. In our fantasies we see our phantom lovers, those knights on prancing steeds, those ideal creatures whom we eventually assimilate with our real friends and lovers and husbands, but who, meanwhile, teach us what we wish to achieve for ourselves. And in our deepest wishes, our most profound prayers, we seek the guidance of our mentors, our spiritual leaders and, ultimately, listen for that awesome voice that connects us with something grander than ourselves.

These images of fathers and brothers, husbands and lovers, mentors and leaders reflect the men we have actually known and observed in our lives. But taken together these images add up to more than the sum of the particulars to create a universal picture of what each of us means by maleness. Jung calls this inner image of maleness the "animus" and sees it as every woman's necessary and intrinsic complement, just as the "anima"—or female principle—is every man's counterpart. For Jung the animus is at once specific and collective. It is both the totality of all the men in a given woman's life and greater than that totality, connecting her—through the deepest channels of dreams and fantasies—to the male archetype in society, culture, and religion. In his essay "The Significance of the Father in the Destiny of the Individual," Jung explains how the shaping of the woman's animus is influenced by her relationship to her father but also by archetypal notions of masculinity that predate their particular relationship:

> . . . the child possesses an inherited system that anticipates the existence of parents and their influence upon [her]. In other words, behind the father stands the archetype of the father, and in this pre-existent archetype lies the secret of the father's power, just as the power which forces the bird to migrate is not produced by the bird itself but derives from its ancestors.[1]

Besides the archetypal nature of the animus, Jung also emphasizes its composite nature. "The animus does not appear as a person, but as a plurality of persons,"[2] he observes and adds,

> Whereas the man has, floating before him, in clear outlines, the alluring form of a Circe or Calypso, the animus is better expressed as a bevy of Flying Dutchmen or unknown wanderers from over the sea, never quite clearly grasped, protean, given to persistent and violent motion. These personifications appear especially in dreams, though in concrete reality they can be famous tenors, boxing champions, or great men in far-away, unknown cities.[3]

In her own essay "Animus and Anima," Jung's wife, Emma Jung, further elaborates on these inner personifications that comprise the animus:

> In dreams or phantasies, the animus appears chiefly in the figure of a real man: as father, lover, brother, teacher, judge, sage; as sorcerer, artist, philosopher, scholar, builder, monk . . . or as a trader, aviator, chauffeur and so forth; in short, as a man distinguished in some way by mental capacities or other masculine qualities. In a positive sense, he can be a benevolent father, a fascinating lover, an understanding friend, a superior guide; or on the other hand, he can be a violent and ruthless tyrant, a cruel task-master, moralist and censor, a seducer and exploiter, and often, also, a pseudo-hero who fascinates by a mixture of intellectual brilliance and moral irresponsibility. Sometimes he is represented by a boy, a son or young friend, especially when the woman's own masculine component is thus indicated as being in a state of becoming.[4]

The animus can make its appearance in both negative and positive guises. On the one hand it can appear as a court of "condemnatory judges" whose pronouncements turn out to be the undigested lessons of our fathers, culled unconsciously from childhood. As Jung describes, they are "compressed into a canon of average truth, justice, and reasonableness, a compendium of preconceptions which, whenever a conscious and competent judgment is lacking . . . instantly obliges with an opinion."[5] "The technique of coming to terms with the animus," Jung suggests, involves a woman's learning "to criticize and hold her opinions at a distance; not in order to repress them, but, by investigating their origins, to penetrate more deeply into the background, where she will then discover the primordial images. . . ."[6] But in addition to its manifestation as a compendium of conventional opinions, the animus also has a positive aspect whose integration expands our vision and possibilities. As Jung explains:

Through the figure of the father, [the animus] expresses not only conventional opinions but—equally—what we call "spirit," philosophical or religious ideas in particular, or rather, the attitude resulting from them. Thus the animus is a psychopomp, a mediator between the conscious and the unconscious and a personification of the latter . . . the animus gives to woman's consciousness a capacity for reflection, deliberation, and self-knowledge.[7]

Keeping in mind Jung's description of the animus—its archetypal and collective nature, its positive and negative guises —I want to conclude by moving from the men in our outer lives to the men in our inner lives, from the bonds with fathers and brothers, the romances with lovers and husbands, the connections with mentors and spiritual guides to the deepest exploration of the self. I want to consider the dreams and fantasies, the memories and projections that transform our relationships with men into our inner vision of maleness. One by one I want to examine the imprint of father and brother, lover and mentor on the psyche, because only by acknowledging and coming to terms with these inner men in our lives will we know ourselves fully as women.

The first and most profound influence on our inner image of maleness is, of course, our father. Inside and outside the home he is a figure of authority, providing an alternative to our intimacy with mother, beckoning us to the thrills and perils of the outside world. He is our point of male reference, our bastion, at his best our shelter. And he comes to represent for us the rules and values, opinions and pronouncements of the outside world. The kind of father he is determines in part our inner definition of his power and our relationship to it. Our dreams and our fantasies will reflect the way we incorporate this paternal power, this male power. If he is a Patriarch, our dreams may show how we fear his power; if a Pal, how we befriend it; if a Bystander, how we struggle to define it; if a Charmer, how we court it; and if he is Absent, how we ambivalently search out his power in our dreams as in our lives.

The twenty-nine-year-old daughter of a Pal father whom she describes as "diligent, emotional, energetic, caring, a short and overweight version of Zero Mostel," dreams, for example, of her father as "a cross between Ready Kilowatt and the Harry Hood dairy character—a small, puppetlike figure bringing cheer and possessing great amounts of energy." For this woman, father's power combines the energy of Ready Kilowatt and the nourishment of the Harry Hood dairy character. *Small and puppetlike,* he appears, in her psyche, to be the same size as her childself; a pal in life, he is also a cheery, ebullient companion in her inner world.

For the thirty-eight-year-old daughter of an Absent Father who was also an alcoholic given to belligerent attacks when drunk, the image expressed in her dreams reflects a more precarious and menacing internal relationship to paternal power. "During the Vietnam War in the mid-sixties," she remembers, "I had a horrible dream about my father that has stayed with me since. I dreamed that my father was really Robert McNamara (in fact, they are not dissimilar—they share the same kind of hairline and hair type), and I was facing him and he opened his mouth and a rat jumped out and at me, viciously, aggressively in attack." In the transformation of the dream language, her father becomes Robert McNamara; the power broker of her private world becomes the power mongerer of the public world. Like McNamara, the secretary of defense in the mid-sixties linked with the policy of attacking Vietnam—the smaller and more powerless country—her father should have been her "secretary of defense," but instead turned on her—smaller and more powerless as well—in vicious, drunken attacks. Both attracted to him—*I was facing him* —and repelled by him—*he opened his mouth and a rat jumped out*— she yearned for him in his absence and felt especially betrayed that when he did appear, he was a drunken, abusive *rat.* She both craved the imagined security of paternal power and yet feared she would be devastated by it.

A thirty-year-old artist, daughter of a hard-driving Patriarch who was also "a loving and giving person who did his best to keep it hidden," shares another dream that is a kind of parable about creativity and its relation to male power:

My dad is inventing film with sound. He's working with a film of Harry Truman giving a speech. The sound, before being incorporated into the film, is in liquid form. He is working in a laboratory next to a gymnasium (in the back of our house). I am working with him. The sound for his film is in a bucket on the other side of the gym, and he asks me to go get it. As I walk across the gym, a little bit of the liquid in the bucket spills out. "Look what you did!" he roars. "You just spilled out 'Hail to the Chief'! I'll have to cut that part out of the film!" I stand back in horror, seeing what I have done.

In this dream the dreamer sees her father as the very creator of what Jung would call Logos, the masculine word. For he is *inventing film with sound,* and the sound is the voice of presidential power, albeit the folksy wisdom of Harry Truman rather than the belligerent saber-rattling of Robert McNamara. His daughter is working alongside him, his helpmate and assistant, for indeed, the feminine is an essential part of this creative task. But when she tries to carry the sound, the masculine narration, over to her father, she spills a bit of it. And what does she spill but "Hail to the Chief"—that paean of praise to the president. Inadvertently—but perhaps with a subtler sensitivity to her own needs—she has dumped "Hail to the Chief," and with it her own posture of obeisance to male power. Although she *stand*[s] *back in horror seeing what* [she] *has done,* she may nevertheless have broken through to another, more balanced kind of creativity, drawing on male energy or male resources but not beholden to them.

The father appears in this dream in a familiar guise—the inner critic, "The Watcher at the Gates," as the German poet

Schiller referred to him. The dream describes the Watcher's vehemence—*"Look what you did!" he roars*—and the daughter's horrified response. But the dream also suggests that resisting the Watcher—spilling out "Hail to the Chief" even while incurring wrath—can lead toward increased autonomy, confidence, and creativity.

The voice of the inner critic is fundamental to the animus, as Emma Jung describes:

> The most characteristic manifestation of the animus . . . comes to us as a voice commenting on every situation in which we find ourselves, or imparting generally applicable rules of behavior . . . this voice expresses itself chiefly in two ways. First, we hear from it a critical, usually negative comment on every movement, an exact examination of all motives and intentions, which naturally always causes feelings of inferiority, and tends to nip in the bud all initiative and every wish for self-expression. From time to time, this same voice may also dispense exaggerated praise, and the result of these extremes of judgment is that one oscillates to and fro between the consciousness of complete futility and a blown-up sense of one's own value and importance.[8]

The inner critic serves as a psychic restraint system that has an uncanny knack for appearing at the very moment we are ready to take a leap forward, as this dream of a thirty-five-year-old woman at a transitional time in her life illustrates:

> I'm attending a seminar on personal growth, and enjoying myself. My father comes up when I'm looking at myself in the mirror. I begin to doubt myself. He criticizes my appearance, and I realize I could get very deflated, depressed, and accept his view of me. It is an easy, habitual thing to do. In the dream it's clear that he isn't going to agree with my definition of success. I look dirty after he has criticized me.

Just at the moment she is enjoying her personal growth, her critic appears to undermine her, challenge her, and criticize her. Although he appears as her father in this dream, he is also part of the reflection in the mirror whom she notices only as she stares at herself. The imagery suggests how the inner critic can be both external and internal. He can be both the sum of the critical male voices of the past—father and grandfather, brother and teacher—and also the voice we have taken to heart and entwined with our own. Although the critic's doubts infect her—*I begin to doubt myself*—she also begins to separate herself from the critic and from his negative, undermining point of view. *I could . . . accept his view of me,* she thinks, as that is the *easy, habitual thing to do.* She also realizes that *he isn't going to agree with my definition of success.* And though the dream ends before the pivotal act of resistance or separation has been accomplished, the dream implies that such a step might well be possible. Turning from the mirror and facing him down, she need not accept the critic's depressing view of her; she can create her own definition of success and continue with her own personal growth. In this way, Jung also felt, dreams can augur and influence the future by opening up the dreamer to possibilities she was not consciously aware of.

In her spirited essay "The Watcher at the Gates," novelist Gail Godwin speculates on the effect of the inner critic on creative work. Calling him "a restraining critic who lived inside me and sapped the juice from green inspirations," she admits that he—and other writers' Watchers—"seemed passionately dedicated to one goal: rejecting too soon and discriminating too severely."[9] She details the "lengths a Watcher will go to keep you from pursuing the flow of your imagination":

> Watchers are notorious pencil-sharpeners, ribbon changers, plant waterers, home repairers and abhorrers of messy rooms or messy pages. They are compulsive looker-uppers. They are superstitious scaredy-cats. They cultivate self-important eccentricities they think are suitable for "writers." And they'd rather die (and kill your inspiration with them) than risk making a fool of themselves.[10]

But having pinned down the insidious qualities of the Watcher, she begins to consider how to confront him, how, even, to capitalize on his critical energy and use it to enhance rather than inhibit creative work:

> Get to know your Watcher. He's yours. Do a drawing of him (or her). Pin it to the wall of your study and turn it gently to the wall when necessary. Let your Watcher feel needed. Watchers are excellent critics after inspiration has been captured; they are dependable, sharp-eyed readers of things already set down. Keep your Watcher in shape and he'll have less time to keep you from shaping.[11]

In a chapter in *Knowing Woman* called "The Animus— Friend or Foe?" Jungian analyst Irene Claremont de Castillejo elaborates on the process of turning the inner critic's carping into something constructive. First she sketches the destructive side of the Watcher, the "animus that is woman's worst bugbear":

> He is the one who tells her she is no good. This voice is particularly dangerous because it only speaks to the woman herself and she is so cast down by it that, as likely as not, she dare not tell anyone about it and ask for help.[12]

But then, like Gail Godwin with her "Watcher at the Gates," Castillejo explains how facing the inner critic can also lead toward facing the strongest, most capable part of the self:

> . . . even this little wretch can also become an asset if only one will face him and say, "Why do you tell me I'm no good, when in fact I have done so and so and achieved such and such, have lived through this and that crisis without wavering?" Gradually one amasses one's good qualities and one's achievements until his "You're no good" looks silly. In other words this poisonous little voice forces one in sheer self-defence to be conscious of who one really is. His poison, like many another poison, brings healing.[13]

As this inner figure is turned from friend to foe, the voice of paternal power and domination is also quieted, and greater independence and growth becomes possible.

If the inner father is the voice of authority, the inner brother is the fantasy of the twin, the equal, the male counterpart to ourselves. He is the path not taken, the complementary course, the self we could have been had we been born a boy. In the poem "Natural Resources," Adrienne Rich invokes "the phantom of the man-who-would-understand," the fantasy of the "lost brother" or "twin" who is part kin and companion and part myth. In her book *On Loving men,* Jane Lazarre explores this "comrade/twin," this seductive alter ego, and "begin[s] to see the promise of his existence in several of the men [she] know[s]" as well as in several literary prototypes:

> I use my friend Judith's brother, Billy. He has always been judged slightly wild by his family, called irresponsible. And in fact, he has been trekking around the world for years, seeking adventure after adventure, playing his guitar, writing novels. . . . To the outline of Billy's face in my mind, I begin to add well-known brothers I've read about: Charlotte Brontë's brother (she wrote her great works of fiction upon his dead body which, like any cannibal, she devoured). I add George Eliot's brother (she repaid his faithlessness and desertion with an abstract devotion made possible only when she actually abandoned him, so that, loving him from afar, she was able to use her energy to become an artist).

To her daytime obsessions, Lazarre adds the images of her dreams, until this fantasy emerges that is so lifelike it is almost warm to the touch:

> He is dark-skinned, like me. But his hair is fair or gray, like my father's. He has a full mustache as my father did in his youth. He is solidly built and wears a crumpled white shirt

tucked carelessly into his worn brown pants. . . . In one dream, he is a fellow student who has found the scholarly texts I have been looking for. We rummage through the index together. (He is wearing a blue lumberjack hat.) In the next dream he is my doctor. I am stricken with a rare virus, the chief symptom of which is that I can in no way communicate with the outside world. My body is paralyzed, my speech garbled because of the strange brain fever. . . . He bends down over my terrified face and swears to devote his life to finding a cure for my virus. The thought goes through my mind that without this man I would be lost forever.[14]

Part family, part fantasy, this "lost brother" is enough like us to share and integrate our past—"dark-skinned like me" with "hair . . . like my father's" yet enough unlike us to make us complete—"without this man I would be lost forever." He is our equal, yet coupled with him, we become greater than ourselves. He is that part of ourselves who dares what we are afraid to dare, expresses what we yearn to express—the madcap fool if we are restrained and controlled, the wild adventurer if we are convention-bound. "I have dreamt of a fantasy brother several times," says a managerial woman at forty. "Generally we are escaping together. We are running to get out of a building and especially running over rooftops of tenement-type buildings." The magic powers of her fantasy comrade allow her to escape the humdrum constraints of her day-to-day existence. Unable to make that leap on her own, she sees herself energized and empowered by the imagined aid of a counterpart who is everything like her, with the additional voltage of being male.

A woman in her late forties, whose relationship with a brother some fifteen years younger is tangled with ambivalence, imagines nevertheless a relationship with a fantasy brother full of delightful harmony and good fellowship:

My imaginary brother is tall and slender, has blond, wavy hair and a cheery smile. He is tan and outgoing and knows how to do things. He takes me places and we laugh a lot, explore hills and woods, and he teaches me about animals and birds and geology and machinery and never forgets to lend an appreciative hand when I prepare a meal. Of course he is a country enthusiast but also a city friend with a sophisticated circle of friends who include me. I have trouble seeing myself as a boy, but truthfully would like to know many things and have both country wisdom and city sophistication. I don't see this brother as an opposite—a male-macho-distant type. I see him as a friend. The other is unthinkable.

Whatever anger or envy, frustration or resentment she may feel toward her actual brother is replaced in her fantasy by pleasure, contentment, and love. For her imaginary brother gives her access to parts of herself that otherwise remain dormant. He is an intermediary between the world of the home and the family and the world of "animals and birds and geology and machinery" beyond. Also he mediates between the simplicities of the country and the sophistications of the city. In fantasy he eases and accelerates her process of integration so that she sees him not as an "opposite" but as a partner and friend.

The fantasy of a secret brother, a male alter ego, often begins in earliest childhood and is shaped by childish wishes and yearnings. A thirty-three-year-old actress who was an only child peopled her inner world with male and female imaginary companions who stood in for the brother and sister she never had. "I always wondered intensely what it would be like to have a sister or brother," she remembers. "When I was five, I had an imaginary friend named Eleanor who had a cousin named Jim Pooplepom. He was sort of like an older brother to me. He was nineteen—to my five—and was quite suave and capable. He knew how to handle things, which Eleanor and I didn't. He dressed nicely, looked a bit like

Christopher Reeve. And of course he loved me, though in a very chaste way. But he disappointed me greatly by growing up to become a minister. I also lost him to another woman and he eventually married her."

This ingenuous girlhood fantasy conjures up the lost brother at his most seductive and unattainable. He is older, suave, capable, and skilled in the ways of the world—a veritable Superman à la Christopher Reeve. But their love affair is chaste, unconsummated, a devotion more reminiscent of father and daughter than of amorous lovers. And indeed she loses him to another woman, just as her father, too, is claimed by someone else. Finally he has that significant spiritual quality—he does become a minister. He, too, serves as an intermediary between the known world of childhood and the world of adulthood ahead, between familiar, daily life and wider spiritual reality beyond.

If the fantasy of the brother can be seen as the masculine complement of the childhood self, then the fantasy of the ideal lover can be seen as the masculine complement of the adult self, and another powerful facet of what Jung considers the animus. But if the vision of the inner brother involves a chaste companionship, the fantasy of the ideal lover is an intensely sexual one, a deep longing for merger, for completion, for a pairing with everything we are not but yearn to be. This ideal too often leads us on the quest for the all-knowing and all-powerful Mr. Right, who repetitively turns out to be the undermining and disappointing Mr. Wrong.

Jungian analyst M. Esther Harding calls him the "Ghostly Lover," who lures his beloved away from reality and into a union with himself. She explains his dynamic pull on the psyche this way:

> . . the Ghostly Lover, in his psychological or subjective aspect, is a living reality to every woman. He holds his power and exerts

his lure because he is a psychological entity, part of that conglomerate of autonomous, or relatively autonomous factors which make up her psyche. As he is part of her so she is bound to him; she *must* find him if she is not to suffer the pain and distress of disintegration. For he is her soul mate, her "other half," the invisible companion who accompanies her throughout life.[15]

For many women the lure of the Ghostly Lover has enormous influence on the real-life search for a mate. Thinking that we have found his face and form and spirit in an actual lover may seem to hasten but may also obstruct our chances of finding harmony with the person we have really found. Sometimes the mistaken conviction we have found a "soul mate" blinds us to what is truly going on. A thirty-five-year-old woman remembers her first lover, a man she lived with for ten years, almost married time and again, but ultimately left: "I had a prescient dream about him about two months before we met. He was a true soul mate. We could talk of *anything,* and it was clear as water between us."

Clear as water between us: The image suggests a calm, quiet pool that can reflect back her own face as it gazes into his, as if into a mirror. And indeed the ideal lover often serves as a kind of mirror, and what we see as we stare at him, whether adoringly or angrily, are our own internal images of masculinity, our own issues and conundrums about maleness projected onto him. What we need for completion but do not feel we can provide for ourselves, we choose our lover to provide for us. What we wish to express yet fear to, we find our lover to voice for us. Power, fame, money, competition, ambition, adventure, strength—for centuries these have been the territories of men, and women have entered them only through their lovers. But even now, as social and cultural options change dramatically, our inner images accommodate more slowly. Often we find ourselves struggling to express what we once defined as only male, as we forge ahead in the ball park or boardroom or courtroom. Yet sometimes we find to our embarrassment that we also still need our lovers to express our deepest desires for us as well.

For one thirty-six-year-old woman within months of getting a hard-won Ph.D. in anthropology, the inner struggle has been around the issue of status in the world. Never married, but having worked on her own "since ninth grade" and supported herself for most of the years since, she defined herself as a professional, as "comma, project director," while never entirely trusting that she carried real weight in the world. For that she looked repeatedly, ambivalently—and unsuccessfully —to her lovers. But when, two months after she began her graduate program, she met her present lover, a carpenter, she felt this issue resonate forcibly enough to herald a change. "The fact that he was a carpenter was a real source of trouble at the beginning. It was a status thing. Was he bright enough? I wondered. But by projecting onto him the thing I needed —primarily status—and seeing that it was not there, I could finally come to grips with how *not* important it was. What's important is his really seeing me as a person and vice versa. And though sometimes I still yearn for a sugar daddy who will provide everything for me, I realize Dan does nurture me— just not in terms of money." For this woman the outer projections and the inner definitions of male and female have gradually begun to realign. What she needs from men and what she feels she can provide for herself have shifted and found another balance. The craving for status she fulfilled through men has considerably subsided. Nor could it be a coincidence that this change was timed with her own academic accomplishment, her own promise of achievement in the world on her own.

For a forty-year-old doctor the complicated inner issue explored in part by projecting it onto her husband is not status in the world but the willingness to adventure. Competent and confident in her career after eleven years of practice and the successful directorship of a training clinic, she realized, at thirty-nine, with two children almost grown, that she finally had the chance to risk the adventures in the world she thought she'd always dreamed of. Instead she found herself pregnant for the third time. A month before the baby is due, she reflects on her choice and on the psychic tug between her internal images of femaleness and maleness. "It turns out that I'm the original Great Base, the psychic base, the love base. Whatever that thing was I first gave to my father—I'm contactable without being dull. But I'd like to be the other—the adventurer. Mark, my husband, is very adventurous and courageous. I'm more timid. I'm not timid about my own head or body. But as far as moving in the world—no. I use men to do that. It's my project in life to do that. But I keep having babies. Will I ever take that crazy trip to Africa, be that hunter-adventurer? I did a big chunk of that in my early twenties, but I got disequilibrated.

"Mark, on the other hand, got up at four A.M. yesterday for a business trip, flew to New York, came back, and is off again today. He's high on the adventure. Whereas I would say, 'Oh no, will it be dark when I get up? Can I make it to the airport? Will I have enough energy for the conference?' Even though I've done it and can do it, I'd mouse along! The difference between Mark and me is that if he gets mad at me, he hikes in the Sierras for three days. Whereas I'd die of fright." Here she pauses to shift her amply pregnant frame. "But I *wouldn't* die of fright, that's the point." The point is that even with this third venture into motherhood, into the known maternal territory, her inner terrain is shifting. Her deepest perceptions of male and female are demanding redefinition, as her expectations of her mate begin to change and her confidence in herself increases.

Clear as water between us: The fantasy of the ideal lover who will simply reflect back our own masculine projections changes considerably as our inner definitions of male and female change. Many years and many lovers later, the woman whose dream foretold of the ideal mate with whom it would be "clear as water" describes another fantasy of an ideal lover. This time her fantasy reflects a corresponding shift in perceptions of herself and her world, a more mature if no less heartfelt desire for that man who will reflect—and share—not the clarity but the complexity of the world she has come to see:

He will be able to perceive not just how slippery reality is, but how poignant all of our attempts to pin it down are. And this with great imagination for other ways of being/ seeing, and with a corresponding respect for other ways of perceiving. I guess the point is that he be both intelligent (more than that) and good—the combination I still despair of finding. Able in the world. Who can be with me when I am dissolved in sadness without having, compulsively, to make it better. Sharing a humor based on affectionate acceptance of human frailty. Also occasionally fighting off the world with a club to win or protect me.

Intelligent as well as good, able in the world as well as a comforting nurturer, accepting of human frailty as well as willing to fight off the aggressions of the world—she imagines in her lover a kind of androgynous ideal who both reflects her own divided longings and begins to help her integrate them.

Again and again when asked to fantasize the ideal lover, the women I interviewed replied not with the macho knight on the prancing steed but rather with this androgynous figure·

I would want my ideal man to be secure about his own professional identity and to grant me freedom and support for my career endeavors. I'd also like someone who likes to cuddle and touch and be playful. I'd like a lot of personal autonomy and identity within a context of abiding and supporting love.

My ideal lover would be a man who was as willing to feel as to produce. He would be like the best women I've known

—strong, assertive, gentle, achievement-oriented but with a priority that was clearly one's relationships.

My ideal lover would be fairly skinny, Jewish, black hair, beard. Sensitive, caring, strong, vulnerable, sexy as hell, smart, funny, career important to him, responsive, exuberant. Good dancer. Bisexual.

The bisexuality of these fantasies of the ideal lover suggests the importance of access in our inner lives to both sides of our consciousness, both the productive and the playful, the assertive and the sensitive, both the side we have always defined as male as well as the side defined as female. What we yearn for in our lovers is the inner union we want to achieve for ourselves.

On the landscape of our inner lives, beyond the figure of father, brother, and lover, there stands the beckoning and inspiring figure of the inner spiritual guide. Like the figure of the inner father, he can provide paternal protection and counsel; like the brother, he can be a constant and ready comrade; like the lover, he can offer us devotion and a sense of completion. By listening to him in dreams or prayers or meditations, we allow him to help us unify and integrate the other parts of our psyche. He both enables us to discover our own highest self and also connects us to something larger and more transcendent than ourselves.

The inner guide is the torchbearer, the mediator, the voice who beckons us to the path we may already be on without being aware of it. Irene Claremont de Castillejo sees his gift as a kind of penetrating and illuminating light:

I personally like to think of my helpful animus as a torch-bearer: the figure of a man holding aloft his torch to light my way, throwing its beams into dark corners and penetrating the mists which shield the world of half-hidden mystery where, as a woman, I am so very much at home.

In a woman's world of shadows and cosmic truths he makes a pool of light as a focus for her eyes, and as she looks she may say, "Ah yes, that's what I mean," or "Oh no, that's not my truth at all." It is with the help of this torch also that she learns to give form to her ideas. He throws light on the jumble of words hovering beneath the surface of her mind so that she can choose the ones she wants, separates light into the colours of the rainbow for her selection, enables her to see the parts of which her whole is made, to discriminate between this and that. In a word, he enables her to focus.[16]

His gift is to help her bring to light what indeed she already knows without knowing that she knows it.

Just as the mentor in our professional lives may take the guise of father, lover, or friend, so, too, the inner mentor may appear in many guises. For one woman he appears in a dream as a deep-sea diver, clad in a wetsuit, ready to help her make the plunge, to take her down to deeper levels of consciousness and understanding. For another woman he appears in a dream as a professor of geography accompanying her on a journey across a vast desert—the inner terrain of her own geography—urging her onward, pointing out the contours of the land. For still another woman he appears in a fantasy and looks "like my father, but skinnier and dressed easier. His advice is 'Pay attention to what's going on' and 'Follow your own path—don't get pulled to someone else's.'"

The most classic vision of the inner guide is the all-knowing and benevolent wise old man whom we also conceptualize as God. Even the most enlightened feminist may be surprised to find the tenacity of this inner patriarchal image, which may yet be transformed but seems meanwhile to be lodged deeper in the psyche than politics:

He's old in a white robe, long white beard (of course). He's immensely powerful, accepting, loving, calm. It's wonderful to be with him. He mainly tells me to trust him. He knows what's best and will take care of me and make everything all right. I can surrender to him. He tells me to be joyful and spontaneous like a child and, like a child, not to worry when I'm sad or mad, but let those feelings get over with and go away.

For a forty-one-year-old nun who had entered the convent at twenty-one, the image of Jesus as lover rather than God the Father was the figure who sustained her inner life and focused her sense of commitment. The daughter of a businesswoman and a mostly Absent Father who left the family when she was nine, Christine thought about entering religious life in high school when she became close to a calm and steady priest who was something of a father figure. "But my real interest came from being alone at night and beginning to rely on the Lord. I began to develop a sense of independence in terms of my religious practice. My family was not very religious. My religious practice came out of wanting to cope on my own."

Although she "dated a lot" in high school and was at one point "practically engaged," the relationship that remained the most powerful and engrossing was the inner relationship with Jesus, her charismatic spiritual guide. "I've always been oriented toward Christ," she explains, "beginning with my name, which derives from his. He had to be my lover when I made the decision to enter the convent. By lover, I mean I see him as present, available, a listener, one who is able to break through that aloneness. He is someone to whom I'm deeply attracted. The difficulty is that he's not tangible enough." For Christine the inner relationship with Jesus both healed the deprivations of early family life and distanced her from them. Autonomy from her old ties as well as devotion to a new tie were made possible by her inner spiritual relationship. But having projected her earliest yearnings for care and security onto the figure of Jesus, she also experiences periodically the frustration that he isn't "tangible enough." Even as she struggles, with Jesus as guide, to transcend the limitations of her own needs and history and move to higher levels of spiritual life, still the shadow of earlier disappointments occasionally comes back to haunt her.

For a thirty-nine-year-old American swami—one of only several women in her order—who once achieved some notoriety as a feminist journalist, a ten-year relationship with a guru she called Baba assuaged her rage and healed the wounds of the past by turning her attention inward to her own highest self. Daughter of a verbal and aggressive journalist who trained her to be both intellectual and dependent, she reveled in his training for a time—married an older, more powerful man like her father—but finally turned away from that posture in disgust. "My own masochism derived from an almost worshipful respect for masculine power," she once wrote, and added in dismay about her younger self, "For a man who could act as my teacher I could be submissive and seductive. I *felt* submissive and seductive; my awe of the male mind translated easily into awe of the male person."

Ironically, it took the ultimate pose of apparent submissiveness—ten years of being a disciple to a powerful and elderly guru—to free her finally from this pose. For even as she cut her ties with the past and accompanied her guru all over the world, as she took faithful notes on his lectures and edited his books, the constant emphasis of his teaching was to turn her attention toward her inmost self. Through meditation she began to look for—and find—a self-awareness that made many of her former angers and difficulties "effortlessly" fall away. Meditation also began to connect her with a kind of cosmic energy more transcendent than anything she had known. "Meditation on the guru," her swami would teach, "is really meditation on the higher self."

Shortly before he died, he initiated her into the small order of swamis who take the vows of poverty and celibacy and dedicate their lives to spiritual teaching. Now, a year or so after her guru's death—"when he left his body" is how she prefers to think of it—she is the co-director of an American ashram. When she lectures to her disciples, she teaches that the "inner guru is the inner self." For this swami, the journey alongside the esteemed spiritual teacher became the journey back to the inner spiritual guide, that teacher who can never be lost because his guidance is our own deepest wisdom.

Integrating the voices of the animus—father's counsel, brother's playfulness, lover's companionship, mentor's spiritual wisdom—is the challenge of a lifetime. Becoming aware of how we project our inner images onto the men in our lives, then learning to release these projections and accept them as part of ourselves, is a complex and profound process that is often accomplished when we are least aware of it, in our dreams, our fantasies, the idle ramblings of our imaginations. Sometimes the lessons of our conscious lives are synthesized and revealed to us only in the imagery of the unconscious. The Jungian analyst M. Esther Harding recounts the case of a woman patient mournful after the demise of a love affair with a man she had hoped was Mr. Right, a man she believed captured all her masculine ideals. But instead of falling into a deep depression, she worked in analysis with the following fantasy, "hoping . . . to understand the significance of the frustration of her love":

Out of the woods into a sunny field I came. . . . I seemed to be in a shallow bowl held high to heaven. I was alone. . . .

Suddenly from the woods behind me galloped four horses, two black and two white. On them rode four knights in armor [which was encrusted with rubies and emeralds and sapphires and topaz].

The four horsemen galloped to the center of the field. They dismounted and, leaving their horses, paced off in opposite directions. . . . At a shout, brandishing their swords in the sunlight, they spurred their horses and dashed headlong to meet their opponents. I fell to the earth and covered my eyes. I heard the heavy impact of the horses' bodies . . . and got on my knees to pray. I must have fainted as I knelt. When I regained consciousness I opened my eyes and there before me in the center of the field was an altar. On it was a shallow bowl of silver studded with rubies and emeralds and sapphires and topaz, in which burned a clear flame which shot to heaven. I staggered to my feet and drew near to the altar, and fell on my knees and bowed my head in prayer. Suddenly I heard a voice. I looked up and there in the flame, poised as if for flight, was a magnificent eagle.[17]

In vivid, symbolic terms this fantasy describes the process by which the voices of the animus are released from projections outward and instead, accepted and integrated within. The fantasy begins in a bowl of the mountains, a kind of inner, contemplative space, an "earth-womb" where the woman has retreated for introspection. Here, in her inner domain, she sees the "heroes, the glorious personifications of the animus, come galloping." To Harding they represent the "four divisions of the microcosm no less than of the macrocosm." I would also see them as the four powerful male figures who preside in the psyche—the father, brother, lover, and mentor.

The clash of the knights represents both an awareness and an annihilation that are pivotal to the woman's inner transformation. "The woman has made many animus transferences before," Harding explains, "but this is the first time she has realized what she was doing *while she was doing it*. The annihilation of the unconscious figures in the conflict is the result of that realization."[18] After the knights clash, they disappear. The woman loses consciousness—for this kind of internal upheaval remains mysterious to the conscious mind. In place of the knights is an altar with a silver bowl, encrusted with the jewels the knights once wore. The jewels of wisdom, the gems of insight and advice that before ennobled the knights now bedeck and belong to the bowl of the woman's own psyche. The magnificent eagle, poised for flight, that appears from the flame in the bowl is a sign of the woman's renewed possibilities and capabilities, the renewed energy—both psychological and spiritual—that has been released and reclaimed as a vital and resourceful part of herself.

Finally, in rather more homely but no less resonant symbolic language, the two dreams that begin this chapter suggest two approaches to the challenge of integrating the male figures within. The first hints of the disappointment and loneliness of rejecting these figures; the second suggests the struggles as well as the riches of accepting them.

In the first dream the inner men appear as a conclave, the composite figure of the animus: Marianne's father and *absolutely every other man* [*she*] *had ever known in* [*her*] *life—including* [*her*] *sons.* Each of them comes to see her—that is, seeks recognition and acceptance—but finding that she does not offer that acknowledgment, they become a *group that excluded* [*her*]. *I was not able to follow,* she dreams, unable to respond to their needs or their teachings, so they leave her behind. Meanwhile her mother is with her, but *oblivious to any of the action.* Her mother is not able to help her with her process of integration, because her mother's *back was turned.* Perhaps a first step for Marianne will be to turn and face her mother and her deepest identification with her mother. Only from that firmer footing in her female identity can she begin to face and accept the inner figures who are male—the father, the sons, and all the men who have come between. In the inner world no less than in the outer world, the relationships with mother and father must be accommodated and balanced to enable the female and male sides of ourselves to come into balance as well.

In the second dream Barbara sees her father *driving* [*her*] *to the store.* He gives her guidance and support, but when they get to the store, he stays behind and lets her negotiate the task herself. The task is *to buy bread*—literal and spiritual nourishment for herself and her family. The transaction, as it turns out, is not an easy feat to accomplish. She must deal with *poor service, getting ready to walk out without paying because the clerk, a young guy, wouldn't come out of the back room.* The clerk—that masculine intermediary—is not obviously and readily accessible to her. Still, she completes the task as best she can. When she returns to the car, in place of her father, she finds [*her*] *friend Ellen waiting behind the wheel.* In order to balance the psyche, the imagery suggests, women must go through rough times, even suffering, to find their strength and individuate. But during those rough times the dreamer has incorporated her father's guidance and made him her friend. Now she can get *behind the wheel*—take charge of her own life—this time accompanied by her female counterpart—her friend Ellen—and *collect* [*her*] *little children and* [*drive them to*] *lunch.* Integrating the inner male—her father's voice this time—with her inner female and maternal side allows her to become a more complete and confident nurturer and protector herself.

This symbolic image of father and daughter driving together to the store recalls Virginia Woolf's meditation in *A Room of One's Own* on a young man and a young woman getting into a taxi on the street beneath her window and gliding off together as if "swept on by the current elsewhere." For Woolf this "ordinary" street sight, like the "ordinary"—and extraordinary—images of our dreams, comes to represent a parallel pairing in the psyche:

> . . . the sight of the two people getting into the taxi and the satisfaction it gave me made me also ask whether there are two sexes in the mind corresponding to the two sexes in the body, and whether they also require to be united in order to get complete satisfaction and happiness. And I went on amateurishly to sketch a plan of the soul so that in each of us two powers preside, one male, one female; and in the man's brain, the man predominates over the woman, and in the woman's brain, the woman predominates over the man. The normal and comfortable state of being is that when the two lives in harmony together, spiritually cooperating. If one is a man, still the woman part of the brain must have

effect; and a woman also must have intercourse with the man in her. Coleridge perhaps meant this when he said that a great mind is androgynous. It is when this fusion takes place that the mind is fully fertilised and uses all its faculties.[19]

Beyond the history with father, the companionship with brother, the intensity with lover, and the apprenticeship with mentor sit this man and this woman in our taxi. They are the man and the woman revealed to us in our dreams, our fantasies, our seemingly most casual musings. We may have met them first in the safety of our families, then deepened our understanding through our love affairs and our work. Now they are waiting to be introduced, be acquainted, be joined, even married, so that they can ride together and move on.

NOTES

INTRODUCTION

1. Simone de Beauvoir, *The Second Sex*, p. 268.
2. John Munder Ross, "The Forgotten Father," in *Psychosexual Imperatives: Their Impact On Identity Formation*, p. 282.
3. Carl Jung, "Anima and Animus," in *Two Essays on Analytical Psychology*, pp. 207 & 209.
4. Emma Jung, "Animus," pp. 5 & 13.

CHAPTER ONE: FATHER-DAUGHTER SINGLES/FATHER-DAUGHTER DOUBLES

1. Ernest Abelin, "The Role of the Father in the Separation-Individuation Process," in *Separation-Individuation*, p. 248.
2. Margaret Mahler in "Discussion of Greenacre's: Problems of Overidealization of the Analyst and of Analysis." Unpublished manuscript, abstracted in *Psychoanalytic Quarterly* 36:637, pp. 8–9, as quoted by Abelin, *op. cit.*, p. 232.
3. Lora Tessman, "A Note on the Father's Contribution to the Daughter's Ways of Loving and Working," in *Father and Child: Developmental and Clinical Perspectives*, Stanley Cath, Alan Gurwitt, John Munder Ross, eds., p. 224.
4. Nancy Chodorow, *The Reproduction of Mothering*, p. 129.

5. Richard A. Gardner, *Psychotherapy with Children of Divorce,* pp. 299–300.

6. Philip Spielman as quoted by Eleanor Galenson, "Psychology of Women: Late Adolescence and Early Adulthood," in *Journal of the American Psychoanalytic Association,* vol. 24, 1976, no. 3, p. 642.

7. Chodorow, *op. cit.,* p. 126.

8. Marjorie Leonard, "Fathers and Daughters: the Significance of 'Fathering' in the Psychosexual Development of the Girl," in *International Journal of Psycho-Analysis,* p. 329.

9. Anne Roiphe, "Daddy's Girls: Women Who Win," *Vogue,* October 1980, pp. 188–189.

10. Lily Pincus and Christopher Dare, *Secrets in the Family,* p. 70.

11. Galenson, *op. cit.,* p. 152.

12. Erik Erikson, *Childhood and Society,* p. 259.

13. *Ibid.,* p. 260.

14. Tessman, *op. cit.,* p. 232.

15. Fritz Redl as quoted by Marjorie Leonard, *op. cit.,* p. 330.

16. Samuel Ritvo as reported by Galenson, *op. cit.,* p. 637.

17. Alvin Winder, "Normal Adolescence: Psychological Factors," in *Adolescence: Contemporary Studies,* ed. Alvin Winder, p. 74.

18. Erikson, *op. cit.,* p. 262.

19. *Ibid.,* pp. 261–62.

20. Erik Erikson, *The Life Cycle Completed: A Review,* pp. 73–74.

21. Dr. Helen Tausend as reported by Galenson, *op. cit.,* p. 645.

22. Tessman, *op. cit.,* p. 238.

23. *Ibid.*

CHAPTER TWO: THE PATRIARCH

1. William James, in a letter to Margaret James, May 26, 1900, as quoted in *The Father: Letters to Sons and Daughters,* Evan Jones, ed. pp. 23–24.

2. Virginia Woolf, *To the Lighthouse,* pp. 10–11.

3. Virginia Woolf, *A Writer's Diary,* p. 135.

4. Study by the Foundation for Child Development, quoted by Letty Cottin Pogrebin in "Gazette News," *Ms.,* October 1979, p. 84.

5. Marjorie Leonard, "Fathers and Daughters: the Significance of 'Fathering' in the Psychosexual Development of the Girl' in *International Journal of Psycho-Analysis,* vol. 47, p. 330.

CHAPTER THREE: THE PAL

1. Helene Deutsch, *The Psychology of Women,* volume I, p. 201.
2. John Munder Ross, "The Forgotten Father," in *Psychosexual Imperatives: Their Impact on Identity Formation,* p. 282.
3. Marjorie Lozoff, "Fathers and Autonomy in Women," in *Women and Success: The Anatomy of Achievement,* ed. Ruth B. Kundsin, pp. 104–5.
4. Ravenna Helson, "Women Mathematicians and the Creative Personality," in *Journal of Consulting and Clinical Psychology,* vol. 36, no. 2, 1971, pp. 210–20.
5. Margaret Hennig and Anne Jardim, *The Managerial Woman,* p. 103.
6. *Ibid.,* pp. 103–4.
7. Margaret Mead, *Blackberry Winter,* pp. 35 & 44.
8. Shirley Chisholm, *Unbought and Unbossed,* p. 55.
9. Jane Fonda as quoted in "Daughters and Fathers" in *Ms.,* June 1979, p. 46.
10. Susan Cheever as quoted by Ben Cheever, "Growing Up Literary," *Savvy,* April 1980, pp. 75–76.
11. John Cheever, "My Daughter, the Novelist," *New York* magazine, April 7, 1980, p. 53.
12. Lily Pincus and Christopher Dare, *Secrets in the Family,* p. 32.

CHAPTER FOUR: THE BYSTANDER

1. Alice Hoffman, *The Drowning Season,* pp. 78–79.
2. Lillian Rubin, *Worlds of Pain,* p. 36.
3. *Ibid.,* p. 37.
4. Gail Godwin, *A Mother and Two Daughters,* pp. 440–41.
5. Shirley MacLaine, *Don't Fall Off the Mountain,* pp. 9–11.
6. *Ibid.*

CHAPTER FIVE: THE CHARMER

1. Sheila Ballantyne, *Imaginary Crimes,* pp. 9–10.
2. *Ibid.,* p. 264.
3. Anaïs Nin, *The Diary of Anaïs Nin: Volume One,* pp. 87–88.
4. Lora Heims Tessman and Irving Kaufman, "Variations on a Theme of Incest," in *Family Dynamics and Female Sexual Delinquency,* ed. Pollack and Friedman, p. 139.
5. "An Epidemic of Incest," *Newsweek,* November 30, 1981, p. 68.
6. Hank Giaretto as quoted by Mona Simpson in "Incest: Society's

Last and Strongest Taboo" in *California Living* magazine of *The San Francisco Examiner,* Oct. 4, 1981, p. 8.

7. Tessman and Kaufman, *op. cit.,* p. 139.
8. Lily Pincus and Christopher Dare, *Secrets in the Family,* p. 89.

CHAPTER SIX: THE ABSENT FATHER

1. Leon Yarrow, "Separation from Parents During Early Childhood," in *Review of Child Development Research,* Martin L. Hoffman and Lois Wladis Hoffman, eds., vol. 1, p. 123.
2. Peter Neubauer, "The One-Parent Child and His Oedipal Development," in *The Psychoanalytic Study of the Child,* vol. 15, pp. 304–5.
3. Ernest Abelin as quoted by Robert C. Prall, "The Role of the Father in the Preoedipal Years," in *The Journal of the American Psychoanalytic Association,* vol. 26, no. 1, 1978, p. 154.
4. Frances Hodgson Burnett, *A Little Princess,* p. 17.
5. *Ibid.,* p. 92.
6. Lora Heims Tessman, *Children of Parting Parents,* p. 472.
7. Tessman, "A Note on the Father's Contribution to the Daughter's Ways of Loving and Working," *Father and Child: Developmental and Clinical Perspectives,* Stanley Cath, Alan Gurwitt, John Munder Ross, eds., p. 232.
8. Tessman, *Children of Parting Parents,* p. 476.
9. *Ibid.,* p. 481.
10. *Ibid.*
11. *Ibid.*
12. Martha Wolfenstein, "Loss, Rage, and Repetition," in *The Psychoanalytic Study of the Child,* vol. 24, 1969, pp. 446–47.
13. *Ibid.,* p. 442.
14. *Ibid.,* p. 446.
15. *Ibid.,* p. 439.
16. *Ibid.,* p. 455.
17. *Ibid.*
18. Gail Sheehy, the "Hers" column in *The New York Times,* Feb. 7, 1980, p. C2.
19. *Ibid.*

CHAPTER SEVEN: MR. WRONG AND MR. RIGHT

1. Andrea Dworkin, "First Love," in *The Woman Who Lost Her Names: Selected Writings by American Jewish Women*, ed. Julia Wolf Mazow, p. 114.
2. *Ibid.*, p. 128.
3. *Ibid.*, pp. 128–29.
4. *Ibid.*, p. 130.
5. *Ibid.*, pp. 132–33.
6. Zora Neale Hurston, *Their Eyes Were Watching God*, pp. 111–13.
7. Anne Roiphe, "Daddy's Girls: Women Who Win," *Vogue*, October 1980, p. 191.
8. Erica Jong, "The Man Under the Bed," *Here Comes & Other Poems*, p. 60.
9. Alice Walker, "Never Offer Your Heart to Someone Who Eats Hearts," *Good Night Willie Lee, I'll See You in the Morning*, pp. 6–7.
10. Anne Sexton, "For My Lover, Returning to His Wife," *Love Poems*, p. 22.
11. "The Big Heart," © Jamie Bernstein and David Pack.

CHAPTER EIGHT: THE MENTOR

1. Georgia O'Keeffe in a letter to Anita Pollitzer, February 1, 1916, as quoted by Laurie Lisle, *Portrait of an Artist: A Biography of Georgia O'Keeffe*, pp. 80–81.
2. Daniel Levinson as quoted by Judith Thurman, in "Do You Need a Mentor?" *Mademoiselle*, August 1981, p. 191.
3. Daniel Levinson, *The Seasons of a Man's Life*, p. 99.
4. Margaret Mead, *Blackberry Winter*, p. 112.
5. *Ibid.*, p. 114.
6. *Ibid.*, p. 127.
7. *Ibid.*, p. 128.
8. *Ibid.*, p. 129.
9. Georgia O'Keeffe in the Introduction to *Georgia O'Keeffe: A Portrait by Alfred Stieglitz* (unpaginated).
10. Laurie Lisle, *Portrait of an Artist: A Biography of Georgia O'Keeffe*, p. 109.
11. O'Keefe in the Introduction to *Georgia O'Keeffe: A Portrait by Alfred Stieglitz* (unpaginated).
12. Laurie Lisle, *op. cit.*, p. 437.

13. Georgia O'Keeffe as quoted by Laurie Lisle, *op. cit.*, p. 136.
14. Laurie Lisle, *op. cit.*, pp. 127–28.
15. *Ibid.*, p. 189.
16. *Ibid.*, p. 272.
17. *Ibid.*
18. Gail Sheehy, *Passages*, p. 192.
19. Levinson, *op. cit.*, p. 334.
20. Pamela Daniels, "Birth of the Amateur," in *Working It Out*, Sara Ruddick and Pamela Daniels, eds., p. 57.
21. *Ibid.*, p. 59.
22. *Ibid.*, p. 57.
23. *Ibid.*, p. 58.
24. *Ibid.*, p. 65.
25. *Ibid.*, p. 61.
26. *Ibid.*
27. *Ibid.*, pp. 61–62.
28. *Ibid.*, p. 66.
29. *Ibid.*, p. 68.

CONCLUSION: THE MEN IN OUR INNER LIVES

1. Carl Jung, "The Significance of the Father in the Destiny of the Individual," in *The Collected Works of Carl Gustav Jung, Volume Four: Freud and Psychoanalysis*, p. 321.
2. Carl Jung, "Anima and Animus," in *Two Essays on Analytical Psychology*, p. 207.
3. *Ibid.*, p. 210.
4. Emma Jung, *Animus and Anima*, p. 29.
5. Carl Jung, "Anima and Animus," p. 207.
6. *Ibid.*, p. 209.
7. Carl Jung, "The Syzygy: Anima and Animus," in *Aion*, p. 16.
8. Emma Jung, *op. cit.*, p. 20.
9. Gail Godwin, "The Watcher at the Gates," in *The New York Times Sunday Book Review*, Jan. 9, 1977, Section 7, p. 31.
10. *Ibid.*
11. *Ibid.*
12. Irene Claremont de Castillejo, *Knowing Woman: A Feminine Psychology*, p. 88.
13. *Ibid.*
14. Jane Lazarre, *On Loving Men*, pp. 118–19.

15. M. Esther Harding, *The Way of All Women,* p. 38.
16. Castillejo, *op. cit.,* p. 76.
17. M. Esther Harding, *op. cit.,* pp. 64–65.
18. *Ibid.,* p. 66.
19. Virginia Woolf, *A Room of One's Own,* p. 102.

BIBLIOGRAPHY

Abelin, Ernest. "The Role of the Father in the Separation-Individuation Process," *Separation-Individuation: Essays in Honor of Margaret S. Mahler,* John B. McDevitt and Calvin F. Settlage, eds. New York: International Universities Press, Inc., 1971.

Altman, Sydney L., and Frances Kaplan Grossman. "Women's Career Plans and Maternal Employment." *Psychology of Women Quarterly,* Vol. 1 (4), Summer 1977.

Armstrong, Louise. *Kiss Daddy Goodnight: A Speak-Out on Incest.* New York: Pocket Books, 1979.

Artson, Barbara Friedman. "Mid-Life Women: Home-makers, Volunteers, Professionals." Berkeley: California School of Professional Psychology Doctoral Dissertation, 1978.

Ballantyne, Sheila. *Imaginary Crimes.* New York: The Viking Press, 1982.

Baruch, Grace K. "Girls Who Perceive Themselves as Competent: Some Antecedents and Correlates." *Psychology of Women Quarterly,* Vol. 1 (1), Fall 1976.

———. "Maternal Influences Upon College Women's Attitudes Toward Women and Work." *Developmental Psychology,* Vol. 6, No. 1, 1972

Bernstein, Leonard. *Findings.* New York: Simon and Schuster, 1982.

Blanck, Rubin, and Gertrude Blanck. *Marriage and Personal Development.* New York: Columbia University Press, 1968.

Block, Jack. *Lives Through Time.* Berkeley: Bancroft Press, 1971.

Brady, Katherine. *Father's Days: A True Story of Incest.* New York: Dell Publishing Co., Inc., 1979.

Brody, Sylvia, and Sidney Axelrod. *Mothers, Fathers and Children.* New York: International Universities Press, 1978.

Broverman, Inge K., et al. "Sex-Role Stereotypes: A Current Appraisal." *Journal of Social Issues,* Vol. 28, No. 2, 1972.

Burnett, Frances Hodgson. *A Little Princess.* New York: Dell Publishing Co., Inc., 1981.

Cheever, Ben. "Growing Up Literary." *Savvy,* April 1980.

Cheever, John. "My Daughter, the Novelist." *New York* magazine, April 7, 1980.

Chisholm, Shirley. *Unbought and Unbossed.* Boston: Houghton Mifflin, 1970.

Chodorow, Nancy. *The Reproduction of Mothering: Psychoanalysis and the Sociology of Gender.* Berkeley: University of California Press, 1978.

Collins, Nancy W. *Professional Women and their Mentors.* New Jersey: Prentice-Hall, 1983.

Daedalus: Journal of the American Academy of Arts and Sciences: "The Woman in America," Volume 93, No. 2, Spring, 1964. Cambridge: the American Academy of Arts and Sciences, 1964.

Daniels, Pamela. "Birth of the Amateur." *Working It Out: 23 Women Writers, Artists, Scientists, and Scholars Talk About Their Lives and Work,* Sara Ruddick and Pamela Daniels, eds. New York: Pantheon Books, 1977.

Dater, Judy and Jack Welpott. *Women and Other Visions.* New York: Morgan and Morgan, Inc., 1975.

"Daughters and Fathers," *Ms.,* June, 1979.

de Beauvoir, Simone. *The Second Sex.* New York: Bantam, 1970.

de Castillejo, Irene Claremont. *Knowing Woman: A Feminine Psychology.* New York: Harper & Row, 1974.

Deutsch, Helene. *The Psychology of Women: Volumes I and II.* New York: Grune and Stratton, Inc., 1944.

Dinnerstein, Dorothy. *The Mermaid and the Minotaur.* New York: Harper and Row, 1977.

Douvan, Elizabeth. "The Role of Models in Women's Professional Development." *Psychology of Women Quarterly,* Vol. 1 (1), Fall 1976.

Dworkin, Andrea. "First Love," *The Woman Who Lost Her Names: Selected Writings By American Jewish Women,* Julia Wolf Mazow, ed. San Francisco: Harper & Row, 1981.

Ekstein, Rudolf. "Daughters and Lovers: Reflections on the Life-Cycle of Daughter-Father Relationships," *Women's Sexual Development,* Martha Kirkpatrick, ed. New York: Plenum Press, 1980.

"An Epidemic of Incest," *Newsweek,* November 30, 1981.

Epstein, Cynthia Fuchs. *Women in Law.* New York: Basic Books, Inc., 1981.

Erikson, Erik H. *Childhood and Society.* New York: W. W. Norton & Company, 1963.

———. *Insight and Responsibility.* New York: W. W. Norton & Company, Inc., 1964.

———. *The Life Cycle Completed: A Review.* New York: W. W. Norton & Company, 1982.

Fraiberg, Selma. *The Magic Years.* New York: Charles Scribner's Sons, 1959.

Frank, Waldo, ed., et al. *Alfred Stieglitz.* New York: Doubleday, Doran and Company, Inc., 1934.

Freud, Sigmund. *The Basic Writings of Sigmund Freud,* A. A. Brill, ed. and trans. New York: Random House, 1938.

———. *Collected Papers, Volume Three: Case Histories,* James Stachey, ed. and trans. London: The Hogarth Press and the Institute of Psycho-Analysis, 1953.

———. *Collected Papers, Volume Twenty-Four: The Ego and the Id and Other Works,* James Strachey, ed. and trans. London: The Hogarth Press and the Institute of Psycho-Analysis, 1953.

Galenson, Eleanor. "Psychology of Women: Infancy and Early Childhood; Latency and Early Adolescence." *Journal of the American Psychoanalytic Association,* Vol. 24, No. 1, 1976.

———. "Psychology of Women: Late Adolescence and Early Adulthood." *Journal of the American Psychoanalytic Association,* Vol. 24, No. 3, 1976.

Gardner, Richard. *Psychotherapy With Children of Divorce.* New York: Jason Aronson, Inc., 1976.

Godwin, Gail. "The Watcher at the Gates," *The New York Times Sunday Book Review,* January 9, 1977, Section 7, p. 31.

Goldstine, Daniel, et al. *The Dance-Away Lover.* New York: William Morrow & Company, Inc., 1977.

Gottlieb, Annie. "Are You Getting What You Need From Your Father?" *Mademoiselle,* December 1980.

Grier, William, and Price Cobbs. *Black Rage.* New York: Basic Books, 1968.

Hall, Nor. *The Moon and the Virgin: Reflections on the Archetypal Feminine.* New York: Harper & Row, 1980.

Harding, M. Esther. *The Way of All Women.* New York: Harper & Row, 1975.

Helson, Ravenna. "Women Mathematicians and the Creative Process." *Journal of Consulting and Clinical Psychology*, Vol. 36, No. 2, 1971.

Hennig, Margaret, and Anne Jardim. *The Managerial Woman.* New York: Pocket Books, 1977.

Hetherington, E. Mavis. "Effects of Father Absence on Personality Development in Adolescent Daughters," *Developmental Psychology.* Richmond, Virginia: American Psychological Association, 1972.

Hoffman, Alice. *The Drowning Season.* New York: E. P. Dutton, 1979.

Horner, Matina. "Toward an Understanding of Achievement-Related Conflicts in Women." *Journal of Social Issues*, Vol. 28, No. 2, 1972.

―――― and Mary Walsh. "Psychological Barriers to Success in Women," *Women and Success: The Anatomy of Achievement,* Ruth B. Kundsin, ed. New York: William Morrow & Company, 1974.

Horney, Karen. *Feminine Psychology.* New York: W. W. Norton & Company, Inc., 1973.

Hurston, Zora Neale. *Their Eyes Were Watching God.* Urbana, Illinois: University of Illinois Press, 1978.

Jones, Evan, ed. *The Father: Letters to Sons and Daughters.* New York: Rinehart and Company, Inc., 1960.

Jong, Erica. *Here Comes and Other Poems.* New York: New American Library, 1975.

Jung, Carl. "Anima and Animus," *Two Essays on Analytical Psychology.* Princeton: Princeton University Press, 1970.

――――. "The Significance of the Father in the Destiny of the Individual," *The Collected Works of Carl Gustav Jung, Volume Four: Freud and Psychoanalysis.* New York: Pantheon Press, 1961.

――――. "The Syzygy: Anima and Animus," *The Collected Works of Carl Gustav Jung, Volume Nine: Aion.* Princeton: Princeton University Press, 1968.

Jung, Emma. *Animus and Anima.* Zurich: Spring Publications, 1974.

Klaich, Dolores. *Woman Plus Woman: Attitudes Toward Lesbianism.* New York: Simon and Schuster, Inc., 1974.

Kohen-Raz, Reuven. *The Child from 9 to 13: The Psychology of Preadolescence & Early Puberty.* Chicago: Aldine-Atherton, Inc., 1971.

Laiken, Deirdre S. *Daughters of Divorce: The Effects of Parental Divorce on Women's Lives.* New York: William Morrow & Company, Inc., 1981.

Lamb, Michael. "Paternal Influences and the Father's Role: A Personal Perspective." *American Psychologist*, Vol. 34, 1979.

――――, ed. *The Role of the Father in Child Development.* New York: John Wiley, 1976.

LaRussa, Georgina Williams. "Portia's Decision: Women's Motives for Studying Law and their Later Career Satisfaction as Attorneys." *Psychology of Women Quarterly,* Vol. 1 (4), Summer 1977.

Lazarre, Jane. *On Loving Men.* New York: The Dial Press, 1980.

Lederer, Wolfgang. *The Fear of Women.* New York: Harcourt Brace Jovanovich, Inc., 1968.

Leonard, Linda Schierse. *The Wounded Woman: Healing the Father-Daughter Relationship.* Athens, Ohio: Swallow Press, 1982.

Leonard, Marjorie. "Fathers and Daughters: the Significance of 'Fathering' in the Psychosexual Development of the Girl." *International Journal of Psycho-Analysis,* Vol. 47, 1966.

Levinson, Daniel. *The Seasons of a Man's Life.* New York: Alfred Knopf, 1978.

Lindgren, Henry Clay. *Educational Psychology in the Classroom.* New York: John Wiley and Sons, Inc., 1967.

Lisle, Laurie. *Portrait of an Artist: A Biography of Georgia O'Keeffe.* New York: Washington Square Press, 1981.

Lozoff, Marjorie. "Fathers and Autonomy in Women," *Women and Success: the Anatomy of Achievement,* Ruth B. Kundsin, ed., New York: William Morrow & Company, Inc., 1974.

Lynn, David B. *The Father: His Role in Child Development.* Monterey, California: Brooks/Cole Publishing Company, 1974.

Maccoby, Eleanor, and Carol Jacklin. *The Psychology of Sex Differences.* Stanford, California: The Stanford University Press, 1974.

MacLaine, Shirley. *Don't Fall Off the Mountain.* New York: Bantam Books, 1970.

May, Robert. *Sex and Fantasy: Patterns of Male and Female Development.* New York: W. W. Norton & Company, 1980.

Malinowski, Bronislaw. *The Father in Primitive Psychology.* New York: W. W. Norton & Company, Inc., 1966.

Mead, Margaret. *Blackberry Winter: My Earlier Years.* New York: William Morrow & Company, 1972.

Medinnus, Gene, ed. *Readings in the Psychology of Parent-Child Relations.* New York: John Wiley and Sons, Inc., 1967.

Miller, Jean Baker, ed. *Psychoanalysis and Women.* Baltimore: Penguin Books, 1974.

Muller, Philippe. *The Tasks of Childhood.* New York: McGraw-Hill Book Company, 1969.

Murray, Saundra Rice, and Martha Tamara Shuch Mednick. "Black Women's Achievement Orientation: Motivational and Cognitive Factors." *Psychology of Women Quarterly,* Vol. (3), Spring 1977.

Mussen, Paul Henry, John Janeway Conger, and Jerome Kagan, eds. *Child Development and Personality.* New York: Harper & Row, Inc., 1963.

Neubauer, Peter. "The One-Parent Child and His Oedipal Development," *The Psychoanalytic Study of the Child,* Vol. 15. New York: International Universities Press, 1960.

Nin, Anaïs. *The Diary of Anaïs Nin, Volume One.* New York: Harcourt Brace Jovanovich, Inc., 1966.

Parsons, Talcott, and Robert F. Bales. *Family, Socialization and Interaction Process.* Glencoe, Illinois: The Free Press, 1955.

Phelps, Robert, ed. *Colette: Earthly Paradise: An Autobiography.* New York: Farrar, Straus & Giroux, 1966.

Phillips-Jones, Linda. *Mentors and Protégées.* New York: Arbor House, 1982.

Pincus, Lily, and Christopher Dare. *Secrets in the Family.* New York: Harper & Row, 1978.

Prall, Robert C. "The Role of the Father in the Preoedipal Years." *Journal of the American Psychoanalytic Association,* Vol. 26, No. 1, 1978.

Rich, Adrienne. *The Dream of a Common Language: Poems 1974–1977.* New York: W. W. Norton & Company, Inc., 1978.

Ritvo, Samuel. "Adolescent to Woman." *Journal of the American Psychoanalytic Association,* Vol. 24, No. 5, 1976.

Rivers, Caryl, Rosalind Barnett, and Grace Baruch. *Beyond Sugar and Spice: How Women Grow, Learn, and Thrive.* New York: G. P. Putnam's Sons, 1979.

Rohrlich, Jay B. *Work and Love: The Crucial Balance.* New York: Harmony Books, 1980.

Roiphe, Anne. "Daddy's Girls: Women Who Win." *Vogue,* October 1980.

Rosaldo, Michelle Zimbalist, and Louise Lamphere, eds. *Women, Culture and Society.* Stanford, California: Stanford University Press, 1974.

Ross, John Munder. "Fathering: A Review of Some Psychoanalytic Contributions on Paternity." *International Journal of Psycho-Analysis,* Vol. 60, Part 3, 1979.

———. "The Forgotten Father," *Psychosexual Imperatives: Their Impact on Identity Formation,* Marie Colman Nelson and Jean Ikenberry, eds. New York: Human Sciences Press, 1979.

———. "Paternal Identity: the Equations of Fatherhood and Manhood," *On Sexuality: Psychoanalytic Observations,* Toksoz B. Karasu and Charles W. Socarides, eds. New York: International Universities Press, Inc., 1979.

Rubin, Lillian B. *Intimate Strangers: Men and Women Together.* New York: Harper & Row, 1983.

———. *Women of a Certain Age: The Midlife Search for Self.* New York: Harper & Row, 1979.

———. *Worlds of Pain: Life in the Working-Class Family.* New York: Basic Books, Inc., 1976.

Sarton, May. *I Knew a Phoenix: Sketches for an Autobiography.* New York: W. W. Norton & Company, 1959.

Scarf, Maggie. *Unfinished Business: Pressure Points in the Lives of Women.* New York: Doubleday and Company, Inc., 1980.

Sexton, Anne. *Love Poems.* Boston: Houghton Mifflin Company, 1969.

Sheehy, Gail. The "Hers" Column, *The New York Times,* February 7, 1980.

———. *Passages.* New York: Bantam Books, 1977.

Simpson, Mona. "Incest: Society's Last and Strongest Taboo." *California Living Magazine, The San Francisco Examiner,* October 4, 1981.

Singer, June. *Androgyny: Toward a New Theory of Sexuality.* Garden City, New York: Anchor Press/Doubleday, 1976.

———. *Boundaries of the Soul: The Practice of Jung's Psychology.* New York: Anchor Press, 1972.

Stewart, Wendy Ann. *A Psychosocial Study of the Formation of the Early Adult Life Structure in Women.* New York: Columbia University doctoral dissertation, 1976.

Stieglitz, Alfred. *Georgia O'Keeffe: A Portrait by Alfred Stieglitz* with an introduction by Georgia O'Keefe. New York: The Viking Press, 1978.

Strouse, Jean, ed. *Women and Analysis: Dialogues on Psychoanalytic Views of Femininity.* New York: Dell Publishing, Co. Inc., 1975.

Swidler, Ann. "Love and Adulthood in American Culture," *Themes of Work and Love in Adulthood,* Neil J. Smelser and Erik H. Erikson, eds. Cambridge, Massachusetts: Harvard University Press, 1980.

Tessman, Lora H. *Children of Parting Parents.* New York: Jason Aronson, 1978.

———. "A Note on the Father's Contribution to the Daughter's Ways of Loving and Working," *Father and Child: Developmental and Clinical Perspectives,* Stanley Cath, Alan Gurwitt, and John Munder Ross, eds. Boston: Little, Brown and Company, 1982.

——— and Irving Kaufman. "Variations on a Theme of Incest," *Family Dynamics and Female Sexual Delinquency,* O. Pollack and A. Friedman, eds. Palo Alto, California: Science and Behavior Books, 1969.

Thurman, Judith. "Do You Need a Mentor?" *Mademoiselle,* August 1981.

Walker, Alice. *Good Night, Willie Lee, I'll See You in the Morning.* New York: The Dial Press, 1979.

Winder, Alvin E., ed. *Adolescence: Contemporary Studies.* New York: D. Van Nostrand Company, 1974.

Wolfenstein, Martha. "Effects on Adults of Object Loss in the First Five Years." *Journal of the American Psychoanalytic Association,* Vol. 24, No. 3, 1976.

————. "Loss, Rage, and Repetition." *The Psychoanalytic Study of the Child,* Vol. 24, 1969.

Woolf, Virginia. *A Room of One's Own.* New York: Harcourt, Brace & World, Inc., 1957.

————. *To the Lighthouse.* New York: Harcourt, Brace & World, Inc., 1955.

————. *A Writer's Diary.* New York: New American Library, 1968.

Yarrow, Leon. "Separation from Parents During Early Childhood," *Review of Child Development Research,* Vol. 1, Martin L. Hoffman and Lois Wladis Hoffman, eds. New York: Russell Sage Foundation, 1964.